Pioneer Doctor

THE STORY OF A WOMAN'S WORK

Mari Graña

TWODOT®

GUILFORD, CONNECTICUT
HELENA, MONTANA
AN IMPRINT OF Rowman & Littlefield

In memory of my mother, Dorothy Atwater Barron

A · TWODOT® · BOOK

Copyright © 2005 by Mari Graña

TwoDot is a registered trademark of Rowman & Littlefield

Distributed by NATIONAL BOOK NETWORK

Library of Congress Cataloging-in-Publication Data
Graña, Mari, 1936–
    Pioneer doctor : the story of a woman's work / Mari Graña.
        p. cm.
    Includes bibliographical references.
    ISBN 978-0-7627-3654-6
    1. Atwater, Mary Babcock. 2. Women physicians—United States—Biography. 3. Medicine—United States—History. I. Title.

R154.A87G736 2005
610'.92—dc22
    [B]   2004059778

Contents

Preface

MY CHILDHOOD WAS FLOODED with exciting legends about my grandmother, Dr. Mary Babcock (Moore) Atwater—Dr. Mollie, as she was known. And nothing was more fun than playing doctor with the wondrous trove of antique medical technology my brother and I found in her old black doctor's bag, which survived in our attic long after her death. Later, realizing there is a kernel of truth in most legends, I decided to see what I could find about the real Mary Atwater. I soon discovered that her life was a part of Montana history from the 1890s, when the new state was still a gold-crazed frontier society, to the Great Depression of the 1930s. Her story is told in newspapers, books, and articles in Montana libraries, and in the archives, clipping files, and eye-crossing microfilms of the Montana Historical Society. Gradually, I began to piece together a life that was extraordinary in human terms, if perhaps not quite the mythic terms of my childhood.

Mary (Mollie) Babcock Moore graduated from the Woman's Hospital Medical College of Chicago in 1887, and worked in the medical field until her death in 1941. Before attending medical school, she worked as a schoolteacher and then as an assistant in her husband's medical practice. Shortly after receiving her degree and practicing medicine side by side with Frank Moore, she realized that though fully degreed and accredited as a physician, she was still his assistant and that opportunities for her as a doctor were limited in their home state of Iowa. In 1890 she left her husband and moved west to Salt Lake City. From there she launched her career as a frontier doctor in Montana, where she lived until the early 1930s, remarrying and raising a daughter.

Many of the medical instruments and treatments that Dr. Mollie used and was familiar with in the 1880s and 1890s are still in use today, but her career was witness to great strides in the advancement of medical theory and practice. Germ theory was a new development in the 1880s; aspirin wouldn't be discovered until 1898; and though the X-ray was developed in the 1890s, it was not available in Montana until much later. Vaccines for common illnesses such as influenza, measles, and mumps were not developed until the 1930s.

In addition to advances in medicine, social policy and politics were perhaps the greatest influence on the career of Mollie Atwater. Her concern for public health and women's health issues flew in the face of conventional wisdom and often put her in conflict with the restrictive Comstock Laws, which permitted the seizure of contraceptive devices and information from the mail. Her story became entwined with that of the suffrage movement as she worked to achieve radical reforms in public health.

The following story is biographical: The actual events and people of Dr. Mollie's life guide the narrative. However, certain elements have been dramatized, or reconstructed, based on the kinds of situations she dealt with, first as a frontier doctor, then later as a militant supporter of women's political and professional rights, and an advocate for public health issues. The reconstructed elements are based on the historical documents as well as on my mother's stories. They are, therefore, realistic portrayals of life as experienced by this remarkable woman. A larger discussion of the world of medicine during Dr. Mollie's career and a full bibliography are given at the end of the book.

Mari Graña
Santa Fe, 2004

Acknowledgments

I WISH TO ACKNOWLEDGE Mrs. Fanny Reynolds, whose stories substantiated those of my childhood. Mrs. Ann Korting directed me around the Marysville area, showing me the old mine sites and places where Dr. Mollie lived and worked. Dr. Volney Steele offered information on early medicine and women doctors on the frontier, and Dr. Friedhelm Kielhorn, Dr. Sherry Wheaton, and Dr. John Talley reviewed the chapters describing Mollie's medical treatments. Barbara Williams of Drexel University Library uncovered the Woman's Hospital Medical College faculty minutes from 1886. Both Joan McDougal of the Beaverhead County Museum and the staff at Bannack State Park provided information about Dr. Mollie in Bannack. Much of the information regarding the suffrage movement, including quotes from the speeches, is from Doris Ward's excellent thesis, "The Winning of Woman Suffrage in Montana." The most important sources of information, however, were the tall tales of my mother, Dorothy Barron, who was Dr. Mollie's daughter. Ginna Fahren provided some pictures of her great-aunt Mollie, and my friend Louise Jones made many helpful comments on the manuscript, as did my colleagues in the Santa Fe critique group of Susan Glodt-Stern and Lynn Stegner.

CHAPTER ONE

An Impossible Marriage

"SALT LAKE CITY—SALT LAKE. Twenty minutes to Salt Lake." The conductor walked down the swaying aisle of the Utah Central coach. Mollie felt the touch of a hand on her shoulder. "Wake up, miss. Next stop is Salt Lake."

Mollie jerked awake and looked around. In the light of the early December morning, the snow-dusted skin of the Wasatch was gliding past the train window. Immediately the anger that had burned in her during the long trip flared again—an anger that had been so long suppressed, the explosion the week before had left her shaking. It had not abated in the days after she moved out of the house and gone to stay with Clara and Charles. And the hurt. Why didn't she realize what Frank's attitude toward her would be even before they started their practice together? At first he had seemed so positive about her going to medical school, yet when she had finally gotten her degree, he had resented it. How could she not have known that side of him?

She opened her purse and took out her compact. Snapping it open, she saw the tiny mirror reflecting deep shadows under her gray-green eyes. She grimaced at the signs of despair and exhaustion, and tapped the powder puff on her cheeks. Even though she had been sleeping on the train, her dark auburn hair still held tight in the bun at her neck. She picked up her hat from the seat next to her and pinned it firmly onto her hair, then gave a last glance at her self-presentation, clicked the compact shut, and settled herself to await her new life alone in Salt Lake City.

Mollie Babcock and Frank Moore had been married almost ten years. They had met in his home town of Osage, Iowa, where he had established his medical practice together with his father, and she was teaching school. Since women were expected to give up their teaching jobs to their single sisters when they married, she had given up her post and become Frank's office assistant and nurse.

At first her marriage had seemed a love affair that would never stop. She enjoyed helping her husband and working with his patients. The experience had led her to the realization that she, too, would like to become a doctor. Frank had encouraged her despite the outrage of his father, the elder Dr. Moore, at the indecency of a woman attending medical school—let alone his own daughter-in-law. Alex Moore, along with many men of his day, considered women—that is, women of the Moores' social class—much too frail and delicate to withstand the assaults on their modesty inevitable in the study of anatomy. Mollie was convinced that this cult of female frailty, which was the vogue among the middle and upper classes, was a conspiracy of male medical professionals designed to keep themselves in business. After all, if women were considered perennial invalids—women, that is, whose husbands had enough money to keep a physician more or less on retainer—the medical establishment could count on a permanent source of income. Of course, this would require convincing the suggestible woman—and her susceptible husband—that she was indeed ill. Mollie and Frank had laughed about such backward attitudes, and talked of practicing together when she graduated.

Mollie's options for a medical education in 1885 were limited. Women were not welcome in most regular medical schools, and Mollie was not interested in the various "irregular" medical procedures that were popular at the time—eclecticism, Grahamism, Thomsonism, magnetic healing, water cures, and such—even though generally these schools accepted women. In 1876 Frank had graduated from Rush Medical College in Chicago, but women were not permitted to attend there. Rush had temporarily rescinded this rule in 1852, and permitted Emily Blackwell—who, along with her sister Elizabeth, was to become one of America's first "regular" woman doctors—to attend a course of lectures. However, because of student and faculty protests, Blackwell was denied admission to a second year, and the Illinois Medical Society had censured Rush for the "impropriety of admitting a woman."

Along with a general conviction of the intellectual inferiority of women, protests and occasional riots by male students, and certain current gynecological theories warning of the injurious effects of intellectual activities on the female reproductive organs, many professors refused to discuss anatomy in the presence of ladies. There were, however, a handful of special women's medical colleges with faculties made up of the few qualified women in the country and those men who were not too squeamish about parts of the body to teach of their tumors and traumas to the delicate sex. Frank suggested they go to Chicago, where there was an excellent women's college and where he had friends from his school days. He was sure that in Chicago he could work in a hospital or with one of his school colleagues.

Mollie was accepted to the Woman's Hospital Medical College of Chicago. The school's only entrance requirement was "satisfactory proof of a good English education." A high school diploma would serve as evidence, but, failing that, an applicant was required to pass an examination in "the branches of a good English education: English Composition, Mathematics and Elementary Physics." Having been a schoolteacher, Mollie had no problem demonstrating a good English education.

The college was directed by Dr. William Byford, a specialist in abdominal surgery and an ardent advocate for the education of women in medicine. Of the college's nineteen faculty members at that time, five were women. The curriculum was a three-year course of study that included guided study in the third year under a regular physician as "preceptor." Frank, who had joined the practice of a school friend from Rush, was Mollie's preceptor. She already had considerable experience working with him in Iowa, and it was easy to slide into the relationship of student to her husband.

Although getting into medical school was easy for Mollie, once there, she had never worked so hard. Her first year consisted of lectures in anatomy, physiology, histology, microscopy, chemistry, and *materia medica*. Laboratory and clinical work connected with these branches was required. Her second year included pathology, therapeutics, surgery, obstetrics, diseases of women and children, diseases of the throat and chest, and diseases of the nervous system. Her third year consisted of a review of the previous subjects plus dermatology, ophthalmology, and dental surgery, with clinical work in a local hospital, overseen by her preceptor. Although the college was strict and exacting with its students, Mollie, if often exhausted, was determined. She was learning to be a physician, and every class and lab session and clinical assignment brought her nearer that goal.

Early in her second year an incident occurred that caused the college to consider expelling her. A student colleague, Isabel Meader, accused Mollie of stealing. A faculty committee determined she was guilty of taking at least one article—a can of tomatoes. The committee requested the secretary "be instructed to inform Mrs. Mary Babcock Moore that the Woman's Medical College cannot receive her as a student from this date." Mollie was outraged; she insisted she had done no such thing, and hired a lawyer to defend her. The faculty postponed its decision to oust her, and set up a subcommittee to investigate the claims on both sides. Finally, in May 1886, the subcommittee issued its report:

> *To the Faculty of the Woman's College, Greeting:*
>
> *Your committee, to which has been referred the case of Mrs. Mary Babcock Moore, desires to submit the following report:*
>
> *The only evidence of misdemeanor brought before us consists of written statements presented by individuals whose character for veracity is unknown to the members of this committee. These accusations are rebuffed by an equally credible denial on the part of the accused. Your committee does not find itself in a position that will enable it to make any conclusive investigation of the matters in dispute: they therefore fail to discover any cause for action in the premises on the part of the faculty of the college.*
>
> *The members of your committee desire also to state that, in their opinion, the only persons amenable to the discipline of the faculty are such members of the institution as may have violated the rules of the college, or may have been justly convicted of misdemeanor before a legal tribunal, or at the bar of public opinion. Otherwise the faculty will find itself compelled to sit in perpetual review of the tittle-tattle of the dissecting room. In the expression of this opinion, however, the members of the committee do not wish in any way to restrict the largest liberty of action by the faculty in the exercise of its discretion when*

called upon to accept any candidate who may present herself for
admission or graduation.
  Henry M. Lyman, MD
  I. N. Danforth, MD
  D. R. Brower, MD

The response to the subcommittee report was a vote of five to three to allow Mollie to continue her studies. She passed her final exams in April 1887, and received her MD degree.

But the injustice rankled—the shame of being almost expelled for a can of tomatoes she didn't steal. Once she had received her MD, except for President Byford, whom she greatly respected and who had not been involved in the committee, she refused to maintain any contact with her alma mater. A few weeks after graduation, Mollie passed her certification exam to work in the state of Illinois.

"Illinois grants me an MD degree," she said to Frank, when she received affirmation of her license. "But will they let me join their elite, gentlemen-only, state medical society? Of course not. How do you explain such hypocrisy?"

"Unfortunately, it's very easy to explain," Frank had said. "As to the justice of it . . . well, let us hope that those men will someday come to realize that women can be helpful to them."

That was not exactly what Mollie had wanted to hear from him. Did he think that a woman worked day and night for three years to become a doctor in order to be helpful to a man? She didn't want to start a fight, so she let his comment slide past. But his remark stayed with her, and it wasn't long after she started working with Frank and his friend that the trouble began.

With her degree and her state license, she had expected to become an equal partner with the two doctors. And in a sense she was, in that she was now able to take on full responsibilities for her patients, prescribing medicines and performing minor surgical procedures. But regardless of the services she provided, at Frank's insistence, the patient always paid him. For the first time he and Mollie began to fight. When she had worked for Frank as his office assistant, she had never questioned their financial arrangements. But now that she, too, had her medical degree, she realized that Frank could not see her—or probably any woman—as his equal. For all his support of her going to medical school, he apparently had not considered that she expected to be accepted as a full-fledged doctor.

Mollie felt demoralized having to ask Frank for spending money. She was angry, yet she knew she had few choices outside of working with him. Aside from internships in Chicago's women's or children's hospitals, it was extremely difficult for a woman to practice alone without the sanctification of a male principal. She was barred from the American Medical Association and from most state medical societies because of her sex, and she knew that male doctors would seldom refer a patient to a woman doctor. She had counted on Frank not only to treat her as an equal, but, when they could afford it, to help her start her own practice as well. Mollie gradually came to the realization that if she was to practice her profession fully, she would have to take on the male-controlled medical world on her own.

Shortly after she had started working, Frank decided they should leave Chicago and set up practice in Calcasieu Parish in Louisiana. He had a friend there who suggested the three of them work together. But no sooner had Mollie been certified to practice in Louisiana than Frank and his friend had a falling-out, and within the year Frank decided they should move back to Osage. At first Mollie was delighted with this decision. She had disliked living in the South, where she felt that professional women were considered uppity and unfeminine. Moving back to Osage meant going home to her family and friends, and perhaps to the happier life she and Frank once had shared. Mollie registered to practice in Iowa, and the couple set up their office.

Since they were starting over again, they lived with Frank's mother, Sarah, to save money. Alex Moore, Frank's father, had died while Frank and Mollie were in Chicago. Sarah Moore was a decidedly opinionated widow who doted on her son, and who considered no woman good enough for him. Not surprisingly, Mollie didn't like her mother-in-law and Sarah didn't like her. Nor was Sarah happy that Mollie insisted on keeping her dog, Willy, in the house with her. There were constant needling remarks about Willy: He got hair all over the furniture, or he spilled water from his dish on the floor. And despite Mollie's efforts to keep the backyard clean, inevitably there would be a mess out there for Sarah to complain about.

Willy had been with Mollie since she was a student in Chicago. She had found him as a pup, nosing around the garbage in the alley behind their apartment. He was hungry and cold and scrawny, no more than a few months old. She had taken him in and nursed him so that he was now a robust dog—a mix of mostly Airedale terrier and several other things. Willy had gone with her to Louisiana and now back to Iowa. Frank put up with the dog with amused indifference. He didn't really mind Willy; he was simply disinterested. He considered Mollie's love of dogs merely one of his wife's many eccentricities.

Sarah sided with Frank in every disagreement that came up between the young couple. Mollie put up with this, hoping that soon she and Frank together would be earning enough to have their own home. But after several months, even with both of them working, that independence still seemed far off.

And there was something more, something beyond all these things, that had begun to disturb Mollie. Since Frank was the more experienced doctor, Mollie tended to defer to his judgment when there was a question about diagnosis or treatment. But twice now, Mollie had been concerned that Frank might be mistaken in his diagnosis of one of her patients. When she questioned him, he became angry and defensive, pointing out that he had been in this business a lot longer than she. His attitude upset her, but at the time she had let it go. Yet in the case of her patient, Mr. Harbison, who was suffering from diabetes, she was convinced that Frank's evaluation of the condition was wrong. She had gone ahead with her own idea of treatment, and simply not informed Frank of her decision.

Then last week Mollie's life blew up. She was in the kitchen cleaning up the breakfast dishes when she heard a yelp of pain. Rushing into the parlor, she saw Sarah glaring at Willy, and Willy, his ears flattened against his head and his tail clamped between his shaking legs, cowering behind a big overstuffed chair. Mollie quickly went to him and stroked his head, speaking softly to calm him. Then she turned and faced Sarah.

"Yes, I kicked him," Sarah snarled. "I'm sick and tired of having this cur in the house, shedding hair all over the furniture and rugs. Last week he knocked my crystal flower vase off the hall table. There was water and broken glass all over the floor. I want him out of here!"

"All right, I'll get him out," Mollie answered in a fury. "And myself as well." She was shocked as she heard her own words. They had come out of her mouth before she could think what she was saying. Sarah stared at her for a moment, then stalked out of the room.

Mollie gently ruffled the fur behind Willy's ears. She knew he loved to have her do this, and that it would calm him down. After a while the dog stopped shaking and began to nuzzle her arm. Then she called him to the front door and put him on a leash. Wrapping herself in her warm winter coat, she took Willy and walked the three blocks over to the house of her friends Clara and Charles. The Bennets had a small enclosed yard in back. Willy would be safe there until Mollie could decide what she was going to do—about Willy, about her mother-in-law, about her profession, about her marriage.

"What a surprise!" Clara said when she opened the door to Mollie's ring. "Do come in, Mollie, and Willy, you come in, too. What brings you both here in the middle of the morning?"

"Would it be all right if I left Willy here with you and Charles for a while? He can stay in the backyard, but he'll have to come in if it gets too cold, and he would have to sleep in the kitchen at night."

"Of course he can stay here, but what's happened?" Clara looked at her friend with alarm. "Come, let's go in the kitchen where we can talk."

Mollie hung her coat on the rack by the door and followed Clara down the narrow hall to the large kitchen at the back of the house. She took a chair at the table and told Willy to sit by her side. Clara put some water on the stove for tea, then sat down opposite Mollie.

"Please Mollie, tell me what's the matter. You and Willy aren't just out for a morning walk."

Mollie explained what had happened with Sarah. Then she confided to her friend the situation with Frank. "I have to ask him for everything, whether I need a tomato to fix dinner or a new pair of drawers. He controls all the money, and he decides how much he will give me. He refuses to have my own patients pay me. I've got to get away from here, at least for a while, but how can I go if I can't get my money from him?" She didn't mention her growing concern about some of Frank's decisions at the office. "Frank and I have gone around and around with this, and I can't stand his attitude any longer."

"You know you can stay with us until you decide what you're going to do," Clara said, smiling brightly at Mollie to reassure her. "And don't worry about Willy. He's a wonderful fellow. We'll keep him as long as you need us to."

Mollie was grateful for her friend's generosity. She had hoped Clara would invite her to stay with them. After what had happened with Sarah that morning, she was too proud to go back.

"I need to go over there and pack some things for the night, but I would like to stay here for a few days until I can think all this through and decide what I really want to do."

"Of course," Clara said, still smiling. "I'll make up the guest room this afternoon, and we'll expect you for dinner at seven. Meanwhile, I'll fix us a sandwich for lunch."

After lunch, Mollie left Clara's and walked down Main to the office. She had a two o'clock patient, Mr. O'Brian, who was suffering from dropsy. She didn't speak to Frank when she went in; he was busy with a patient in his examining room. She knew Sarah would tell him what she had said before she would even get the chance.

Michael O'Brian, a man in his late fifties, was officially Mollie's patient. He always came to the Dr. Moores' office accompanied by his live-in mistress, a music teacher named Rita. Rita gave violin lessons at O'Brian's apartment. She boldly informed Mollie at their first meeting that she and Mr. O'Brian were not married, but that she would be taking care of him. Mollie guessed Rita must be in her late forties. Her appearance was startlingly dramatic. She emphasized her high cheekbones with gold dangle earrings, and she braided glass beads into her dark hair. She wore dark-colored, revealing dresses. None of this was to Mollie's sense of taste and decorum. Coming from a proper, straitlaced New England family, Mollie had initially disapproved of Rita, of a woman living with a man not her husband. But over the weeks that O'Brian and Rita had been coming to the office, Mollie began to admire the woman's self-determination and forthrightness, the kindness and warmth she showed to O'Brian in his illness. Here was a woman who dressed as she pleased, took what she wanted in life, and let society be damned. Different as they were, the two women came to admire each other and were soon friends. Occasionally, if Mollie had some free time from her patients and Rita could get away from her violin pupils, the two would meet for afternoon tea in one of the tearooms along Main Street.

Mollie was so distracted, she found it hard to concentrate on her patient. She dreaded the scene she knew was coming that evening. She couldn't just go to Clara's without first facing Frank. When she finished examining Mr. O'Brian, Rita walked outside to talk to her while O'Brian was dressing.

"You're upset, I can tell," Rita said as they stood outside the office door. "Is there something I can help you with? Please, Mollie, please feel you can talk to me if you wish."

Despite her determination to remain professional in encounters regarding her patients, Mollie was desperate. She said to Rita: "Frank's control of the money makes it impossible for me to establish myself independently, either here with him or on my own. I need to get away for a while, and I need Mr. O'Brian to pay me his bill directly." As Mollie had hoped, she had touched Rita's womanly empathy, her sense of independence.

"I've been there, too, Mollie," Rita said, sympathetically. "I know what it is to be dependent on a man. I had to leave a marriage. But I can support myself now with the violin lessons, and Michael makes no demands on me. That's why I love him, and why I'm willing to take care of him. Because it's my choice." Rita smiled at her friend. "What you need is some money to get you on your way, Dr. Mollie. I'll see that Michael pays his bill to you. Come over to our place in the morning about ten, all right?"

O'Brian came out of the office, and Rita slipped her arm in his.

"Tomorrow," she said, nodding to Mollie as she and O'Brian turned to go down the stairs to the street.

The anger that had come out at Sarah in the morning exploded that evening at Frank. To test him one last time, Mollie said: "I've been going over the accounts received for last month, and I believe that the total for my services in this partnership is approximately $120. I would like to have that money now."

"Must we go over this again, Mollie?" Frank exclaimed, exasperated. "You know perfectly well the practice is mine. You are my assistant. And an excellent assistant you are, my darling, but of course the patients pay me. If you need money for something, just ask me. You are my wife. Don't I always give you money if you need it?"

The response was what she had expected; she had heard it enough times. "Frank," she said, trying to remain calm, "I can no longer tolerate this situation between us. I'm going now. Please tell my patients that I won't be able to see them tomorrow."

Frank sat back in the overstuffed chair that was officially "his," according to Sarah, and glowered at Mollie. "What do you mean?"

"I'm going to Charles and Clara's tonight. Willy is already there. You can tell Sarah that she need no longer worry about dog hair on her precious furniture. I'll talk to you about this tomorrow."

Mollie went upstairs to their bedroom and picked up the overnight bag she had packed earlier. As she passed the parlor on her way out, Frank was still sitting in his chair. He seemed to be reading the paper and didn't look up. Outside on the cold sidewalk, she looked back once at the house and saw Sarah watching her from an upstairs window. Something in Mollie made her turn and wave with a grin.

Next morning Mollie walked to the end of town, where Rita and O'Brian shared rooms in a large house they had converted into two apartments. She had been there once before on one of her afternoons with Rita. Rita answered her ring with a wide smile.

"Come on in, Mollie, Michael wants to talk to you."

Mollie followed Rita through the entry hall into the living room. Michael O'Brian was sitting in a rocking chair by the window, a quilt draped over his legs. His heavyset face was pale.

"How nice to see you, Dr. Moore. Please excuse me if I don't get up. Do come and sit down here." O'Brian pointed to a chair close to him. As Mollie sat down, he reached over to a small table next to him and picked up some papers. "I have your bills here for the past two months. I was meaning to pay these on my next visit, but Rita tells me you would like me to pay you now—today." He reached into his breast pocket and pulled out a small folded piece of paper. "I believe this will cover what I owe you to date." He handed the check to Mollie. "I understand that I won't be able to continue with you, and I want to tell you that I regret that very much. My condition has improved considerably in the past couple of months, and I'm very grateful to you for your help."

Although she felt it was appropriate for her patient to pay her directly, Mollie was embarrassed about collecting her bill at his house, and she was eager to bring the conversation to an end. "Yes, you have improved considerably, and I'm sure that if you wish, Frank will continue to care for you." She stood up and thanked him. "I need to go now. I do hope you will be well soon."

As Mollie turned to leave, Rita, who had been standing at the window while Mollie and O'Brian were talking, came forward to accompany her to the door. As they entered the front hall, Rita put her finger to her lips and took hold of Mollie's arm.

"I have something for you," she whispered. She reached into her bosom and drew out a small packet wrapped in a handkerchief. "This is a loan from me, Mollie. It's my money, not Michael's. It's from the violin lessons. You can pay it back when you get yourself settled and are working again." As Rita opened the front door, she pressed the packet into Mollie's hand and wished her good luck.

Mollie didn't open the packet until she had walked a few streets away. And then her eyes clouded with tears. Rita had loaned her $300! She couldn't ask her own mother for money, if she knew that with it Mollie would run away from Frank. She pulled out her handkerchief and dabbed at her eyes, overcome by Rita's kindness to a friend.

Late that afternoon, Mollie went to the office to wait for Frank to finish with his last patient. The office was upstairs, over the Mitchell County Press on Main Street. She and Frank had been concerned that the stairs would be difficult for some of their patients, but at the time there hadn't been another office available for rent. Sitting in the waiting room like a visitor, she looked around at the place she had worked for the last few months. She had decorated the waiting room herself, picked out the light green patterned paper and the quiet prints of mountain scenes on the walls. The chairs were not what she had wanted, but they had been able to buy them inexpensively from the former tenant. At least the beige upholstery didn't compete with the wallpaper. She had bought the lace half curtain for the window that looked down on the street, and hemmed it herself. Yet it was Frank's office. She had shared it, but it never was hers. She had fooled herself into thinking there could ever be an equal partnership with Frank. She couldn't be both professional and wife, and if she couldn't be one, she couldn't be the other. The thought that she had refused to face for so long was now obvious: To be Frank's wife at the expense of her own career was not enough for her.

Frank ushered his last patient out of his office and stood chatting with him for a moment at the top of the stairs. Then he came back to the waiting room and sat down opposite Mollie. Neither spoke for a few moments. Finally, Frank said angrily, "What do you think you're doing, moving out of our house?"

"It's not *our* house, Frank. It's just yours and Sarah's. You know that. But that's not what this is about. I told you last night that I can't tolerate this situation. I had hoped we could work together on an equal basis, but I can see this is not possible. I cannot be your wife any longer under these circumstances."

"I see," said Frank, his face grim. "This is what I get for letting you go to medical school?"

"What do you mean, 'letting me go'?" Mollie charged. "I went to school because I wanted to go, not because you 'let' me."

"So leaving my practice here and moving to Chicago so you could go to school was nothing. Is that it? I had nothing to do with that? Hell, I thought you would really be able to help me once you graduated." Frank's face was red with fury. "Ever since you got that damn degree, you've been acting like you know more than God Almighty. And now you think you can go out on your own? Is that what you want? Well, lots of luck, little lady." Frank slammed his fist down on the table, knocking a stack of magazines to the floor. He got up and stormed out the office door. Mollie could hear him stomping down the stairs to the street.

Mollie waited at Clara's a couple of days before going back to Sarah's house to pack her clothes. She picked a time when she knew Frank would be at the office and Sarah would be out at her Shakespeare Club. She went upstairs to their bedroom and began to lay out her clothes on the bed. She took the framed pictures of her mother and father, her brother and sister off the top of the highboy. Her father, Samuel Babcock, had died several years before when the family lived in Wisconsin. Samuel had been a member of the Ceresco agricultural commune in Ripon in the 1840s, before he had married Adelia. When he had become ill, he had wanted to return to Ripon, where he still had many friends. This was the only photo she had of him.

She wrapped the frames in some underclothes and packed them in her suitcase. On the dressing table was the cut-glass perfume bottle that Frank had given her for her birthday the first year they were married. She had been so happy that day. Frank had borrowed his father's carriage, and they had driven out to the ruins of the old Batchelder Mill where Sugar Creek flowed into the Cedar River. Mollie had packed a picnic, and Frank had given her his present. After they had eaten, they found a secluded spot to sit among the willows on the riverbank. Frank had wanted to make love to her. She had laughed, embarrassed that someone might see them, but he had insisted. She poured the contents of the bottle into another container and wrapped it in a scarf; she would take it with her.

There were a few precious articles her family had given her over the years: a tiny silver horse her father gave her when she was a little girl; an ivory dresser set, a Christmas present from her mother; a set of hand-embroidered handkerchiefs Sadie had made for her. They squeezed at her heart. Clearly she couldn't stay in the same small town with Frank, but leaving Osage meant leaving her mother and Sadie and her brother, Jason.

Mollie had no idea where she would go. Suddenly she felt a fear so intense, she started to shake. She crumpled onto the edge of the bed and put her head in her hands. The career she had worked so hard for in Chicago now seemed ephemeral. Could she possibly succeed alone in a world so prejudiced? Could she live without Frank's love? A wave of grief passed through her and caught in her throat with a sob. She would have to. The price of Frank's love was one she could no longer pay. Not now, not after all that had happened.

The sound of the front door opening below jerked Mollie back to the moment. She jumped up and hurriedly continued packing her clothes. Sarah came up the stairs and stood in the bedroom doorway, as if barring it.

"And just where do you think you're going, young lady?" Sarah asked, her voice tight with anger.

Mollie didn't answer. In grim silence she finished packing her clothes into two large suitcases. She picked up the first one and pushed past Sarah down the stairs to the front entry. When she came upstairs to get the other, Sarah had disappeared into her own bedroom.

Mollie shoved the two suitcases up against the wall of the entry hall. "I'll have a man come around to pick these up tomorrow," she called up to Sarah as she opened the double front door.

The train moved slowly into the Salt Lake station. Mollie knew there was no going back even if she wanted to. Yet she had to admit that she was afraid. How was she going to start a career in a city where she had no professional relationships, nothing more than the address of her friend Edna Tuttle, whom she had met at medical school in Chicago?

Mollie had not wanted to go back to Chicago; there were too many memories there. And her brief stay in Louisiana with Frank had convinced her that the South was still fighting the Civil War, and she was too much of a Yank to find entrance into that partisan society. She didn't want to go back east: Two of her friends from school had written her how difficult it was to break into the male medical establishment in the eastern cities. To Mollie, the logical place to go was west. The West was still new, was still becoming. The society, she reasoned, was bound to be more open than in the East. She had had to decide quickly, and since

Edna appeared to be doing well in Salt Lake City, Mollie hoped she would find the same opportunity there as her friend had. Salt Lake seemed as good a place as any to start her new life. She had written Edna a quick note to say she was coming.

She was concerned about the scandal she had created back home: By now the whole town would be chattering like monkeys about her. Running away from one's husband simply "wasn't done" in the circle of her family and friends, a circle that included Frank's family, too. Not that she cared what Sarah thought, but she had embarrassed and shamed Frank. The day before she was to leave, he had come to Charles and Clara's and begged her not to go. She had tried to be calm with him, to tell him that she felt sure her leaving was better for both of them. But even as she tried to talk to him, his anger had flared at her again, and he had slammed out of the house.

And then there was what she had done to her mother. Her dear mother—so proper and conventional, so concerned about the "correct" way to behave. Adelia Sophia Babcock had tried to impress on her daughter the importance of living up to her background, to her "heritage."

"You come from staunch Revolutionary stock," Adelia would tell Mollie proudly over and over again. On one occasion Mollie had snapped back at her mother: "I guess that's why I'm the way I am. It must be that staunch Revolutionary stock."

It was bad enough when she had told her mother she was going to medical school. Her mother had protested—just as Alex and Sarah Moore had—that a woman had no business in medical school. It was absolutely unladylike. And now a divorce! No one in their family of "Revolutionary stock" had ever gotten a divorce.

She had asked her brother, Jason, to get her clothes and other things she had left behind at Sarah's, and to keep them at her mother's house until she could send for them. Jason could handle Sarah. She didn't want to embarrass her mother or Sadie by asking them to go over there. And Clara was a dear friend to keep her beloved Willy for her. She must send for him as soon as possible.

With a squeal of metal on the rails, the train slowed to a stop.

"Salt Lake City," the conductor called out.

Mollie picked up her purse and her overnight grip and precious medical bag. After Frank had stomped out of the office last week, she had gone into her examining room and retrieved the bag. She would need it to work. If she could work. Clutching her various bags and packages, she let the porter help her down to the platform and walked over to the baggage master's office to wait for her suitcases to be unloaded.

Clara's husband, Charles, had given Mollie the name of a proper ladies' boardinghouse near the downtown. Charles was in the insurance business and often made trips to Salt Lake. He had inquired of his clients about appropriate lodgings for Mollie. She had telegraphed to the boardinghouse, and a response confirming an available opening had reached her by messenger at Clara's. The price was $4.00 a week for board and room—a little steep, but thanks to Rita she could afford it for a while.

Mollie hailed one of the carriages waiting at the station and gave the cabbie the address of the boardinghouse. He picked up her suitcases and packages and stacked them in the space in the back of the carriage, then helped her up to the seat beside him. The horse snorted clouds of hot breath into the cold December morning as Mollie rode through the unfamiliar streets. A covering of white crystals had fallen in the night, and the tracks of hooves and wheels crisscrossed on the road in front of her. As the carriage passed a row of shops, she saw Christmas decorations in the windows. She felt in her purse again to be sure Edna's address was safe.

CHAPTER TWO

A Job in a Mining Camp

THE LADIES' BOARDINGHOUSE that Charles had recommended was located near the downtown of Salt Lake on Fourth South. It was a large, white-painted structure that had come down in the world somewhat since its transformation from family home to boardinghouse. But the rooms were clean, the food more or less passable, and indeed—as Charles had assured Mollie—the home was proper. The landlady, Mrs. Schwantes, a widow of some sixty years, insisted that her young ladies be indoors no later than ten o'clock on weeknights and eleven on Saturdays. The house rules reminded Mollie of the year she had spent in boarding school—except now she knew better than to sneak cigarettes. If Mrs. Schwantes knew that Mollie not only was married but was contemplating a divorce as well, she would have had a conniption. Introducing herself to the establishment as "Dr." Moore allowed Mollie to avoid presenting herself as "Miss" or "Mrs." She wasn't about to explain why she was there without her husband.

There were four other young ladies living in the house. Two were sisters from Provo, working in the ZCMI department store, and the other two were schoolteachers from Pocatello. Since Mollie had once been a schoolteacher, she tried to engage these two in a discussion of school curriculum in Salt Lake. But they were intensely shy, intimidated by Mollie's apparent sophistication and presumably by the *Doctor* title. From what they did tell her, she found their classroom emphasis on what she considered the strange dogma of Mormonism distasteful. When all five ladies were at the table, the conversation, along with the repast, was utterly boring. She knew she must find another place to live as soon as possible, but she would have to put up with Mrs. Schwantes and her lady inmates until she could find employment.

Finding employment, however, was turning out to be difficult. In her haste to get away from Frank, she had not had time to learn much about Salt Lake City, relying on the brief information her friend Edna had written her over the past two years. Edna had developed a small gynecological practice in Salt Lake. As soon as Mollie arrived, she had asked her friend if there was any possibility of working with her.

"I'm terribly sorry, Mollie," Edna had answered, "I would love to have you work with me, but I've not been able to develop my practice to the point that I could take on another doctor. I've got a woman assisting me part time as a nurse, and for now that's all I can afford."

"I understand," Mollie assured her friend. "I managed the business affairs of Frank's practice, and I know well how careful one must be not to overcommit to another person."

Although a liberal anti-church group had recently been elected to the municipal government, Salt Lake City was still controlled by the Church and Kingdom of Jesus Christ of Latter Day Saints. Mollie was discovering that to a large extent, job opportunities in professional fields were also controlled by the church, either directly by the mysterious Council of Fifty—an anonymous group that ran the affairs of the church and its adherents—or through the social network of church members. Edna had told her in Chicago that she was from a Mormon family. But Edna was something of a rebel, which was why she was in Chicago at all. The two women had discussed religion early in their friendship. Mollie allowed that she was a member of the Protestant Episcopal Church and attended services because it was the tradition in which she was raised; she felt grounded by her weekly participation in the ritual. For Edna, the Mormon religion was a matter not of personal faith, but of close relationships in a family of several siblings, offspring of her father's three wives. Neither of the two women were believers in the doctrines of an organized religion. Nevertheless, Edna had been able to establish her practice because, on paper at least, she had the proper religious credentials for Salt Lake City. Mollie did not.

Mollie pored over the weekly classifieds in the *Deseret News* and the *Salt Lake Tribune*. There were several ads for nurses to attend invalid patients in their homes—certainly not what she wanted. Once there was an opening for a doctor at the city hospital. She made an appointment for an interview, but she needn't have bothered. The hospital already had two women doctors on staff, and was not hiring another woman. If she would be interested in applying as a nurse, they told her, there might be some openings coming up. Mollie desperately hoped it would not come to that. She didn't want to settle for the job of nurse, a position she had held in Frank's office long before she went to medical school.

Mollie's fear at not finding employment advanced in inverse proportion to the rate at which Rita's money was diminishing. She walked the often muddy streets to save the cost of fare on the mule-drawn streetcar; she never allowed herself a meal out of the boardinghouse, nor would she stop in a shop for a cup of tea and a tasty on a cold afternoon. Even Mrs. Schwantes, a paragon of housekeeping parsimony, was impressed with Mollie's frugality.

Except for the three years in Chicago, Mollie had lived all her life in the country or in small rural towns: first as a little girl on the family farm near Concord, Vermont; then, when she was twelve, in the little town of Ripon, Wisconsin; and last, after her father died, in the small town of Osage, Iowa. When Mollie got her teaching position in Osage, her mother had followed with Sadie and Jason. Chicago had been a shockingly new experience: The city had close to a million people in 1885 when she and Frank moved there. Because the O'Learys' cow purportedly kicked over the lantern that started the Great Fire of 1871, most of Chicago was new or newly rebuilt. Sanitary sewers and water mains had been installed, and the streets were paved. Salt Lake City, on the other hand, was filthy, and the longer she stayed there, the more she grew to hate it. The streets of the downtown, including the one in front of Mollie's boardinghouse, were being plowed up to install sewer pipes. The gigantic Mormon temple, a few blocks away on Temple Square, was still in construction—a colossus that had been under way for almost forty years. All this digging and building meant that pedestrians were constantly sloshing through mud and filth. The city had constructed water mains a few years before, but the system generally fed municipal fire hydrants. Much of the population still drew household water from open ditches and wells. And given the thousands of outhouses in a city of 45,000 people, there were recurrent epidemics of typhoid. In the overcrowded miners' quarters, tuberculosis was rampant.

If all this was not bad enough, the air was so filthy that on some days Mollie avoided leaving the boardinghouse at all. Hundreds of copper, silver, gold, and lead mines had been developed in the canyons along the Wasatch Front, and huge smelters refined the ore. These spewed particulate and smoke into the air above the city, visibly damaging the plants in the parks and residential areas. As a doctor, she was quite aware what this filthy air would do to her lungs.

Aside from her discussions in Chicago with Edna about religion, Mollie had not come into contact with the Mormon Church before coming to Salt Lake City. She was repelled by the church's advocation of polygamy. Such a thing was abhorrent to her straitlaced New England background. To Mollie's mind, the "Sacred Covenant," as the Mormons called their doctrine of plural marriage, was nothing more than the sanctification of male sexual self-indulgence. In the desire to convince Congress that Utah was ready for statehood, as well as deter the U.S. government from its plans to confiscate church property, Mormon leader Wilford Woodruff had officially issued his "manifesto" of a few months before: All church members were to obey the U.S. anti-polygamy laws. This was the official position, but Edna told Mollie that unofficially the church permitted and even encouraged polygamous marriage. The practice, she said, was alive and thriving throughout the Utah Territory and surrounding Mormon settlements.

One evening at dinner, Mollie was appalled at the conversation going around the table. One of the shopgirls from ZCMI announced that she would be leaving soon. She would be marrying an older man who already had a wife. The man apparently had taken a fancy to the young girl, and had approached her parents for their approval of the union. The family felt it was a good chance for their daughter, since the man was well thought of in the community and was certainly not without means. Mollie felt sorry for her. The girl seemed complacent about the arrangement, as if she had nothing to do with it. Her role was to comply with the wishes of her elders.

Mollie had held her peace during the dinner conversation, but the next afternoon she walked over to Edna's office to discuss this.

"She's nothing but a piece of meat," Mollie had growled at Edna. "And when she's produced the sons he needs to feed his ego, he'll tire of her and get himself another. The prostitutes down on Commercial and Franklin are in a better position than this poor girl. At least they get paid for their services."

"Calm down, Mollie," said Edna. "I can understand your disapproval, but it's not always awful for the women. I grew up in a very loving family, and my father's wives were like sisters to each other."

"I'll take your word for it," Mollie said with a shrug, "but I find that hard to believe. It seems to me the women would just naturally be jealous of each other."

"Yes, sometimes they are, and sometimes plural marriage is indeed just a form of licentiousness on the part of the men. But don't forget, Mormons are a religious people. They consider these marriages sacred."

Mollie was not convinced, but she let it drop. She knew Edna was not a believer, but she also knew that her friend was very close to her Mormon family. Edna was the only person in Salt Lake who knew she was married. Frank and Mollie had met her when Mollie and Edna were students, and it was a great relief for Mollie that she had a friend in Salt Lake in whom she could confide, with whom she didn't have to pretend. Although she knew Edna agreed with her about many things, including her concerns about Mormonism, she knew she had to be careful not to offend her friend, who had a divided mind when it came to her family.

Within this turmoil of the city's physical and social environments and her straitened financial circumstances, Mollie had to face inner demons as well. At times she was appalled at what she had done—to Frank, to her mother and Sadie and Jason, to herself. Running away, leaving scandal and hurt behind her. At first it had seemed easy to blame Frank for the problems between them. But now that she was alone in this new and strange and ugly place, she had the time to question her own motives, her own conduct. And the questioning brought her up short. Yes, there was Frank's attitude about the bill payments. Yet she was guilty of making assumptions about their business relationship that she should have discussed with him at the outset. And was she using this disagreement as an excuse to leave him? He had indeed left his practice in Iowa to move to Chicago so that she could go to medical school, certainly a professional as well as a financial sacrifice for him. Her concern over his diagnoses: Was she so sure of herself, fresh out of school? Did she really know what she was doing? Was she being arrogant as Frank had charged? Indeed, she had been concerned about some of his decisions, but perhaps more concerned about his defensiveness when she had questioned him. Were the domestic issues with Sarah all that important? They would have disappeared once she and Frank were able to live on their own. Sarah had, indeed, opened her house to them and provided a place to live at no cost so that she and Frank could save for a future together.

But then she reminded herself that Sarah's attitude toward her had been intolerable. How that woman had treated Willy! Mollie could concede that some people didn't care about animals in the way that she did. But abusing a dog, kicking a dog, was another matter. Was she considering divorcing her husband because she didn't like her mother-in-law, because the woman had kicked her dog? And, of course, the ever-present question: Could she make it on her own as a physician? The prospects were looking dim.

Then Mollie would rally with fierce determination: She would do it; she must do it. Something would come along; it would have to. She would be damned if she was going back to a nursing job after all she'd been through.

These thoughts chased one another through Mollie's mind in nights of little sleep and days of increasing discouragement. And as she mulled them over, one realization gradually emerged: Whatever her responsibility was for what had gone wrong in her marriage, and for the sorrow she had created for Frank and for herself, somewhere in the events of the last ten years, the love that had once seemed so strong, so lasting, so full of joy, had slipped away.

Mollie had arrived in Salt Lake City in the middle of December. That Christmas was the lowest point of her life. At the boardinghouse the two schoolteachers had gone home to Pocatello for several days; the ZCMI girls were in Provo. Even Mrs. Schwantes was spending the day with friends. Edna had invited her to Christmas dinner with her family, but Mollie had no stomach for it. She spent the day in her room, sewing a rip in one of her dresses and reading. Late in the afternoon she went down to the kitchen, where Mrs. Schwantes had saved some leftovers for her in the larder.

The year turned from 1890 to 1891, and still Mollie had found nothing. By April she had interviewed several doctors in the hope that they would hire a woman medical assistant. But no luck. She was running into the same prejudice in this western city that her friends were experiencing back east, but in Salt Lake it was compounded with the religious concern. Indeed there were a couple of women on the staff at the Deseret Hospital, but they were Mormon doctors. The other two hospitals in the city, one run by Episcopalians, the other by Catholics, were not interested in hiring a woman physician. Rita's money had dwindled to perhaps enough for another month or so. She didn't know what to do. She couldn't go back to teaching school in this city of Mormons.

For all her peppy words to boost her resolve, the reality of her situation was finally coming home. There was no opportunity for her in this city, and it looked as if there never would be. And now she didn't even have the money to get out of there. And where would she go if she could? There was no longer any choice. She would just have to take a nursing job after all. If she could do that, at least she could pay Mrs. Schwantes. After all of her work in school, after breaking with

Frank to go her own way, there she was, back where she'd been almost ten years ago.

Still, having faced this decision, Mollie actually felt relieved. Taking a nursing job meant she could stop this daily discouragement, this fruitless searching for a job that just wasn't out there—at least not for her. At any rate she would be able to pay back Rita's loan, and, if she was careful, put a little money aside. Once she had a nursing job, she could decide later how to get out of Salt Lake.

One of Edna's patients was an elderly woman with chronic gout. Edna asked Mollie if she might want to take on a nursing job looking after the woman days.

"It means getting Mrs. Clendening up in the mornings, bathing her, and fixing her breakfast and lunch. If the weather is good, you'll need to take her out in her wheelchair. You don't have to stay there nights; there's another woman who comes in at dinnertime and sleeps there. The day nurse she has now is leaving, she's moving out of Salt Lake."

Reluctantly, Mollie had agreed. She had never felt so depressed. She envied the day nurse who could simply pack up and leave.

Caring for the woman was not so bad as she had feared. Mrs. Clendening, although seriously ill, was friendly and still had her wits about her. Mollie soon discovered the woman was quite intelligent and well read, and continued to read even though it seemed to strain her eyes. Mollie began to enjoy talking with her.

One of the books Mollie found her patient reading was a treatise on witchcraft. Mollie asked her if there were some special reason she wanted to learn about witches.

"Only that one of my ancestors was a prosecutor at the Salem witch trials," Mrs. Clendening answered. "And I've always been fascinated how this murderous antagonism to women, especially elderly women, came about. Do you realize that historians now estimate that in

Europe, maybe as many as a hundred thousand women were burned or hanged as witches in the fourteenth and fifteenth centuries, even up into the so-called Age of Reason? Actually, the last woman accused of being a witch was burned in Switzerland only a hundred years ago. The main complaint against them was that they were healers. And if they were any good at it, it was assumed that they got their powers from consorting with the Devil."

Mollie was shocked. "No, I had no idea. A hundred thousand women! I'm interested that your ancestor was a Salem prosecutor. One of mine was, too—Nicholas Putnam. Is he mentioned in your book?"

"No," replied Mrs. Clendening, "he must have been one of many. But what happened in Salem was such a small event compared to what the Catholic Church, and then later the Protestant church as well, allowed to happen to those women. In Salem they only hanged nineteen, and pressed one to death. In Toulouse four hundred were burned in a single day."

"It rather reminds me of male doctors' attitudes toward women healers today," Mollie said, grimly. "Of course, they can't burn us anymore, so they just ridicule us, which, I suppose, results in the same— that is, clearing the world of competitive women."

"Yes, Doctor," Mrs. Clendening said, "I'm afraid you're right. But for what it's worth, I do greatly appreciate your help. Do you think a male doctor would do all you have to do to help me? I highly doubt it. Actually caring for someone, especially if it involves bedpans, is woman's work. Am I right?"

Mollie could only nod in agreement.

One afternoon while her patient was resting, Mollie picked up the May issue of *The Ladies' Home Journal* she found on the kitchen table. Leafing through it, she came across an article titled "Women's Chances as Breadwinners: The Man's View." Under the circumstances, the title was bound to catch her attention. A Dr. George Shrady was giving his views on women in the medical profession:

> *Far from intending any discourtesy to the female sex, I am striving to pay it a compliment by saying that the reason why woman is not fitted to medicine is because she is too delicate and good for its rougher and harder work. . . . Woman's real place for woman's work, the place for which she was intended by God and man, where she can do the greatest good in the best possible way—is Home. . . . Would it not be more in keeping with our smart little Mary, who is studying typhoid in a distant hospital, to be home nursing her sick brother, smoothing the pillow for her invalid mother, or perhaps cooking a dainty for her overworked father? What recompense would there be even in the discovery of a new bacillus or the writing of a prize thesis, when husband and children may be suffering neglect at home?*

Mollie slammed the magazine down on the table. What recompense, indeed! She was sick and tired of those arrogant doctors. Since they could no longer accuse women of fornicating with the Devil, suddenly women were delicate butterflies whose only purpose in life was to fluff pillows and cook dainties. What in hell were they so damn afraid of? That maybe "our smart little Mary" would discover a new bacillus before one of them did?

The noise of the magazine slamming onto the table had awakened her patient. Mollie heard her call from the bedroom.

"I'm so sorry, Mrs. Clendening," Mollie apologized as she hurried into the room. "I was reading an article in your magazine, and it made me so angry, I forgot for a moment you were sleeping. Please forgive me for waking you."

"It's all right, my dear." The woman's watery eyes could still hold a smile. "I think I know what you were reading. Was it that article in the Journal about woman doctors? I read that, myself, this morning. You know, Dr. Moore, if I had the energy, which alas I don't, I would write to that magazine and tell them what wonderful doctors you and your friend Dr. Tuttle are. That foolish man doesn't know what he's talking about."

"Thank you," Mollie said. "It's encouraging to have someone say that. Trying to get the world to acknowledge that a woman can be competent seems an endless struggle."

To Mollie's surprise Mrs. Clendening lived into late fall. But then it was over, and once again she was out of a job.

Mollie was at bottom. She put on her coat and left the boarding-house to walk off her despair. As she picked her way through the mud the workmen had left from the pipe trenches they were still digging, she thought she might as well pick up the paper down on Temple Square. Maybe there would be something in it that day.

As Mollie walked along the dirty streets, the fresh breeze in the brisk air made her feel better. Although the year had started into December, it had not yet begun to snow. When she got to the huge square, she stopped at a newsstand and bought copies of the *Deseret News* and the *Tribune*. She put the papers in her bag and walked over to the construction area. The great temple had risen to an amazing height already, and the workmen were now building the last of the six massive spires. She watched them maneuvering the large granite stones up the trolleys. It seemed to her that within a few months, maybe a year at most, the edifice would be completed. While she was staring up at the trolleys, some sixth sense made her turn around. For a moment she thought she was hallucinating. Standing there, just a short distance behind her, was Frank. He, too, was watching the stones rising on the trolleys.

In a flash Mollie realized that Frank had not yet seen her. Her mind started to race. What was he doing there? Was he looking for her? Clara and Charles wouldn't tell him where she was living. But her mother? Her mother knew where she was. Could she keep her secret from Frank if he pressured her?

The last thing Mollie wanted was a confrontation with Frank. She couldn't bear to have him see how she had failed. Yet the sight of him standing there behind her had shaken her in a way she had not expected. As if by instinct her immediate reaction had been to turn to him. Fortunately, her better sense stopped her.

Mollie ducked through the crowd and headed back to the boardinghouse. She knew that if Frank was aware where she was staying, he would come after her; if he didn't yet know, she might be safe there for a while.

Over the next two days, Frank did not come to the boardinghouse. For fear of running into him, she didn't dare go out. On the third day of this self-imposed incarceration, Mrs. Schwantes knocked on her door and said there was a message for her. The delivery boy was waiting downstairs. Full of trepidation, she followed Mrs. Schwantes down to the front door, took the envelope from the boy, and gave him a dime. She asked him to wait a few minutes and took the note up to her room to read it:

> *Dear Mollie,*
>
> *Come to my office Saturday next at 2 o'clock. I've been invited to tea at the home of some friends of my family, and I want you to accompany me. I'll explain later.*
> *—Edna.*

That was all. Mollie was so relieved, it took her a few moments to reflect how odd it was that Edna would include her in an invitation in this manner to the home of strangers. She felt much too miserable to put on a social face for a tea party. She was ready to send a message back to Edna saying she couldn't accept. But then she considered: Edna didn't know that Frank was there, but she did know how depressed she was. Maybe Edna was just trying to cheer her up; then again, it might be something really important. She scribbled a note of acceptance, found an envelope, and went back down to give it to the messenger.

On Saturday, Mollie, dressed in the brown gabardine town dress and feathered hat she had bought in her Chicago days, splurged a dime on a mule-car ticket to travel across the city to Edna's office, a modest little house on Tenth North with an apartment behind. The apartment was rented by someone else; Edna lived out of a room in back of her office.

Edna opened the door to Mollie's ring. "Come in, come in, I'm so glad you decided to come," she said excitedly. "We're invited to the Longmaids'. John Longmaid is a friend of my father's. They're in the mining business together. John's son, J. Henry, and his wife are visiting Salt Lake from Montana, where he's the manager of a gold mine. I've known J. Henry and his little sister, Annie, for years. And Mollie—he's here in Salt Lake looking to hire a doctor for the mining camp."

"Edna!" Mollie exclaimed. "Are you suggesting that a man is going to hire me—a woman—to work in a mining camp? You must be joking."

"Well, why not?" Edna's voice was impatient. "You aren't getting anywhere here in Salt Lake. If any woman is tough enough to handle a job like this, you are. Don't worry, I haven't told them you're a doctor looking for work. You've got to figure out a way to get an interview with J. Henry, and then convince him you're the woman for the job. But whatever happens, we're invited to the Longmaids' for tea, and I certainly don't want you running out on me after I've wangled this invitation for you. They're expecting both of us."

Mollie was skeptical, but of course she wouldn't think of being so impolite as not to honor the Longmaids' invitation. Nor would she disappoint Edna, who had maneuvered this meeting.

"Mr. Longmaid will be sending his carriage for us here at the office," Edna said. "He said to watch for it at three o'clock. Look at it this way." Edna eyed her friend intently. "If nothing happens about a doctor job, at least you will have met some new friends here. Believe me, Mollie, these friends are very influential in Salt Lake, even if they aren't Mormons. They're in mining, and I want to tell you, 'being Mining' is almost as important in this city as 'being Mormon.' At least both groups seem to be equally interested in making money."

At three o'clock sharp the Longmaids' driver stopped in front of Edna's office. The two women were waiting outside for him, and he helped each of them up the metal step into the carriage. As they set out, Mollie's spirits picked up.

"This will be fun," she said. "I haven't been out like this since I left Iowa."

"I know you will like the Longmaids," Edna responded. "And if I know you, you're going to be a mining camp doctor."

Mollie was not convinced, but she settled back in the carriage, determined to enjoy the afternoon. After a few minutes the driver turned onto South Temple, a wide avenue lined with elegant homes built in the last few years by wealthy mine owners. The carriage turned up the circular drive in front of a large, gracious mansion.

"Definitely a 'good address,'" Mollie said as she looked about at the manicured grounds of the Longmaids' home.

"I told you these are people you want to know," Edna said, smiling at Mollie. "No matter what happens, I want you to meet my friends."

The driver escorted the ladies to the front door, where the butler met them, took their wraps, and announced their arrival to the group assembled in the drawing room. On seeing Edna, Annie Longmaid jumped up from her chair and ran to embrace her.

"Oh, I'm so glad you could come! I'm home from school for Christmas vacation, and I was so hoping I'd see you before I have to go back." Then, remembering her manners, she turned to Mollie. "You must be Edna's friend. I'm Annie." Annie held out her hand to Mollie. Edna spoke up quickly.

"This is Miss Mollie Moore," she announced to Annie and the family. Introductions were made all around. The two were invited to sit down, and Edna caught up on family gossip with Annie and the elder Longmaids while Mollie chatted with J. Henry about his life in Montana. After a few minutes two maids came in, one wheeling a mahogany tea wagon covered with an embroidered cloth laden with cups and saucers and a silver tea service, and behind her a girl bearing a tray of tiny delicate sandwiches and elegant chocolate and vanilla petits fours. Other than once in a shop window, Mollie hadn't seen such treats since she had come to Salt Lake. She felt she could eat the whole trayful. Unfortunately, etiquette required that a lady take only one dainty as the tray was passed to her.

As the others were talking, Mollie asked J. Henry if there were any special reason he was in Salt Lake at this time.

"Why, yes," he responded. "I'm looking for a doctor. We had a doctor in Bannack until recently, but he's returned back east. Actually, I think the primitiveness of the place, along with the primitiveness of most of the people, finally drove him out."

"It must be challenging, living in such a remote place, and working so hard under difficult conditions." Mollie had no idea where Bannack was, just that he had described it earlier in the conversation as a

remote settlement in southwestern Montana. "I suppose when someone gets sick, it's a pretty serious matter, since there are probably no
hospitals for miles."

"Yes, it is, Miss Moore, and especially for my wife. She is here with
me now, but is feeling very much under the weather. She wanted me to
be sure to give you and Edna her apologies for not joining us. She is
expecting in July—our first child. Actually, I want her to stay here in
Salt Lake until the baby comes, but she won't hear of it. She insists on
returning to Bannack with me. So you see, I need to find a doctor right
away. Not only for my men, but I'm afraid my wife may need help with
this baby."

Indeed, Mollie did see. For the first time in weeks she felt a spark
of hope. If she could convince him that a woman doctor would be a
help to his wife, *and* that she could handle the miners . . .

The tea party was drawing to a close. Mollie and Edna had stayed
the appropriate length of time, and Edna announced that they really
must be on their way. Mollie thanked her host and hostess and said
good-bye to Annie. Then she turned to J. Henry.

"I know someone who might be interested in your job. An emi-
nently qualified physician who is looking for a little adventure in life
right now. I think that camp doctor at Bannack might be just the thing.
Perhaps we could make an appointment now for an interview, and I'll
pass the information along."

"By all means," said J. Henry with enthusiasm. "Bring him to
Father's office tomorrow at two. It's 415 Second North. I'll look forward to meeting him."

Mr. and Mrs. Longmaid ushered the two women out onto the
front porch, where the carriage was waiting for them under the porte
cochere. As they settled themselves into the carriage and the horses
started down the drive, Edna exploded with laughter.

"You're a genius, Mollie! J. Henry is going to have the surprise of his life when you show up there tomorrow alone."

Mollie laughed. "When he told me his wife was having some trouble, I thought I might just have a chance. We'll see tomorrow. Did you hear? I didn't lie, I never said the doctor was 'he.' What I have to do now is work out my plan of attack. I've got to convince him I can handle a crowd of crusty miners."

"That you can indeed, I have no doubt," Edna said, laughing. "The question is, can you handle J. Henry? You must let me know what happens."

The driver dropped Edna at her home and drove on to Mollie's boardinghouse. She was so excited at dinner that evening, she actually managed to elicit responses to her lighthearted conversation from the two timid schoolteachers. Then she retired to her room to concentrate on what she was going to say to J. Henry.

The next afternoon at two o'clock Mollie stood outside the offices at 415 Second North. She had spent close to an hour in front of the mirror in her room, trying on dresses. She wanted to look elegant, but certainly not frilly—maybe even a little staid. She had already worn her brown gabardine to tea. It was perhaps the most appropriate, but she didn't want J. Henry to think it was her only dress. He probably wouldn't notice anyway, she thought. Men seldom do. Still, she didn't want to take the chance. She decided on her gray velvet suit with the black trim. A plain white blouse would dress it down enough, and a single strand of jets would pick up the trim on the jacket. She tried on her black hat—no feathers this time, just a gray ribbon around the brim. Black, high-button shoes completed the black-and-gray effect.

After she had decided on the clothes, Mollie studied her face in the mirror. She had just passed her thirty-third birthday in January. Her dark hair, gathered in a bun in back, still showed no hint of gray. It swooped along the sides of her head from under her hat. "Well, Doctor, you certainly look old enough to be serious and experienced," she said to the mirror. "On the other hand, you're still pretty enough to turn a head. And that's never a disadvantage." The final touch was to apply powder to take the shine off her nose, and just the faintest blush of rouge on the line of her cheekbone. She decided against perfume. "This is a job interview, not an assignation," she said aloud, grinning at herself in the mirror.

Suddenly she felt a flash of panic. She had been so excited about the coming interview, she had forgotten for a moment that Frank was somewhere out there looking for her. She couldn't let him find her like this. She would just have to convince J. Henry that she could handle the job. She got up from the dressing table and opened the roll of papers she would take to show him: her medical diploma from Chicago and the papers from Illinois, Louisiana, and Iowa showing she had passed her state certification examinations. She put the diploma and the certifications into a large carpetbag, along with some testimonial letters from patients. This was her chance for a future. She had to get that job.

Mollie announced to the receptionist that Miss Moore was here to see Mr. Longmaid. Implying that she was unmarried made her feel even more duplicitous, since Moore, of course, was her married name. J. Henry rose as the receptionist ushered her into his office.

"And where is your doctor friend?" he asked, as he invited Mollie to take a seat.

Mollie put on her most engaging smile. "There is no doctor friend, Mr. Longmaid. I must ask your forbearance with this little ruse, but it was necessary for me to have a private interview with you. *I* am the doctor who is applying for the position."

"My dear Miss Moore . . . ," J. Henry began.

"*Doctor* Moore," Mollie corrected him with a smile. "I've brought my papers to show you. I have four years' experience both as a physician and as a surgeon." She didn't mention Frank. She opened the packet of papers she had brought. "Here are my licensing credentials and several letters from patients. I would be happy to leave them for you to read over."

"But, Dr. Moore"—this time J. Henry was careful to get the title correct—"this job is in a *mining camp*. There's syphilis and snakebites and gunshots and amputations and the usual plague of epidemics that run through these camps. Surely a woman couldn't—uh—wouldn't want to work under such conditions."

"Mr. Longmaid," said Mollie evenly, "all those conditions you just mentioned I have dealt with in my practice. If you are concerned whether I can deal with the problems of men, please rest assured. I am quite experienced in treating men's maladies, as you will see from the letters I've brought. And in addition to the afflictions you've just mentioned, I have considerable experience in gynecology and obstetrics. I am sure that even in mining camps there are childbirths and women's problems that need attending to." There; she had put out the bait.

J. Henry seemed taken aback by the encounter. Mollie's forthrightness had caught him off guard, as well as the surprise of her appearance in his office alone. "I'll have to think about this, Dr. Moore. I'll look at your materials here and let you know." He appeared eager to end the interview.

"Thank you, Mr. Longmaid. I look forward to hearing from you. I'm lodging in a house on Fourth South. The address is there in my papers." Mollie stood up and smiled at J. Henry as she took his extended hand. "Please forgive me for my deviousness regarding this interview. It was indeed a trick, but I knew no other way to approach you."

For the next few days, Mollie was in hell. She didn't bother with the newspaper; she couldn't think about looking for a nursing job now. She knew she was pinning her hopes on a very slim chance, but she couldn't help it. She had to get that job and get out of Salt Lake before Frank found her.

And then three, four, five days went by. J. Henry still had not contacted her. Was he so rude as to simply ignore her? Or was he too spineless to tell her no? Once more she felt the despair of the past months flooding over her. Why wouldn't he at least answer her, one way or another. Finally, she decided she couldn't stay hiding in the boardinghouse, worrying Frank would see her. She had to get out and go for a walk. She grabbed her coat and stormed out into the fresh air.

Careful to avoid the temple area where she had seen Frank, Mollie walked toward the office at 415 Second North. Of course she wasn't planning to enter, but she felt drawn to the street. As it happened, when she turned onto Second North she realized with a start that J. Henry was walking a short distance in front of her. She kept a way behind him and tried to appear nonchalant, in case he should turn around and spy her. She was curious to see where he was going.

She assumed J. Henry would go into one of the many offices along the street, but to her surprise he went into a small florist shop on the corner. She stood studying a store window, her back to the florist shop, and waited for him to come out. He came back in her direction, passed without noticing her, and, farther down the street, entered the building where his father's office was located.

When she was sure J. Henry was out of sight, she hurried to the florist shop and entered. "Did a Mr. Longmaid just order some flowers from you?" she asked the woman behind the counter.

"Why yes," the woman said. "They're to be sent to his wife over on

South Temple. Apparently she is not feeling well."

"If you don't mind," said Mollie sweetly with a wide smile, "I have a message I'd like you to put in the bouquet for me. It's just a little get-well message for his wife."

"Of course," said the saleswoman. "Here are some notes and envelopes for messages." She handed Mollie a piece of floral notepaper and a small envelope. Mollie sat down at a little writing desk and dipped the pen in the inkwell. Her missive was simple and straightforward:

> *I am still waiting to hear about the job.*
> *—Mary B. Moore, MD*

"Here," Mollie said, handing the clerk her note, tucked into the tiny envelope, addressed, and sealed. "Please, just put it in the bouquet with Mr. Longmaid's message." Mollie hurried back to the boarding-house to wait to see if there would be a response to her cheek.

Later that afternoon, a messenger came to the boarding house with a note:

> *Dear Dr. Moore,*
> *Would you be so kind as to call at my father's office tomorrow at ten o'clock? I have something I would like to discuss with you.*
> *Sincerely,*
> *J. Henry Longmaid*

Mollie immediately forgot she was angry that he had taken so long to contact her. If he was going to turn her down, she reasoned, he would have done so much sooner—probably just sent a polite note. She gave him that the decision to hire a woman as camp doctor was certainly irregular, and of course he would have to take time to give it serious consideration.

Mollie presented herself the next morning at the office at 415 Second North. The receptionist smiled as she recognized her. "Yes, Miss Moore, Mr. Longmaid is expecting you." And again Mollie was ushered into J. Henry's office.

"Please do sit down, Dr. Moore." J. Henry indicated a chair opposite his desk. He was unsmiling, serious, and Mollie felt a cramp of fear grab her stomach.

"I've read the papers you left here with me, and I must say, they are indeed an impressive testimony to your competence as both a physician and a surgeon. Let me return these to you." He handed over the sheaf of papers to her. "Now tell me, honestly, why would you want to take a job in a frontier mining camp instead of one, for example, in a city like this, or some other large urban area? Certainly you understand the conditions are exceedingly primitive."

Mollie was careful to be positive. The man was waiting for her to convince him. She hoped he didn't know about Frank. "Mr. Longmaid," she said, "I grew up on a farm. That may not be as primitive as your mining camp, but it is certainly very different from living in a city. I know how to drive a buckboard, and I am an excellent horsewoman. You have read my qualifications. I presume I don't need to reiterate them here unless you would like me to. But I imagine your main concern is whether I can handle the men. I assure you I can. I have become a doctor in a man's world, Mr. Longmaid. In medical school some men jeered at me, but I am still here, and I have succeeded in what I set out to do."

"Yes, I rather think you have." And for the first time, J. Henry smiled at her. "I must tell you, I've discussed this with Edna. I suspected she would be in on your tricks. Now I understand why she was so eager to bring you to tea the other afternoon. Anyway, Edna was adamant that you could hold your own in a mining camp—or anywhere else, for that matter."

Mollie held her breath. She had to get this job. She had to get out of this horrible town. She was sure Frank would never think to look for her in a Montana mining camp.

"I must confess, Dr. Moore, I admired your creative little subterfuge the other day. And my wife was delighted that you slipped that note in with her flowers. Frankly, as you know, I am concerned for her health right now, and I know she would be more comfortable with a woman doctor. As for the men, yes, they will be surprised, to say the least. But I do indeed think you can handle them. In the years I've known Edna, she's never been wrong in her estimation of someone. So I speak for my wife as well as for myself in saying that we would be pleased if you would join us in Bannack."

Mollie suppressed her joy and relief behind a proper professional smile.

"The mine is the property of the Golden Leaf Mining Company," J. Henry continued, "which is owned by a London syndicate. The miners pay a monthly medical fee to the company. It's a kind of insurance. The camp doctor works for the mining company, not for the individual patient. Your fees would be covered by the company at $75 a month. Would this arrangement be acceptable to you?"

Mollie stood up and held out her hand to J. Henry. "When do I start?"

"As soon as you can, Doctor," J. Henry replied, his smile breaking into a laugh. "If my wife is feeling well enough, she and I will be leaving tomorrow. Do you think you could be on the train to Dillon a week from today? That should put you in Dillon a day later. Unfortunately, the Corinne Hotel by the station burned down a few months ago, but I'll make a reservation for you at the Magnolia. You can spend the night there, and I'll send the wagon to take you to Bannack in the morning."

A week from today. Mollie could hardly restrain herself from skipping down Second Street. She was eager to get to the boardinghouse to tell Mrs. Schwantes she would be leaving. Dear Edna, this was her doing. She would miss her. And Frank. She hoped she could avoid him. She would have to deal with the divorce soon, but not now. She just wanted to get out of Salt Lake City.

CHAPTER THREE

The Ride to Bannack

THE PORTER PICKED UP MOLLIE'S SUITCASES and set them in the train. She was about to mount the steps when she saw Edna rushing toward her along the station platform.

"I was afraid I would miss you!" Edna said breathlessly. "I couldn't find a cabbie for the longest time."

"I'm so glad you came," Mollie said, hugging her friend. "We still have a few minutes."

"Tell me, Mollie, did you manage to avoid Frank?"

Mollie's smile vanished. "Of course not. I suspected that sooner or later he'd show up at Mrs. Schwantes's. Was she ever surprised when he inquired if his wife was living there. Not that it mattered any longer."

"I do hope there wasn't a scene."

"I don't know if you'd call it a scene, exactly," Mollie said. "We went for a walk. I didn't want to talk to him at the boardinghouse. Mrs. Schwantes would have been snooping outside the door.

"He begged me to come back to him. Told me that he'd found a place for us, that he'd already moved out of Sarah's house. And he told me he had not understood how important it was for me to earn my own living as a doctor, even if we were partners together. And that of course from now on my patients would pay me directly."

"But isn't that what you wanted from him?"

"Edna, I was so discouraged that if he had come two weeks earlier, I might well have gone back to Iowa with him. It would have been both a great relief—and a bitter defeat. And in the long run a mistake. It's too late for Frank and me now. It's not the job, Edna, it's Frank. I'm not trading a career for Frank. I don't want this marriage any longer."

"So what did he say—what did he do?" Edna looked at her friend worriedly.

"It was horrible. He started to cry. I didn't know Frank knew how to cry. I thought I couldn't stand it, seeing what I was doing to him. But I don't have a choice. When he finally understood that I wouldn't come back to him, that the marriage was really over, he accepted it. He calmed down. He wasn't angry, just quiet. I suppose he had spent all his anger earlier. I told him we couldn't discuss divorce now, that I would write him. Do you know, he never even asked me where I was going."

"I'm so sorry, Mollie. That must have been so painful for both of you."

"Yes." Mollie looked at her friend with a smile. "It's been a sad time. But here I am, ready to get on this train for a new place, a new life. So it's a mining camp—I don't care. It's my first professional job on my own. And I thank you so much for making this possible."

Just then the train whistle blew. Mollie hugged her friend. There were tears in both women's eyes. "I'll write you, Edna, and promise you'll come visit me in this godforsaken place I'm off to?"

"Of course I will. I can hardly wait. Now hurry, Mollie."

Mollie grabbed her overnight case and her black medical bag. She climbed up the iron steps to the train car and waved good-bye to Edna. With a jolt and a screech of metal against the track, the train moved slowly out of the station. Mollie settled herself by a window, and rejoiced as she watched Salt Lake City receding into the past.

Mollie had to transfer to the Utah & Northern Line at Ogden. The train stopped for the night at Pocatello Junction, where she joined the other passengers for dinner and accommodations across from the station at the Yellowstone Hotel. She needed to be up before dawn to catch the northbound for Dillon.

The U&N was much slower than the transcontinental on which she had arrived in Utah the year before. Slower and infinitely less comfortable. The train carried both passengers and freight. It stopped at tiny stations every few miles, and occasionally when someone flagged it down. There was already snow on the grain and potato fields as the train puffed northward, crossing the Snake River at Idaho Falls and gradually climbing toward the Continental Divide, which separated Montana from the new state of Idaho.

The slow progress of the train gave Mollie much time to go over the events of her stay in Salt Lake. Her difficulties finding work still rankled, and yet if she hadn't gone to Salt Lake where Edna was working, she wouldn't be on this train now headed for an adventure she could scarcely imagine. The memory of the scene on her walk with Frank persisted with a dull pain, like a headache at the base of her brain. For all their fighting that last year together, had he perhaps needed her more than he had let her know? But would it have made any difference? It wasn't just the fighting—the fighting was only a sign that the marriage had already begun to sour. As Mollie thought back over their years together, she realized that something had changed as soon as she had graduated from medical school, almost four years before. They had begun to lose the sense of intimacy that had once been so strong; their lovemaking occurred less often, was more perfunctory. She considered that perhaps Frank, too, like so many other doctors, unconsciously harbored an antipathy to women in his field. It's true he had encouraged her. Yet could she expect him to be immune to the cultural attitudes that prevailed among his male colleagues? She looked out at the mountains moving slowing past the window. The train was approaching the Continental Divide. Enough of these questions. It didn't matter any longer.

Mollie had never seen such a landscape. To the east the Centennial Range rose, snow-covered, like gigantic white teeth ready to bite at the sky. And to the west the vast, cold Beaverhead Mountains towered in the distance, lower foothills enclosing the valley as the little train climbed toward the narrow Monida Pass into Montana. For a flatlander from Iowa, the land was awesome, even frightening, but with a majesty that dazzled her. Although she had passed through high mountains on the transcontinental route coming into the Salt Lake Basin, she had been too preoccupied with the turmoil of her thoughts and emotions to pay attention to the scene beyond the train window. Now it seemed like she was seeing the world outside for the first time in months.

Occasionally along the tracks were small settlements—Spencer, Humphrey, finally the Divide at the town of Monida. Now and then Mollie could see a ranch house and barns in the distance and cattle huddled together in the snow-covered fields. She wondered how people could survive the isolation and loneliness of such a life. The scene made her shiver, as if the cold were penetrating the train window.

Beyond the pass into Montana, the tracks followed along the Red Rock River, came to a lesser pass at Clark Canyon, and then leveled out along the Beaverhead River. Unlike the vast, barren coldness of the

Idaho side, the snow in the Montana river valleys was lighter. The willows and cottonwoods along the icy banks stretched their bare arms toward a winter sun. Huge redrock cliffs rose up from the valley, too steep to hold the snow. Mollie felt a sense of wonder stirring in her. This silver land, which promised her future, stunned her with its beauty.

It was late afternoon when the train pulled into the U&N station at Dillon. Mollie asked the porter to deliver her suitcases to the baggage master; she would claim them the next day. As the train left the station to continue its run up to Butte, Mollie spied the hotel J. Henry had mentioned across the tracks and a block down Montana Avenue. She picked up her overnight case and her medical bag and crossed over the tracks to the street. The hotel clerk was expecting her.

"You must be the new doc at Bannack." The clerk looked her over in a way that hinted at his curiosity—and maybe something more. "Mr. Longmaid said you was a woman." He was young, hardly out of his teens. Not old enough to deal with the surprises that might present themselves at his desk, such as lady doctors. "Mr. Longmaid said to tell you the wagon will pick you up around eight. Ol' Billy's already in town, stayin' over at his brother's place. Dinner is served in the dinin' room startin' six thirty. Breakfast anytime seven to nine." The boy pointed to the long hall that ran from the reception area to the back of the hotel. "Privy's down there and out the back." Mollie took the room key and thanked the boy with a smile.

The furniture in the room was sparse: a wardrobe with mirrored doors, the mirrors already veined with age, a washstand with an enamel pitcher of water and a basin, a night table with a kerosene lamp. The room was clean, but a musty smell of previous inhabitants hovered in the air, and she immediately opened the window. The only thing that interested her was the bed. She made her way in the cold out to the privy, then came back to lie down until dinner. She had been up since the middle of the night, and the train ride had taken ten hours.

Mollie was surprised to find it was early morning when she awoke, still wearing the petticoat in which she had lain down to rest. She had been so tired she had slept through dinner and on through the night. She was hungry. She washed and dressed and went down to the dining room for breakfast, then to wait for the wagon to Bannack.

A few minutes after eight, the young desk clerk from the night before came into the dining room to tell her that Billy was outside waiting for her.

"Please tell him to go over to the station and get my suitcases from the baggage master. I'll be ready in a few minutes."

She finished her breakfast, gathered her bags, and went out to the front of the hotel. Billy was just coming back across the tracks with her luggage.

"We got a ways to go, ma'am," he said as he helped her up onto the seat beside him. "'Bout 25 miles to Bannack." He slapped the reins on the horse's flank, and the wagon turned west out of town. They moved out onto a broad, lonely plain. An early snow had melted, leaving a bleak, winter-dead scruff of greasewood and grass. In the distance the cone-shaped Baldy and the silver peaks of the Big Hole Divide reflected the morning sunshine. The road was rough, and Mollie was grateful the buckboard seat was stuffed with horsehair. She had been afraid that she might have to ride 25 miles sitting in silence, but quickly discovered that Billy was a talker. He was full of stories about Bannack, and she was eager to hear them.

"Been here nigh onto thirty years," Billy said in answer to Mollie's question. "Me and my brother, we came here in the first rush, back in '62. We panned the Grasshopper and did pretty good for usselves for a while there. But then Jimmy—that's my brother—decided to go over to Alder Gulch by Virginia City with just about everyone else. I stuck around and panned some of the other creeks. But then the big guys came in with their hydraulics and stamp mills and all, and I decided it were a lot easier just to run this here livery business. Jimmy, too. He's a blacksmith by trade, and he made a good livin' over in VC. But 'bout ten years ago when folks left over there he come here to Dillon. He got hisself a nice wife, and he's doin' real good for hisself blacksmithin'."

Billy drove on in silence for a while. Then he turned to Mollie: "You heared about what happened in Bannack back in the '60s with them road agents?"

Mollie confessed she didn't know who or what a road agent was. "Tell me about them, Billy."

"Well, I reckon folks all over Montana knows what happened here when the vigilantes went after them road agents. You see, this feller Henry Plummer come to town in '62. And he acted real nice and friendly to everyone. Why, he was even friends with Judge Edgerton, the chief justice when this was part of Idaho Territory, invitin' him an' his missus to dinner and all. But then he got in a fight with Hank Crawford. Hank was sheriff here then, and he shot Plummer in his trigger arm. Well, some of Plummer's friends took him over to Doc Glick's place to get his arm fixed up. They told the doc, 'If Plummer dies, we'll blow your head off.' The doc fixed him okay, but Plummer had to learn to shoot with his left hand. Meanwhile Hank didn't wait around for Plummer to get even. He hightailed it out a here back to the States.

"Well, that left Bannack without a sheriff, and folks here abouts thought Plummer was so nice they elected him. And as sheriff he got to know what was goin' on, when the stage was carryin' gold out, or when somebody was goin' to be ridin' along the road to VC. Well, Plummer had this gang of road agents, see, and he'd tell the gang to rob the stage and kill the travelers to get the gold. Folks say Plummer and them road agents killed over a hundred men in less than a year. But don't you worry, ma'am. That was a long time ago. The vigilantes caught most all of 'em."

"So what happened to them?" Mollie asked.

"Hanged 'em. All except a few what got away when they seen what happened to their friends. The gallows is still up on the hill there waitin' for 'em."

"Well, I'm glad to know the town's still ready for them," Mollie said, laughing. "But tell me, what's going on in Bannack now?"

"Why, Bannack's a mighty fine little town now. Respectable-like. We've got a school and a church and a fine Masonic lodge. And two hotels. The Meade, that's where J. Henry's fixin' to put you up. You'll like the Meade. It's real fancy now it's been painted up new and all. Used to be the courthouse, before they moved the county seat to Dillon." Mollie idly wondered what "real fancy" might mean to Billy. "And a couple a doors up is the Goodrich," Billy went on. "My livery's behind the Goodrich. I reckon you're gonna need a horse for ridin' around to sick folks. Well, you just come back to my place, Doc, and I'll fix you up with a good 'un. And I got one of them special lady saddles you can use."

"Thank you, Billy. I appreciate that." Mollie sat back and laughed to herself. So this must be the "Wild West" she had always heard about.

"Of course you gotta be careful ridin' around here by yourself," Billy continued. "You're gonna need your gun with you just in case."

"What do you mean 'just in case'? In case of what?"

"Well, ma'am, I don't mean to be worryin' you or nothin', but sometimes some of them prospectors out in the gulches . . . well, you know, ma'am . . . maybe they ain't seen a woman for a while . . . you know. . . ."

Mollie was considering how to respond when the wagon suddenly lurched to the side, making her grab for the seat rail. Before she could see what had caused the commotion, Billy had pulled a revolver from his pack on the seat and was shooting at the ground. The horse jumped around at the sound, jerking the wagon back and forth. A noise like an electric buzzer cut the air and then stopped.

"Got 'im!" Billy was exuberant. "Just a minute, ma'am, I'm gonna have me that snake for dinner." He jumped down from the wagon. "Funny he's out so late. Most of 'em are holed for the winter. He's so big, though, he must a got hungry, come out lookin' for somethin' to eat."

Mollie gave a shudder as she watched him coil the 6-foot rattler and put it behind the seat. The idea of eating the thing was revolting. She realized this was something she'd have to get used to. After she was settled, she'd ask Billy to show her how to use a gun.

The excitement over, the horse resumed his steady pace. Mollie turned to Billy: "You were telling me about Bannack, Billy. Please go on."

"Well, Bannack ain't nothin' like it use to be back in the rush, when Jimmy and I first got there. Folks say there was maybe 3,000 miners in town in those days. Of course there weren't no good houses back then, just shacks and tents and all. But then almost everyone just plum up an' left 'cause a the strike in Alder Gulch. Now there's only a couple hunnerd folks livin' in town, but it's a real nice town with nice houses. Fifty or so of those folks work for J. Henry. That English company he works for bought a bunch of mines last year: the Wadams and Golden Leaf and French Excelsior and Wallace. The Golden Leaf mine's got electricity inside, too. They built a new mill down below town on the Grasshopper where the old Shenon plant use to be. And they run the big Golden Leaf general store in town. There's lots of families now, lots more than in the old days. Miss May Coll, the schoolmarm, has her hands full, I'm tellin' you. She must have 'bout fifty or so children in that schoolhouse."

Mollie made a note of the name. As a former teacher herself, she knew that the schoolteacher was the one who probably knew the most of what went on in a town.

"Ain't no unmarried ladies like you here, Doc. Except Miss May, but she's fixin' to git hitched to some feller back east as soon as school's out, or so I heard. And there's some young girls growin' up in the families that ain't so real young anymore. Then there's the girls in Ma Stewart's boardinghouse who work either at Minnie Sanders's place, or upstairs at the Bank Exchange Saloon. But they ain't ladies like you. No, ma'am."

So—she would not be only an oddity as a woman doctor, she would be an oddity because she didn't have a husband. She hoped they would get used to it.

The wagon crossed Rattlesnake Creek, and in a short time Mollie saw a road leading off the main wagon road to the right.

"That there's the road to Argenta." Billy motioned with his arm. "There's a heap a silver come out a there. You see that smoke up there?" Mollie saw a billowing rising up from the basin to the north. "That's W. A. Clark's Tuscarora smelter." Mollie wondered if she was supposed to know who W. A. Clark was. The smoke from the smelter reminded her of Salt Lake, except that in this clear mountain air, it dispersed into the ether. "The Tuscarora's the last smelter up there now," Billy continued. "Mostly folks ship their ore to the big smelters in East Helena and Glendale."

A little after noon, Billy stopped the wagon. He climbed down and held up his hand to help Mollie. "I reckon it's time to give Charlie Horse here a rest, and for us to get some eats." Mollie had been getting hungry for the last hour, but it hadn't occurred to her to bring any food. She was feeling foolish; she hadn't even thought about how many miles it might be from Dillon to Bannack. Billy reached up into the wagon and brought down a water jug and a small box wrapped in brown paper.

"Folks back at the hotel fixed us some eats to take along," he said, handing Mollie the box. "J. Henry thought you might not remember to bring food, so he had me order up some for you when I stopped by there yesterday."

Mollie was relieved, but embarrassed that she had not thought to bring food. She would have a lot to learn. One didn't travel around in country like this without carrying food and water.

In the box were some slices of bread, thickly spread with butter, some jerky, and two apples. Plenty for both of them. Billy reached into his pack in the wagon, brought out two fairly clean enamel cups, and poured Mollie some water.

She found a rock to sit on and ate her lunch. After resting a few minutes, Billy climbed back up on the wagon and reached a hand down to Mollie. "We better git goin'. We ain't more'n halfway there yet, ma'am."

The sun moved slowly west with the wagon. Toward late afternoon it was shining in their eyes, hanging just above the tops of the Big Hole, casting long shadows on the land. Although Mollie was wearing her heavy coat, she was cold. Billy told her to pull the blanket out from behind the seat. Since that meant moving the deceased reptile, she decided she wasn't so cold after all. Despite the horsehair in the wagon seat, her back was aching from the constant jostling. That was another thing she would have to get used to. She had told J. Henry she could ride all over those hills. He had taken a big chance with her; she couldn't let him down now.

Finally, over a rise she could see that a fork bent off to the south.

"We're almost there, Doc. The road straight ahead goes on up to

Big Hole Pass. That there's the fork to Bannack." Billy pointed to the turn. "We got just another 4 miles." She was relieved: Her back felt about ready to give out.

Just then they heard the stage coming up behind them.

"You could a come on the stage," Billy said, "but it goes out of the way up to Argenta. It's a mite faster than Charlie Horse here, but we'll get there almost the same time." The stage was the only vehicle they had seen on the road all day. They waved to the driver as Billy pulled over to let him pass.

The road soon joined the edge of a wide creek. "This here's Grasshopper Creek what started it all back in '62," Billy said. "A couple a fellers from Colorado were just passin' through and stopped to pan the creek and found a pile a gold."

Mollie looked at the devastated creek. Pieces of old wooden sluice boxes were scattered along the bank, and rusting metal sculptures stuck up out of the ground, the arms and legs of some abandoned apparatus. Their use she couldn't imagine. The devastation, however, was what had been done to the land along the banks. Hydraulic hoses had stripped off the sage and greasewood, and eaten into the dirt and rock along the sides, leaving humps and mounds of debris at intervals along the banks. The detritus of hope and greed, and probably disillusion for some—those who didn't get in on the rape fast enough.

A little farther along they passed some granite markers and a few forlorn rectangles of picket fence. "That there's the new cemetery," Billy said, following Mollie's gaze. "The old one's up by the gallows."

Not the most inviting entrance to a town—death and debris to welcome the weary traveler. Not far ahead, under a broad, looming mountain, Mollie could see smoke rising from a small settlement.

"Here we are, ma'am. This here's Bannack." The road widened into a main street, lined on either side with boardwalks. Several small wooden houses were set back on both sides, with commercial buildings adjacent to the boardwalks. The air was heavy with the smoke of woodstoves. From the raucous noise coming from one of the storefronts, Mollie surmised it must be a saloon.

"That there's the Bank Exchange Saloon," Billy said, confirming Mollie's thought. "And over here's Skinner's Saloon." He pointed to a small building with two large paned windows on either side of a central door. "It's not a saloon anymore, more like a general store nowadays, but folks still call it that. Dunno why—they hanged Skinner over in Missoula 'bout thirty years ago. And this here next to Skinner's the Meade. J. Henry said to take you to the Meade. Said he and the missus would be meetin' you there at dinnertime. I reckon that'd be in a couple a hours from now. Gives you some time to settle in and all."

Billy stopped the wagon in front of a two-story brick building with a broad front porch and a balcony above. Mollie surveyed Bannack's gesture to elegance as Billy helped her down from the wagon and then followed her up the front steps with her suitcases. As she entered the hotel, she could see immediately what Billy had meant by "real fancy." The hotel had been recently painted. Mollie could see into the dining room, where the tables were covered with white linen cloths and set with elegant china. Sturdy wooden chairs were set around the tables, and the walls were freshly papered in a deep red pattern. A woman came forward from the back of the hotel to greet her.

"Why, you must be the new doctor for the Golden Leaf Company," she said, looking at Mollie with obvious curiosity. "Mr. Longmaid said you would be traveling alone. I'm Mrs. Meade, and my husband, John, will be in to say hello right away. We're pleased to have you staying with us."

The woman's greeting was cordial enough, but something in her tone put Mollie on her guard. Clearly, they were not used to a woman traveling alone.

"I'm Dr. Moore," Mollie said formally, accepting Mrs. Meade's extended hand. "You have a lovely hotel here. I'm sure I'll be very comfortable."

"You must be exhausted, Doctor. It's a long ride from Dillon. You go on up to your room and rest. I'll have John bring your bags up in a few minutes. Mr. and Mrs. Longmaid will be joining you for dinner at seven."

Mollie turned to Billy, still standing in the lobby. "Thank you, Billy, for all your help and for telling me so much about Bannack. I'll be around to your livery to talk to you about a horse in a day or two when I get settled. And enjoy your dinner," she added with a laugh.

"Thank you, ma'am." He grinned back at her. "I will. That's a fat 'un." Mollie's smile didn't let on what she thought of Billy's dinner. She picked up her handbags, took the key from Mrs. Meade, and climbed the stairs to her room.

CHAPTER FOUR

The New Doc Is a Woman?

A FEW MINUTES LATER JOHN MEADE brought Mollie's suitcases up to her room. Tired as she was from the long ride, she didn't want to fall asleep as she had the night before. She was eager to meet J. Henry and his wife and discuss what her duties would be. She spent the time until dinner unpacking, hanging her wrinkled dresses in the wardrobe, and putting things in the highboy. The room was attractively furnished with a comfortable bed, a flowered china pitcher and basin on the washstand, the wardrobe and mahogany highboy, and a dainty writing table and chair. The walls had been freshly papered with a soft pink-flowered design, and a tall, lace-draped window looked out onto the balcony and the street below. Mollie found the elegance of the room an astonishing contrast from what she had expected when she and Billy had driven up the rutted Main Street past the small clapboard bungalows, the mortared log cabins, and the wooden, false-fronted stores. The Meade's proprietors clearly entertained grandiose expectations for their newly refurbished establishment.

At seven o'clock Mrs. Meade knocked on Mollie's door. "The Longmaids are waiting for you in the dining room," she said when

Mollie opened the door. An enticing smell of roasting meat wafted up the stairway.

"Please tell them I'll be right there." Mollie combed out her long hair and pinned it up in back, put a finishing touch of powder to her nose, and went down to greet her new employer.

J. Henry rose as she entered the room. "How nice to see you again, Dr. Moore. And this is my wife, Janette." Mollie shook hands with them. She could see that the young woman wasn't feeling well. She was pretty, with light blond hair braided into a bun and pale blue eyes, but her face was drawn, and a puffiness about the eyes suggested that she was retaining water. She looked to be only about twenty, several years younger than her husband.

"I do hope you're feeling better, Mrs. Longmaid. I'm sorry we couldn't meet in Salt Lake."

"Oh I do feel a bit better now, Dr. Moore. But I want to make an appointment with you as soon as you're settled."

"I hope your trip in the buckboard wasn't too tiring," J. Henry said as he held out Mollie's chair. "You could have come in on the stage, but it makes a detour up to Argenta on the way. Since I needed Billy to go into Dillon for some supplies, I thought it would be easier for you to come back with him."

"It was tiring, but Billy's company was so enjoyable I hardly noticed. I now know a good deal of the history of Bannack and a little bit about who's who in western Montana."

"I rather thought you two would get along," J. Henry said, laughing. "Billy's an institution around here. He's been here longer than anyone else in town, knows everyone and everything."

There were only two other parties at table in the dining room: a couple with a young child, and an older man sitting alone. Mollie noticed that J. Henry nodded at both of them.

Dinner at the Meade was whatever the cook was preparing that day, and Mollie was delighted to learn that the delicious smell that had come up the stairs earlier was roast lamb with mashed potatoes. J. Henry asked for a bottle of California wine from the private stock he kept at the hotel. Janette just picked at her dinner and refused a glass of wine, but Mollie was hungry. Since breakfast in Dillon, she had eaten only bread and jerky and an apple all day. The wine was delicious and it quickly warmed her to her new friends, to her new home.

"Mr. Longmaid . . . ," she began.

"Please call me J. Henry. We're very informal here in Bannack."

"Of course. And you must call me Mollie. Now, J. Henry, when you have some free time in the next few days, I would like you to show me around the mines. I want to understand the working conditions of the men who may become my patients. And I especially want to see the mill. Billy told me about your new mill. He said you have twenty stamps there now."

"Indeed," said J. Henry, "the new stamp mill has made an enormous difference in our production. I'll be glad to give you a tour. I should have some time for that next week. But I'd like to see you before then, I hope tomorrow afternoon. We need to discuss where you'll be working. The Matthews house is currently for rent. I think it would be a good place for your office, and big enough for you to live in as well. I'll take you there tomorrow, and, if you think it appropriate, the company will contract with Mr. Matthews.

"As for the working conditions, our major mine, the Golden Leaf, is recently enlarged. The addition of electricity has cut down on the kinds of accidents that can occur from inadequate lighting. But a big problem here is alcohol. We watch the miners carefully to make sure they aren't drinking in the mine or that they don't come to work with whiskey on their breath. But the problem is more social. Saturday nights can get pretty rough in Bannack, and the drinking can be hard on the wives and children, who are often the victims. There doesn't seem to be much one can do to control this, and the women are usually afraid to ask for help. I am hoping that as both a doctor and a woman, you'll be able to talk to them. You can expect to be pretty busy on Saturday nights, since that's when the gunshot cases will be brought to your door."

"I guess that cuts me out of the Bannack nightlife," Mollie said, laughing.

"Oh, you'd be surprised just how much nightlife there is in this little town," Janette said, entering the conversation for the first time. "We have socials and dancing parties, sometimes two or three a week, and the children are welcome, too. And now in winter there are skating parties."

"Those are usually on Saturday nights, though," J. Henry added with a grin, "but you might get in a few turns around the pond before the shooting starts." Mollie laughed, aware he was teasing her. "Most of our miners live here in town," he continued. "But occasionally you'll be called out. The company, of course, will cover all your expenses relating to our people. Billy will fix you up with a horse."

"Yes," Mollie said, "he and I have already discussed that. I told him I'd be around to the livery as soon as I got settled."

"Of course," J. Henry continued, "you'll need to make your own arrangements for payment from people not with the company. Don't be put off by the looks of things around here. Even though conditions are primitive, some of these folks are doing all right for themselves."

"Thanks for the warning. I'll remember that."

When they had finished their dessert—Mrs. Meade's specialty, a deliciously smooth lemon custard—Mollie could see that Janette was tired. The young woman had said very little during dinner; it was clear that she wasn't feeling well. And she was rather shy, speaking mostly to her husband.

"I think it's time for me to retire," Mollie said. "It's been a very long day. I thank you for this delicious dinner." Turning to Janette, she added, "I'm so glad to meet you. We must get together as soon as I'm settled and talk about that baby."

J. Henry stood up as Mollie rose to leave the table. "Until tomorrow, then. I'll come around about two."

Although she was exhausted from the long ride, Mollie couldn't sleep. As she lay in bed, the events of the day washed over her. Clearly she was going to have to defend her status as a single woman and a doctor here. The coldness in Mrs. Meade's greeting rankled her. And Billy's commenting that she was the only single woman in town with the exception of the soon-to-be-wed schoolteacher, a few teenagers, and the soiled doves over the Bank Exchange Saloon meant that she would be viewed as an oddity, perhaps even as prey.

Well, what did she expect? She would be an oddity. Whoever heard of a woman doctor in a mining camp? But she didn't really care what people might think: She had taken the job, and she intended to see it through. She would carry a riding crop, and if she needed to use it on some old cuss—he'd better watch out. She wasn't sure she was ready to take up Billy's suggestion that she tote a pistol, however.

And then, as he did every night, Frank invaded her consciousness. He brought with him the lovemaking that was once so precious to her; he brought his anger at her in Osage, his tears on the street in Salt Lake. And she worried again over the letter she would have to write. The letter must have the right tone, let him know she was firm in her decision, but gentle and careful of his hurt pride. And grateful, too. She was grateful to Frank. For all their disagreements, he had indeed made sacrifices to help her. As she lay there sleepless, the words of her letter whirled into sentences and the sentences into paragraphs. And then the paragraphs rewrote themselves over and over into the night. It wasn't until early morning that she finally fell asleep.

After a late breakfast, Mollie had some time before J. Henry would take her to see the Matthews place, and first off she needed to attend to some business. She had brought a few medical supplies with her, but she needed to find out where best to procure a continuing supply.

"Could you tell me if there's a post office in Bannack?" Mollie asked her hostess.

"Of course there's a post office," Mrs. Meade responded in a slight tone of annoyance. "My husband gave up the postmaster job just last month to spend more time at the hotel and his pharmacy. The post office has moved temporarily to Athol Wright's general store up the street until a new postmaster is appointed."

Mollie found the store a few doors up Main Street, next to the Goodrich Hotel. Athol Wright was in the back discussing the relative merits of different brands of calf weaners with a customer, and paid no attention to her when she came in. After five minutes of waiting, Mollie started to fume at this "western" rudeness. Finally she broke into their conversation to inquire if Mr. Wright would be so kind as to provide her with some information. Athol Wright seemed startled at the edge in Mollie's voice and abruptly hurried over to her.

"I wonder if you could give me the address of the Central Pharmacy in Dillon. I will need to order some medical supplies."

"Why, ma'am, you must be the new doc." He didn't immediately answer Mollie's request. "I'm Athol Wright. Pleased to meet ya." Mollie politely took hold of Athol's extended hand. She realized she had better be careful. No need to make an enemy. Maybe time was measured differently in the backwoods of Montana.

"Sure, I'll get you that address, but John Meade has a drugstore right here in Bannack. I'm sure you can get anything you want at John's place."

"Oh, I'm sure I'll need many things from Mr. Meade"—Mollie smiled sweetly at him—"but still I would like to write for their catalog." Mollie realized she was undoubtedly stepping on some toes, but she sensed she should not be doing business with the Meades in matters of personal medicinal needs. Neither one of them had been very friendly toward her when she arrived yesterday. And during their dinner last night, J. Henry had recommended dealing with the Central Pharmacy in Dillon in order to maintain a degree of privacy for her patients. In a town of 200, anyone's business was everyone's business. Since Bannack had recently installed telephone connections with Argenta and Dillon, Mollie reasoned she could call the pharmacy and her supplies could be put on the next morning's stage. Even here, though, she knew she would have to be careful; the phone line was not private. Athol supplied her with the address, and Mollie sent off a letter requesting their catalog and expressing her desire to open an account. This first bit of business behind her, she bought some toiletries in the store and, having still an hour to spare, decided to take a walk around the town. The sky was a threatening gray; it would be snowing soon, but she was warm in the fur-lined coat she had brought from Iowa. She had known Montana would be cold, but until now she hadn't thought any place on earth could be as cold as Iowa.

Her first Bannack encounter was with a swarm of schoolchildren returning after lunch to their classroom in the Masonic temple opposite the Meade. Someone new in town was an exciting event, and the children stared at her, whispering to each other. As a former schoolteacher, Mollie was fond of children. Their tendency to giggle and whisper didn't rile her as it had some of her teacher colleagues. She and Frank had determined early in their marriage that they would not have children of their own. Or was it just she who had decided that? She had asked herself this more than once in the past few months. Children would be the end of her career. She couldn't have a medical practice and be a mother at the same time, and she had made her choice. Frank had agreed about the children, or at least he'd said he did.

As she passed the Bank Exchange Saloon, a row of men sitting on the bench out front stopped talking about whatever it was they were talking about, and stared.

"I reckon that must be the new doc Longmaid hired," she heard one comment. "She ain't bad lookin', but why in hell did he hire his-self a woman?"

"Probably 'cause a that fancy New York wife of his'n," said another. "Wait'll that she-doc has to deal with them Krauts and Bohunks he's got workin' in the Golden Leaf. If she thinks they're gonna let her look up their assholes—well that'd sure as hell be fun to watch." Naturally, all of this was spoken loud enough to ensure that Mollie could hear.

J. Henry was waiting for her on the porch of the Meade. He had the key to the Matthews house, and they walked the short distance down and across Main Street. The little whitewashed structure was set back, shaded by large cottonwoods, and separated from the street by a white picket fence. An acorn pattern of trim decorated the edge of the roof. It was small, as were nearly all the houses in Bannack, consisting of a large room in the front of the house, a kitchen in the back, and a bedroom with a door connecting back to the front room. Shuttered windows opened on either side of the front door. A small potbellied stove stood in one corner. The bedroom contained a primitive bed and a scattering of odd chairs. In the kitchen was a large woodstove and a table with three chairs.

"I think this will be fine," Mollie said to J. Henry. "I can use the front room for my office, although I'll need a bed to put in there and cupboards and shelves for medicines and equipment. I could use another table and some more chairs, and the bed needs a better mattress."

"That's no problem," said J. Henry. "I'm sure we can find what you need. I'll check over at the Golden Leaf store and at Wright's. Athol always knows who's coming and going from town and who wants to sell their household things."

Within the week J. Henry had acquired what Mollie had requested to furnish her office and living quarters. And he had ordered a cord of stove-cut firewood delivered to the back of the house. Mollie was glad to move out of the Meade. She didn't feel comfortable there, although she had to admit that her room in the hotel was more elegant than what she would have at the Matthews house.

Looking around her new home, Mollie couldn't help laughing. The little house was a far sight from her family's home back in Iowa: the parlor with its horsehair sofa and side chairs and the little, marble-topped mahogany tea tables; the dining room with its rose-patterned wallpaper and the ornate hand-painted gas lamp that hung over her mother's large dinner table; the silver tea set on the sideboard—it had been her job to polish it every Saturday morning. She knew Adelia Sophia would be appalled if she could see her daughter's new home in the Wild West.

Mollie tried out several of Billy's horses until she found one that suited her, a four-year-old chestnut mare. She stopped by the livery every day that first week, and if the mare was there, she'd give her a treat, a lump of sugar or an apple; if she had time, they would go for a short ride. Mollie had grown up with horses, and she knew it was important for the horse to bond with her.

"She's a wonderful horse, Billy," Mollie said to the liveryman as she dismounted from a ride and tied the mare's reins to the hitching post.

"I can't promise she'll always be here when you need her," he said. "But if you know ahead of time, I'll keep her back for you."

Over the next weeks, winter set in with teeth-chattering ferocity. The *Dillon Tribune* reported that one night it was twenty below in Bannack. The Longmaids had invited her to Christmas dinner at the Meade—a much happier Christmas than the one she remembered from the year before, alone in Mrs. Schwantes's house—and Mollie met some of the other mine owners and their families at the event.

Since she had arrived, a few of the more outgoing women had stopped by the office to visit. There had been one childbirth, but otherwise business was slow—too slow. Clearly, it was going to take some time for the men to get used to a woman doctor. She had sought out the schoolroom in the Masonic lodge shortly after her arrival and introduced herself to May Coll. Mollie sensed immediately that May was a woman she could talk to, and she invited her to visit that evening—her first guest. Although May was somewhat younger, Mollie felt the two would become friends.

May was from Kentucky. She had answered an ad for a schoolteacher in Montana. "I thought it would be an adventure, coming up here," she said to Mollie on the evening she stopped by for a visit. "And it certainly has been. But it's hard, too, being away from my family and friends for so long. I've been here three years now, although I've gone back summers. I've got a fiancé in Kentucky, and I'm going back at the end of the school year. Jim's just been appointed to a teaching position in Lexington, and we're going to be married in the fall. They haven't found my replacement yet, and that worries me—worries me for the children. I'm concerned about several of them. An awful lot of drinking goes on."

"Yes," Mollie said. "J. Henry told me about that. He, too, is concerned about the children."

"I know your job here is to look out for the Golden Leaf miners," May said. "But if you ask me, it's the women who need help. Some of them seem to get pregnant every year. They're exhausted. Two women died last year in childbirth, leaving a whole batch of children. I think they just wore out. Some of them came here years ago as mail-order brides, and their fate was to become baby-making machines. We've always had a man doctor either here in Bannack or coming in from Dillon, and either men don't know anything about how to stop women from having so many children, or they don't think it's proper to give them the information. I don't know. But unfortunately, you're going to find cases of self-induced abortions."

"What I hope to do," Mollie said, "is to get the women to talk to me. I know I can help them if they'll let me. A couple of women have stopped by, not to discuss any problems, but just to find out who I am. And I suppose to find out if I can be trusted. But since I've been here, I've had only one man come to my office. He'd broken his finger. I set it for him and put a cast on it. It will hurt for a while, and he'll have to be careful, but he'll be all right. I gave him a strong tea and sent him home. I hope he'll spread the word that even if I'm a woman, I can at least fix a broken finger."

"Don't worry," May said. "Wait till something awful happens. They'll come running. Two years ago we had the Russian flu through here, and the doctor was busy night and day. I think it was that flu epidemic that drove him out of here earlier this year. He just wasn't going to handle an onslaught like that again."

"Well, one good thing about this freezing weather," Mollie said, "it keeps the bugs down. Let's hope we have till spring before the germs unfreeze."

Mollie had had a lot of experience with childbirths in Chicago and with the women who'd come to Frank's office. She knew what could go wrong and how to handle the situation. But the kinds of epidemic illnesses that often ran through these camps—typhoid, diphtheria, smallpox, cholera, flu—made her apprehensive. She had seen these before. Flu was an annual occurrence, although in some years the strain was more virulent than in others. Diphtheria had hit Osage just a few years before, and she and Frank had worked night and day. They hadn't been able to save everyone, but at least there was a hospital they could send their patients to. Except for a small establishment run by Dr. Pickman in Dillon, the closest real hospital was Saint Joseph's in Deer Lodge— too far to be of any use in an epidemic. Here she'd be on her own.

Shortly after Mollie settled into her new office, Janette Longmaid stopped by for a social call and to make an appointment. The young woman was not so shy as she had been at dinner that first night. A native of New York, Janette admitted that her first sight of Bannack was a shock.

"J. Henry warned me," she said, laughing, "but still I couldn't imagine such a place." Mollie surmised that her shyness at dinner the other night, in addition to her not feeling well, was perhaps a reticence in the presence of her older and clearly more worldly husband. They agreed on the next day as a time for an examination.

"You don't know how relieved I am that you're here," Janette confided when she arrived in the office the following day. "I was too embarrassed to see one of those doctors who would come here from Dillon. I haven't been feeling well with my pregnancy, but I couldn't bear to have some man touch me in the way that doctors do." Mollie smiled at Janette's embarrassment. It was clear to her that Janette was the reason she was in Bannack. J. Henry must have told his wife that a woman had applied for the job, and no doubt Janette had talked her

72

husband into hiring her. Not that Mollie was to be the private physician to the Longmaid family. There were still those fifty employees of the Golden Leaf Company and their families.

While Janette went into Mollie's bedroom to undress, Mollie pulled the curtains and locked the front door. It wasn't the ideal setup for a doctor's office, but it was what she had. At least she could offer her patients a modicum of privacy. Janette came out of the bedroom wrapped in the sheet Mollie had given her and lay down on the office bed. The bed was as close as Mollie could come to an examining table, but at least it was firm. She had asked J. Henry to bring her some boards to put under the mattress, and they had raised it higher by nailing planks to the wooden legs.

Mollie took her stethoscope and listened to Janette's heart, then measured her blood pressure. It was a little higher than it should be. She felt along the belly—too early to tell much. It was the slight swelling around Janette's ankles and arms and the puffiness in her face that concerned her. Janette was retaining too much water, and this, along with her slightly high blood pressure, could lead to toxemia later on.

"So far everything's normal," Mollie said when she had finished her examination. "However, I want you to get rid of that water you're hoarding. I'm going to give you some diuretic pills. Although I don't have a scale here yet, I think you're heavier than you should be, and it's mostly just water. You've said that you are feeling nauseous much of the time. I think you have more than the usual gastric reaction. Your nausea should go away soon. I know it's such an awful nuisance, but it usually lasts only into the third month. Still, I do want you to get rid of that excess water."

"I'm so relieved to hear you say that," Janette said. "This is my first, and I just didn't know what it would be like. I will certainly take those diuretic pills."

Janette climbed down from the high bed and went into the bedroom to get dressed. When she emerged, she said: "Now I want to talk about something else. J. Henry and I are very happy to be having this child, and we want to have more, but not right away. I see these women around here—one after another. I don't want that, and I'll need your help."

"Of course," said Mollie, "we'll talk about it when the time comes. Don't worry. There are lots of things you can do."

"Thank goodness," said Janette, collecting her things to leave. "And I have a couple of friends I may be sending to you."

Mollie unlocked the front door. "Please do that, Janette. I'll look forward to meeting them."

As a married woman who had determined not to have children, Mollie had no sympathy with the exceedingly influential "purity" writers of the day, many of whom were doctors. Their attitude toward the wife was that she should either accept the inevitability of constant pregnancy or simply avoid the marriage bed. What particularly riled her was that some of the purity pundits were women doctors. Despite their own professional ambitions, they advocated that the only proper place for a woman was in the home.

Not only the purity marriage manuals, but even the professional medical journals were full of opinions about women: Frigidity was a virtue to be cultivated in that it kept the male disinterested and protected him from squandering his "vital forces." Mollie had laughed out loud when she read this. The prevailing fear of those writers was that the use of contraceptives would bring the ways of the licentious prostitute to sully the hallowed halls of the home. They seemed less concerned that virtuous frigidity might well drive men out of the hallowed halls to sully more sporting establishments. She was angry that just getting contraceptive supplies was difficult ever since Anthony

Comstock—a fanatical prude, in her opinion—had managed to get legislation passed that forbade the use of the U.S. mail to send contraceptive devices.

Mollie didn't want to deal with John Meade or anyone in Bannack for supplies. She would need to take the stage into town soon and make contact with the right person in the Dillon pharmacy. A few days before, she had received the catalog in the mail. One of the ads read: *"A full line of rubber goods at the Central Pharmacy."* This was the commonly acknowledged code that contraceptive articles were available. She would have to set up an agreement with the Dillon pharmacist to have them sent.

From what she was hearing, she might be spending more time ministering to the Golden Leaf wives than to the Golden Leaf miners.

If Mollie was concerned that the miners were too embarrassed to deal with her, or that, because she was a woman, they doubted her competence, this situation was remedied one freezing February night. She was awakened around midnight by a loud banging on the door. A young man, tottering from drink, was hollering something about a stabbing. Mollie told him to wait outside, then rushed to put on her boots and button her heavy fur-lined coat over her nightgown. Grabbing her bag, she opened the door and followed the man up Main Street to the Bank Exchange Saloon.

When she entered, she was blasted by the heat from two roaring woodstoves and the heavy smell of whiskey breath on the air. A crowd of men was hovering over something. She pushed her way through and found a man laid out on a billiard table, bleeding from the neck. She didn't need to ask what had happened.

She knew she would have to deal with this fast. There was no time for antiseptics. But then, the poor man probably had enough booze in him to kill anything from the inside out. The man stared up at her with the eyes of a frightened animal. As she applied pressure to slow the blood, she could see that fortunately the knife had just nicked the artery.

"You'll be all right, " she assured him. "It's not a deep wound."

Momentarily clamping off the blood flow, she managed to suture the cut. The man cried out in pain as the needle knit his life back together. Then she put some disinfectant on the wound and bound the neck with the bandage material she always carried in her bag. It was an unbelievable place to perform an operation, and she prayed there would be no infection. At least her tools were always kept sterilized for just such an emergency.

"You men make a stretcher," she ordered the crowd of onlookers. "Find a table or some planks and carry him home—and gently! He can't stay here on this billiard table. I'll check on him in the morning." She packed up her tools and left the saloon. She had no idea who had perpetrated this act, and she knew it was not her place to ask. If the victim survived, and she was sure he would, the men would probably find no reason to mention the affair to Sheriff Rose in Dillon.

J. Henry dropped in at her office the next afternoon.

"I understand you've been initiated into Bannack nightlife," he said, grinning. "I just stopped by to tell you that last night you established yourself. The men are very impressed. They were all buzzing about it when they showed up at the mine this morning."

"Well, it's only because that fellow, Kurt—I didn't learn his name till a couple of hours ago—has survived. He'd already lost some blood, but fortunately the wound wasn't all that bad. I went to see him earlier today—had to ask the bartender where to find him. He'll be all right, but he'd better lie low for a while for more reasons than one. Someone was pretty mad at him last night. And he sure made a mess of that billiard table," she added with a laugh. "The bartender isn't too happy with him, either."

"Well, the men think you performed a miracle last night, so let's just hold on to the rumors as they are," J. Henry said, smiling. He got up to leave and offered her his hand. "I knew I hadn't made a mistake when I hired you."

CHAPTER FIVE

A Boy with a Broken Leg

ONE AFTERNOON IN EARLY SPRING, as Mollie was walking home from the Golden Leaf store, her arms full of groceries, she saw a buckboard hitched to the fence in front of her house. A tall, thin man, unshaven, wearing somewhat ragged clothes, was walking toward her door. Mollie called to him: "Are you looking for me?"

The man turned and hurried toward her. "Are you the new doc?" he asked breathlessly.

"Yes. I'm Dr. Moore. Is something wrong?"

"It's my boy. He was up in the barn loft shovelin' hay down for the horses and tripped on a pitchfork and fell through to the floor. His leg's broke. Please, you gotta come right away. He's awful hurt."

"I'll be right there. Just let me put these groceries in the house and get my things." She went quickly into the house, set down the groceries, took a notepad and pencil, and went to the door.

"Where are we going?"

"It ain't far," was the reply. "Just down to Spring Gulch, 'bout 5 miles from here."

Mollie scribbled a note and pinned it on the door:

Have gone to Spring Gulch. Back tonight.—Dr. Moore

She had no idea where Spring Gulch was, only that it was 5 miles away. She grabbed her coat and scarf and her bag, and locked the door behind her.

The man gave Mollie a hand up to the wagon seat. "'Scuse me, ma'am. I didn't git around to sayin' my name. I'm Jeb Cartwright. And my boy's Davey." Jeb flicked the reins and the horse set off at a clip. "Me 'n Davey live alone down at Spring Gulch now the missus is gone. Davey's almost fourteen now. He's got a job sweepin' up for J. Henry at the mill. He was just finishin' up with the horses before goin' to work this mornin' when he fell. I didn't find him till a while ago."

"Where is he now?" Mollie asked.

"Me 'n Harry, we carried him into the house and laid him out on the bed. Took off his boots and pants. Harry's my brother, lives down behind us. We gave him whiskey so's it wouldn't hurt so much." She was immediately concerned—too much alcohol wasn't good for a young boy—but she said nothing. There was no point.

The road followed south along Grasshopper Creek, past the stripped dirt of the creek embankments and the persistent thumping of the Golden Leaf stamp mill that pounded her eardrums. The snow had only recently melted, leaving the road a muddy set of tracks. Jeb said very little as they drove. Mollie sensed his worry, which made her more apprehensive. She knew that this was another test. She had been lucky with the knifing at the Bank Exchange, but if she failed this time, she'd be back to zero with the miners. It had been hours since the accident occurred—she feared what she might find.

The two drove on into the cold of the dying day. Mollie had not yet explored this far south of Bannack. The land along the creek verges was littered with implements of the exploitation of hope, now carelessly abandoned to rust in the damp air. By the time the wagon reached Spring Gulch and then turned west for another quarter mile to the farm, the day had lost the sun behind the Big Hole.

Jeb pulled up the wagon in front of a cabin of rough logs. Behind it was a small barn, some horses, a cow, and a calf in a corral. At the far end of a stubbled hay field Mollie could see another cabin.

A middle-aged man with a grizzled beard emerged through the low doorway. "He's sleepin' now, Jeb. I gave him a good lot of whiskey, but he threw it back up. That leg don't look good."

Mollie grabbed her bag, jumped down from the wagon, and hurried into the cabin. In the fading light from the window, she could see the boy stretched out on the bed. His face still had traces of vomit. She sat down on the edge of the bed and drew back the soiled blanket that covered him. His shirt was filthy, and his skinny body smelled of sweat. It was obvious his clothes hadn't been washed for weeks, and by the smell of the blankets, they hadn't seen fresh air in years. She didn't bother to ask if there was a clean sheet in the house. She felt along the leg. The pitchfork had broken the skin, and dirt and some dung into which he must have fallen had penetrated the wound. Still, she was sure it wasn't a compound fracture. Her problem wasn't going to be the break, but rather the possibility of infection.

"Bring me some light," she ordered the two men, "all the lamps that you have, and set them on that shelf over the bed. Then you, Jeb, you hold one close here so I can see what I'm doing."

The boy stirred and began to whimper with pain. Mollie put her hand gently on his forehead.

"You're going to be all right, Davey. I'm a doctor and I've come to fix your leg."

81

"Mama," mumbled the boy. "You've come back." Tears had washed in streaks down the sides of his face. Mollie turned to Jeb, her eyes questioning him.

"He's never got over his mama leavin' us," Jeb whispered. "Sometimes I hear him cryin' at night. It's time he growed up and gets over it. Damn bitch. She ain't worth not one a his tears. No, ma'am. Not one . . ."

"Shhh." Mollie put her finger to her lips, her eyes warning Jeb to keep quiet. "Stoke up that stove." She turned to the man she presumed was Harry—the men had been too distracted to introduce her. "I need hot water. And get me a board. We've got to splint this leg."

Harry built up the fire under the kettle on the stove, then disappeared out the door. There was the sound of nails being yanked out of wood, and he returned in a few minutes with a short piece of rough-sawn 1-by-4 plank he had pulled from the side of the barn.

"That will work just fine," Mollie said as she pulled several small jars, some clean towels, and a roll of bandage material from her bag. She took a flask of antiseptic soap and one of the towels and went over to the bucket of water and basin on a table next to the stove and washed her hands. She motioned to Harry to do the same. Then she drew out some peroxide of hydrogen, sterile cotton, and a small flask of chloroform. She poured a few drops of the chloroform onto a towel and held it a couple of inches above Davey's nose. Davey began to relax, and Mollie counted his pulse.

"Jeb, I want you to hold the lamp so I can see. And Harry, cleaning out this wound will hurt Davey a lot, so I want you to hold the chloroform above his nose, just enough so you can see he's not feeling anything. I'll keep an eye on you. It doesn't take much. Can you do that?"

"I'll try, ma'am." Harry moved to her side and took the cloth.

Carefully, Mollie swabbed down the bruised and broken skin with the peroxide. Davey jerked at her touch, and Harry jammed the chloroform down on his nose.

"Gently!" Mollie barked in a loud whisper. "Be careful! Keep it off his face. He doesn't need to be put out." She was glad Davey had already thrown up the whiskey.

When she had cleaned the wound, she took a roll of muslin bandages and a small sterile dish from her bag. Taking some hot water from the stove, she poured it into the dish, added several ounces of laudanum, and immersed the bandage in the mixture. Gently but firmly, she wound the laudanum-soaked bandage around Davey's leg. Then she took a pillow from the bed, placed it on the board Harry had fetched, and set them under Davey's leg. With adhesive plaster she bound the leg tightly to the board and pillow.

Mollie turned to the men and motioned them to step outside with her. "The fracture isn't severe," she said when she was sure they were out of earshot. "It should heal in a few weeks. My concern is that the wound doesn't become infected. His leg took a nasty tear from that pitchfork. I've cleaned out his wound as best I can. I'll come down tomorrow to change the dressing and give him a bath. When he needs to, help him up so he can urinate. He seems to have lost contact with reality and he thinks I'm his mother. Please, Jeb, don't try to argue this with him right now. He's sick. He doesn't need any correcting from you. Whatever he says in his pain, just ignore it."

"Yes, ma'am," Jeb said, hanging his head. "I know you're right. I just hate to see him sufferin' over that damn bitch."

"We need to watch that wound so he doesn't get a fever. I'm leaving you some paragoric solution. It will help his pain. I want you to give him a teaspoonful every hour or so if he is awake and in pain. And please don't give him any more whiskey. The paragoric is better for him."

"Yes, ma'am. I'll do what you say."

"And Jeb . . ." Mollie steadied her eyes on him. "The boy needs some clean clothes. You've got to do some washing. You can't have him going around filthy like that."

Jeb seemed to hang his head even farther. "I know, Doc. It's just there's so much work to do around the place, and now that she's gone I just ain't had the time to do much washin'."

"Well, I left some carbolic soap on the table next to the stove. This evening I want you to boil up his clothes with that soap. Rinse them thoroughly and hang them out here in the fresh air."

"Yes, ma'am." He shifted his eyes back to the ground.

"Now it's late, and I have to get back."

Harry spoke up. "I'll take you back, Doc-ma'am. Jeb here's pretty tired and upset."

Mollie went back into the cabin to collect her coat and medicine bag. Davey was lying quietly. She went over to check and saw that he was asleep.

"Sleep well, son," she whispered. "I'll see you tomorrow."

Riding back in the buckboard with Harry, Mollie asked what had happened that Davey's mother had left them.

"Well, Doc-ma'am," Harry said slowly. "It ain't easy to say. Jeb's my brother and all, but in my opinion he didn't treat his wife good. He'd get to drinkin', and then he'd get mad and hit her if she said somethin' about it. One night 'bout four years ago there was such a row over there so loud I could hear 'em clean over at my place. I went over there and Jeb was drunker'n a skunk and beatin' up on Jill and she was cryin' and Davey was standin' there cryin' and beggin' Jeb to stop. Well, the next day I was walkin' over there and I seen her come out a the house. She was all bruised all over and was carryin' a big bag a somethin'. Clothes I guessed it was. She didn't say nothin' to me, just walked past me and went into the barn and saddled up the mare and tied that bag behind and took off down the road toward town. Next day I heard she'd took the stage to Dillon. Jeb had a pile a dust stashed in the house that he'd panned over on Horse Prairie. She took it while he was sleepin' off the drunk and plum disappeared with it. I don't blame Jill for leavin', Doc-ma'am, but it's been hard on poor Davey."

Mollie's heart sank into the gloom of the darkness around them. This was what May had been talking about. The drinking. She would have to ask her about Davey. School wouldn't be out for another month. Why wasn't he in school? He shouldn't be working at the mill at this time of year.

"Jeb's really not a bad sort, ma'am," Harry continued. "It's just he can't hold his liquor and then he gits mean. But he loves that boy, I know he does."

She didn't answer. She didn't put much stock in Jeb's ability to love if he treated his wife as Harry had described. And it was obvious he was keeping his son out of school, probably for the pittance Davey could earn.

Mollie was no teetotaler like the WCTU women who were agitat-ing to close down the bars and prohibit the sale of alcohol. She came from a family where wine was served from a crystal decanter for Sun-day dinner when friends came to visit. Yet when she heard stories like this one, she had to consider that maybe those women were right. She'd be sorry to forgo the Sunday wine, but if shutting down alcohol would stop people like Jeb from indulging himself in the contents of the liquor cabinet, she'd gladly pay the price.

The problem was that Mollie didn't believe the Women's Christian Temperance Union or the Anti-Saloon League or any reform group would be able to stop the Jebs of this world from getting hold of a bot-tle. And what's more, she was suspicious of the motives of some of the women. The WCTU was responsible for much of the "purity manual" misinformation about sexual behavior and contraception, literature that Mollie believed to be extremely damaging, especially to women. It seemed to her that although they were right to decry the effects of demon rum on American society, as well as the scourge of prostitution, many of them felt they had the right to impose their beliefs about what was appropriate behavior in all aspects of social and personal life. And with this Mollie strongly disagreed. She was particularly riled by Dr. Mary Wood-Allen, the national superintendent of the Purity Department of the WCTU, who cautioned a woman to endure the attentions of her husband without a particle of sexual desire, so as not to arouse immodest responses in him. It was the wife's duty to ensure through her sexless passivity that the marriage relationship would attain a level of platonic bliss. In a sense, the anti-sex argument was the same as the anti-alcohol argument: The woman's shining example of moral purity would deflect the man from indulging himself in the liquor cabinet.

Mollie thought that the "purity" people would more likely drive a man to drink. She had recently come across such an article advocating sexual passivity in a current issue of *The Ladies' Home Journal.* She wondered how a woman who claimed to be a physician could write such hogwash. Not only was such an attitude a disgrace to her profession, but this writer and her kind were driving a generation of women crazy.

Harry tied the buckboard to the picket fence and walked Mollie to her door, then waited while she lit a lamp in the front room.

"Thanks for bringing me home, Harry. I'll ride down tomorrow afternoon. Make sure that Jeb gives Davey that paragoric, but only one teaspoonful an hour. And remember what I said about no whiskey. Better be careful that Jeb doesn't take any, either. He's got to watch out for that boy."

"Yes, ma'am, I'll look in on them when I git back."

The next day at noon, Mollie stopped by Billy's livery. "I'd like to have the mare in about a half hour if she's available."

"She sure is, Doc," Billy answered. "I'll have her saddled and ready for you."

Then she crossed over to the Masonic hall to see May. She found her sitting outside in back on a bench, eating her bag lunch. Several of the children were sitting on the ground near her.

"Do you have any time now?" Mollie asked. "I have something I'd like to talk to you about."

"Run along and play, children," May said to the group near her. "You still have twenty minutes before we go back inside. Sit here, Mollie," she said, moving over on the bench. "What is it?"

Mollie told her about Davey's leg, and what Harry had said on the ride back. "Why isn't Davey in school? Did Jeb take him out?"

"I'm afraid so. Davey's a bright boy. He was doing well in class. But once he'd learned basic reading and writing and had a pretty good grasp of numbers, Jeb thought there was no need for Davey to spend any more time in school. I argued with him, but Jeb himself is only semi-literate; he couldn't understand the importance of Davey's continuing past the primary level. So the boy's been sweeping out that mill for the last year and a half.

"And I'm concerned about Davey for other reasons," May continued, looking out into the yard where the children were playing. "He was pretty upset when his mother left, and from what you just told me, he still is. Jeb has no idea how to deal with a complicated boy like Davey. I worry what's going to happen to him. I can't blame Jill for taking off like that. Living with Jeb's drinking was impossible. And she knew she couldn't take Davey with her. Jeb would just come after her, and God knows what would have happened to her when he found them. I don't think there's much money there. Jeb was working for

Longmaid for a while, but I heard he quit a while back and spends most of his time now over on Horse Prairie. I guess he's got a strike there that pays something.

"Look, Mollie," May said, turning to her friend. "This is something you're going to have to get used to. Like me, you're going to watch these children suffer. And you've got to be tough with yourself. There's nothing we can do but hope they'll be able to get out of here before they get sucked down into the booze just like their fathers—or worse." May had stood up from the bench and was pacing angrily back and forth. "I'm sorry, Mollie, but now I've got to call my brood back to school. We can talk more later."

As May rounded up the children, Mollie crossed the road to the livery. Billy was just bringing out the mare on a lead.

"I've got her all ready for you, Doc," he said as he tied the lead to the saddle and handed Mollie the reins.

"Thanks, Billy. I'll stop by my office to leave a note on the door and pick up my bag. I should have her back late afternoon."

The sky was flirting with a storm: sun-bright one minute, brooding-dark the next. Shadows formed on the Grasshopper, then disappeared, then returned. As she rode along the muddy wagon road to the gulch, May's words rang in her ears: *You're going to watch these children suffer and there's nothing you can do.* Davey Cartwright was probably just her first exposure. May had said there were several children who were victims of their parents', or at least their fathers', intemperance. Much as she disapproved of the temperance women's puritanical attitudes, she had to admit that they were indeed trying to do something on the political level about situations like Davey's. And that was probably the level on which one could best approach the problem. The only alternative would be to take a child like Davey under her own wing. And she couldn't do that; where would it stop? Her wings weren't broad enough to shelter all the hurt in the world, or even just the hurt here in Bannack.

The nacreous sky was oppressive, and Mollie watched it nervously. It seemed to be bearing down on her. She had experienced already the viciousness of Rocky Mountain storms. A few weeks earlier one of the Golden Leaf miners had been killed by lightning as he ran across the meadow toward his shack. Mollie had had to write a death certificate for the charred body.

She beat the storm to the cabin and called out to Jeb. There was no answer. Unhooking her leg from the saddle horn, she jumped down, tied the reins to a fence post, and went over to the door and knocked. Since there was no response, she entered the cabin. She stopped short in shock: The room stank of urine and whiskey. The stove was out and the room was cold. Davey lay on the bed moaning. His shirt was twisted around him, and he was wet with the sweat of fever. She hurried across the room and saw immediately that the bed was drenched in urine. He was unconscious; the water and paragoric she had left were still on the chest across the room, untouched.

"Jeb!" Mollie yelled, "Jeb!" There was no response. She rushed into the back room of the cabin. Jeb lay passed out on a bunk, an empty whiskey bottle near him on the floor.

"You goddamn fool!" she screamed at him. Jeb grunted and turned to the wall. She went back to the main room and picked up a half-full water bucket. She carried it into the back room and threw the water at Jeb's head.

Jeb screamed and sat up. Glaring at Mollie, he struggled to his feet and lunged toward her. "So you've come back, have you? You damn bitch. I'll teach you to take my gold!" Halfway across the room he tripped on his own feet and sprawled on the floor. For a moment he tried to get up, and then fell back with a groan and lay quiet.

Shaken, Mollie turned, ran out of the cabin, and grabbed the reins of her horse. Then she stopped. She realized Jeb wasn't coming after her. The enormity of the situation terrified her. She had to get Davey away from Jeb. But how? She had to get that fever down. He would catch pneumonia, lying there wet and cold. He was too sick to move, but if he stayed there with that maniac, he would die for sure. Maybe Harry . . .

She spied a man moving about outside the cabin at the end of the field. She untied the mare, mounted, and galloped across the field. The snow had started, and sleet hit her in the eyes.

"Has something happened?" he called in alarm as Mollie reined in her horse.

"Quick! I need your help!" Mollie was breathless. "Davey's bad and Jeb's drunk. He's delirious, too . . . thinks I'm Jill . . . threatened me."

Harry ran to the small barn behind his cabin. In a flash he had bridled his horse and thrown on a saddle. He galloped behind Mollie back across the field.

Jeb was still out cold when they got to the cabin. "Good," Mollie said, looking at the body on the floor in disgust. "At least that will keep him out of the way."

"Damn! I should a stayed here," Harry growled. "I should a know'd he might do this. I looked in on 'em when I got back last night. Davey was asleep, and Jeb said somethin' about he was gonna wash some clothes. I figgered everything was okay. I was just fixin' to come over when I saw you ridin' across the field."

"Never mind that now," Mollie barked. "Help me get Davey cooled down. Go get another bucket from the well. Hurry."

While Harry went out into the snow to get the water, Mollie eased the shirt off the unconscious boy. She felt his forehead. It seemed to burn her hand. She cursed herself for throwing water on Jeb, but then realized he was in no condition to help her anyway. "Help me hold him up," she said as Harry came in with the bucket. "We've got to get his fever down." Mollie poured some water into a basin and dipped Davey's shirt into it. She squeezed it out and began to mop the perspiration off of Davey's chest and back while Harry held him. Again and again she dipped the shirt into the water, wrung it out, and wiped the cool, damp cloth across Davey's skin. She pulled off his urine-soaked underwear and wiped the lower part of his body. "I wish we could immerse him, but I don't dare get that leg wet," she said to Harry. Finally Davey's eyes fluttered open. Mollie put her hand on his forehead. His temperature felt at least three degrees cooler.

"All right, get the stove going. We can't let him get chilled now that his temperature's down. And then get my saddlebag off the mare."

Harry went over to the wood box. It was almost empty. "Damn Jeb," he muttered as he lit the fire with the scraps. "Can't even keep the goddamn wood box filled." In a moment the fire flamed, and he went out to get Mollie's bag.

"We need to get him off this wet bed," Mollie said. "Bring that chair over here and let's try together to lift him over to it."

She turned to Davey: "We're going to help you stand up so you can move over to that chair. Then I want to take your temperature with this thermometer." She showed him the mercury-filled tube. "But it's made of glass so you must be careful not to bite down on it."

Davey gave a faint nod and then whispered, "My leg . . ."

They each grabbed the boy under an arm and lifted him over to the chair; Harry held him steady. Having nothing clean, Mollie wrapped the dirty sheet around his nakedness. Then she slipped the thermometer into his mouth. While Harry held Davey steady in the chair, Mollie dragged the filthy bedclothes off the bunk, took them out in the fresh air, and spread them on the damp dead grass. She was in luck: The snow had stopped; the storm clouds had moved on toward the Big Hole, and the sky over Spring Gulch was clearing.

Mollie came back into the cabin and took the thermometer from Davey's mouth. The fever was down to 102. She went into the back room. Stepping over Jeb, still sprawled on the floor, she pulled the bed-clothes off the bed. "They're not very clean," she said as she carried them back into the main room. "But Davey's mattress is wet. I'll hold him steady in the chair. You go out to the barn and get some hay we can spread on the mattress to keep him dry. We'll put these blankets on top of the hay."

In a few minutes Harry returned with a bundle of hay in his arms, and Mollie fashioned a dry bed. Together they helped Davey to lie back down. She spread Jeb's dirty sheet over him and turned to examine his leg, worried at what she suspected she would find.

"Harry, get some more wood. I need hot water. Put just a little water in the kettle so I can wash my hands as soon as it gets warm."

Harry found some pieces outside on the woodpile. While Mollie waited for the water to heat, she took the alcohol and laudanum and bandage material out of her bag and began to unwrap the splint.

Suddenly there was thumping and banging, the sound of someone staggering, coming from the back room. She and Harry looked at each other in alarm.

"He's crazy!" she whispered. "He thinks I'm Jill. Don't let him in here. He tried to attack me."

Harry rushed into the back room. Mollie heard Jeb growl: "Where's that bitch? I'll show her! Thinks she can come back here . . ."

Mollie heard a crack and thump of something falling on the floor.

Harry came back, rubbing the knuckles of his right hand. "I had to do that, Doc-ma'am. Had to keep him out a here. He'll be out for a while."

"Thank God you did!" Mollie breathed with relief. She poured the water that was now warm into the basin and washed her hands with disinfectant.

As she feared, the leg was infected. The bandage was wet with pus as she unwound it. Once again she asked Harry to hold a chloroform cloth over Davey's nose, and she cleaned the wound again as she had the day before. She wrapped the leg in a fresh bandage and bound the splint on again.

Then she turned to Harry: "We've got to get him away from Jeb now. He has to go to Dillon. I know it's 30 miles and he's in no condition to travel, but if he stays here, he'll die. Dr. Pickman has a place where he can stay. I wouldn't call it a hospital exactly, but it's the best Dillon has to offer. There's no adequate hospital until Deer Lodge, and that's too far to try to take him. The storm has passed, it'll be a clear night, but cold. You hitch up the wagon and lay a mattress of hay in it. I'll look for a shirt and underwear and some pants for Davey."

She remembered there had been some fairly clean clothes in the chest she had searched the day before. Davey had lost consciousness again, and his thin, feverish body was deadweight as she struggled to get clothes on him. She dressed him in all the sweaters and coats she could find.

Harry came back with a wagonload of hay. He spread Jeb's blankets over the hay, and then together he and Mollie carried Davey out of the cabin and lifted him onto the wagon. Then they piled more hay on top of him and the rest of the blankets.

"Jeb's going to go crazy when he comes to and finds Davey gone."

"I don't give a damn what he does," Mollie muttered under her breath.

"There's a shortcut from here over to the stage road. Cuts off going back to town first. Saves about 5 miles."

"Good," Mollie said. "I'll ride on back to Bannack and put in a call to Dr. Pickman. I'll tell him to expect you."

Mollie watched as the wagon headed east out of the gulch. A wave of apprehension made her feel light-headed. She knew it would be a miracle if Davey survived the ride. In a moment she gained control of herself and went back into the cabin. She gathered the filthy bandages into a sack and took them outside. She was in a hurry to get away before Jeb woke up. There was no time to burn the bandages.

As she was tying her bag onto the mare, she heard a roar from the cabin. Tossing down the sack of bandages and throwing on her coat, she grabbed the reins, hurriedly mounted, and urged the mare out of the farmyard.

As the horse settled into a steady trot along the road back to Bannack, Mollie became aware that she was shaking. The reaction to her near fight with Jeb, and the horror of Davey's condition, was pressing down on her. The boy needed more help than she could give him. All she had been able to do was clean him up and bring down the fever, at least for a while.

The 5-mile ride seemed twice as far as it had a few hours earlier. The night was full of noises that pricked at her consciousness. If she had believed there were any point in prayer, she would have prayed for Davey. But she knew she could not.

She stopped at Athol Wright's store. It was closed this late, but she roused him and put in the call to Dillon.

CHAPTER SIX

A Deadly Pregnancy

WHEN MOLLIE FINISHED EXPLAINING Davey's condition to Dr. Pickman on the telephone, she walked the horse over to the livery and hitched her to the post in front. She was so tired, she decided not to bother fixing dinner—just go straight to bed. She untied her saddlebag and was turning to leave when she saw Billy hurrying toward her from the barn.

"Dr. Mollie, wait!" Billy called, catching his breath as he reached her. "May Coll was by here just a few minutes ago lookin' for you. Askin' if I knew when you'd be back. Said one of her children's mothers is awful sick over on Yankee Flats. She left you this note." Billy reached into the pocket of his overalls and handed Mollie a folded piece of paper:

Mollie,

I'm over at the Braunfelses' place on the Flats. Therese has taken too much of something and I think she may have poisoned herself trying to deal with her latest problem. Come quickly, she's bad. Third cabin to the right after the bridge.

—May

Mollie immediately understood what May was suggesting; the note was written in such a way that Billy in his nosiness wouldn't catch on.

"Never mind putting her down," she said to Billy as she stuffed the note into her pocket and tied her saddlebags onto the mare again. "I've got to ride her over to the Flats right now."

She untied the reins and mounted. She kicked the horse to a gallop and headed across the Grasshopper bridge to the Flats. She knew there would be no chance to sleep now for hours.

Therese Braunfels had called on Mollie a couple of weeks before. In the course of her visit, Therese had casually mentioned that she was having some menstrual problems. The woman was in her middle forties, and the conversation had turned to the change of life. Mollie had suggested that most likely that was the cause of her irregular menses. It hadn't occurred to her that Therese was sounding her out, trying to determine if she could talk about an abortion.

Mollie was furious that she had failed to pick up on what Therese really had wanted. As a physician, she would not advocate abortion unless she thought a woman's life might be endangered by her pregnancy. While she certainly endorsed methods of contraception, and she herself had avoided conception during her own marriage, she could never accept abortion as a method of birth control. Yet she knew that abortion was all too common in every social class, a practice that often destroyed not only the fetus, but the woman as well. She was well aware that if Therese wanted an abortion, she would find a way to do it.

Women over the centuries had used natural herbs—tansy, rue, ergot, savin, pennyroyal, fennel, as well as stronger poisons of strychnine, calomel, iodine, or prussic acid—to induce "accidental miscarriages." Many of these substances were now made into pills and sold as "menses regulators" or "menstrual stimulators" or some such subtle code name that a woman could use with her pharmacist or her mail-order contact. Some of the mail-order companies even sold uterine probes and catheters to help a woman relieve her "female complaint." Doctors were reluctant to discuss abortion with their patients, either because of their own moral positions or for fear of litigation, leaving the woman to experiment on her own. The results were often disastrous. Mollie felt it was criminal for a mail-order company to advocate that a woman use some kind of probe on herself. She wished she had been able to warn Therese, at least to tell her what *not* to do. She berated herself for being so deaf to what the woman had been suggesting.

Mollie was familiar with the numerous reports of women who died from self-induced abortions, and of young, unmarried women, afraid of social condemnation, who destroyed their physical capability of ever having children. She blamed the moral prudery that seemed to grip the nation and had resulted in punitive legislation regarding dissemination of contraception information. She had read that the U.S. Post Office had confiscated 60,000 "rubber articles" in a single year. She wondered, grimly, if that represented 60,000 unwanted children being born—or maybe aborted? She also held culpable the unregulated pharmaceuticals industry that was not required to reveal the contents of the nostrums subtly advertised in women's magazines. The tragedy of all this was that either women continued to have unwanted children, at sometimes great physical and psychological expense for all involved, or they procured an illegal abortion or attempted self-abortion risking possibly worse consequences. And the irony was that prostitutes seldom got pregnant. They knew perfectly well how to avoid conception. It was the middle class, and sometimes working-class wives as well, who were the focus of all this hullabaloo about purity in marriage.

Mollie spied May standing in front of the Braunfelses' cabin, waving at her. She reined in the mare, jumped down, and tied her to the hitching post.

"Thank God you're here," May cried. "I was so worried you wouldn't get here in time. I hope you *are* in time! I made Maria—she's the oldest—get the children out of the house. They were crying, terrified. They don't know what's wrong with their mother, and of course I couldn't tell them. They've gone to a neighbor."

"Good they're not here. Now I'm going to need your help." Mollie grabbed her saddlebag and rushed into the house. Therese, her face a sickly pallor, lay on the bed. She seemed half conscious. Now and then her body gave a convulsive jerk and her limbs trembled. She was muttering as if responding to hallucinations. Mollie touched her forehead. It was cold. Her whole body was cold.

"Has she vomited?" Mollie asked.

"Yes, a little."

"A little isn't enough. We've got to keep her awake. Is there any mustard in the house?"

"I don't know."

"Well, we don't have time to look for it. There's some hot water on the stove. Pour me about a pint and cool it down to lukewarm. I've got some ipecac here that will make her vomit."

While May poured the water, Mollie lifted Therese to a sitting position and shook her. "Wake up, Therese. You mustn't sleep!" Therese opened her eyes and stared at Mollie in blank, unfocused fear. Mollie took her wrist and counted her pulse. The beat was rapid and much too weak.

May came over to the bed and handed Mollie a large cup of water. Mollie put several drops of ipecac into the cup.

"Now, Therese, I want you to drink this." Therese turned away from the cup.

"Drink this!" Mollie ordered in her most martial tone. "Now!"

Therese slowly began to sip from the cup. Then she tried to push it away, but Mollie forced it between her lips. "You must drink!" she ordered the woman. Therese swallowed and swallowed again. Suddenly she gave a loud burp and a groan of nausea.

"Quick, bring that basin over here," Mollie said pointing to an enamel basin on the washstand.

May rushed the pan to the bedside just as a stream of vomit erupted from Therese's mouth. When the waves passed, Mollie pressed more of the ipecac water on her. Again, the reaction was a watery vomit. When Therese had drunk all the solution, Mollie forced her to swallow plain lukewarm water. Therese would vomit the water and Mollie would force her to swallow again. Finally, when there was no longer a need to continue forcing the vomiting, she gently lowered Therese back down on the bed. Her body was still cold, and she was convulsively jerking and twitching. Mollie pulled the covers away, but there was no sign of blood.

She turned to May. "Dump this basin outside. Things are really going to get messy now that we've got her stomach empty. I've got to give her some calomel. Maybe I can purge the poison out of her. Did you manage to get her to tell you what it was she took?"

"I don't know," May said. "She mumbled something about pills. But what kind I don't know."

"Well, look around here!" Mollie snapped. "See if you can find the bottle." May hurried to do as she was ordered. It was not the time for niceties and politeness.

On a shelf above the washstand, May found a bottle with the name SIR JAMES CLARK'S PILLS on the label.

"Damn it!" Mollie cursed. "I might have known. Those things are deadly. How many did she take? See how many are listed on the label, and then guess how many are left in the bottle."

May measured out ten pills and then compared the amount in her hand to what was in the bottle. "The label says there were a hundred in the flask, and it looks like there's maybe thirty left. Of course we don't know how many she took. Maybe someone gave her the bottle, which may not have been full."

"Let's hope she didn't take them all," Mollie growled. She took her stethoscope and listened to Therese's heart.

"Whatever she's got in her, it's restricting her arteries. Where's Braunfels, anyway. Doesn't he know his wife is sick?"

"No, he doesn't," May answered. "Maria said he left early this morning on the stage to Dillon. He had some business at the bank there. He probably won't be home till tomorrow evening."

"I guess she figured to take care of her problem while he was away. Those children are going to be coming back soon, and you've got to go home and get some sleep tonight. Take my horse back to Billy's. Tell him to bring a wagon over here. We've got to get Therese over to my place. He and I can handle that. You just go on home."

"Sure, Mollie. I'll come by before school in the morning and see how it's going." May picked up her coat and went out.

Mollie heard her ride away, then settled down in a chair beside Therese to wait for Billy. She knew there was enough ergot and savin in a bottle of Clark's pills to abort a horse, but she didn't know how many the woman had taken or how long ago. If it was just after the children went to school, and she could find someone to watch the baby, it might be as long as five or six hours ago, and the poison would be well into her system. If less than that, maybe there was hope. If the calomel purge was effective, the ergot would probably do its job as well. She hoped Therese wasn't more than a month or so pregnant.

Mollie leaned back in her chair and closed her eyes, trying to rest without falling asleep. The tension of what she had just gone through with Davey and now Therese, as well as the 10-mile ride to the Cartwright place and back, made the muscles in her back and shoulders ache. When she felt herself nodding off, she stood up and paced the floor of the cabin to keep alert. She opened the cover on the gold watch she wore around her neck. Almost eleven. Harry should have gotten to Dillon by now.

She looked down at Therese. She hardly knew the woman. She didn't feel the sense of closeness she had felt for her patients in the past back in Iowa when she and Frank had worked together. For a moment the images of Rita and Michael O'Brian flashed across her mind. She thought of the office she had decorated for Frank and herself. There her skills and knowledge as a doctor were wrapped up in a package of elaborate presentation: the lace curtains, the soft color of the walls, the politeness, the discretion, the propriety of it all. Illness, especially among her middle- and upper-class women patients, was often a retreat from the boredom of their lives. Yet at the same time, both the men and the women often camouflaged the reality of their suffering, perhaps with alcohol, perhaps with just such pills as Therese may have taken, certainly by the easily accessible compounds of opium and morphine. All they had to do was send for the stuff and for the moment their troubles were over. The occasional deaths were of course lamented by all, explained as a matter of age, a deplorable accident, the inevitable toll of disease. The funeral orations invariably spoke of the deceased as "a pillar of the community" or "the strength and joy of all who knew her" or some such epithet of civic and familial honor. Never any mention of his alcoholism or her opium addiction or that she died by her own hand, scraping out her uterus.

Mollie might have gained a wider perspective on human suffering from her work in the Chicago hospital, but there she was merely a student observer, and the people who suffered there were strangers. Their diseases or traumas were objectified; any other aspect of their individual lives did not appear on the chart at the foot of the bed.

In Bannack, though, she had begun to understand her role of doctor in the community as something quite different from the easy class compatibility of Iowa or the disengaged objectivity of the Chicago hospital. She was beginning to understand that pain and disease and suffering were not separate from the lives of the people, not something that could be cured, made to go away. Any treatment she might offer would have to be tempered to the circumstances of the patient's reality. Thus Davey's broken leg was the result of his working in the barn instead of sitting in school, where he should have been. But Davey had an alcoholic father who felt school was irrelevant, who had driven Davey's mother away so that now there was no one to care for him, even to the extent of seeing that both he and his clothes were clean. And then Therese, a mail-order wife sent over from Germany years ago. She might die before the morning, trying to protect herself from the onslaught of humanity's emissaries emerging one after another from her womb, their exponential demands pushing her beyond her ability to cope. Therese simply couldn't make room for another body, no matter how small, in the bed the children all shared. Mollie realized that in this case, Therese's ignorance was caused in part by her limited knowledge of English, and in part by a society that purported to dictate moral behavior to a woman, as if it had any idea of the reality in which Therese Braunfels must live and move and try to have her being. It was the same with the alcoholism she saw all around her, hounding the men who had sought an easier life than the one they had fled, but who found that they'd brought with them from afar the habits that would ultimately kill them in the loneliness of that primitive world. It was the same with the miners' consumption, the "white plague," pushed out of sight as hopeless by those who would protect the afflicted. Mollie was sure the disease was caused by the toxic dust of the underworld in which they worked—a holocaust of lungs and life offered up to the god of greed. She was beginning to understand that arrogance and ignorance were the parameters of despair.

She looked again at the time: half-past eleven. She could never open the watch without the image of Frank flashing across her mind. It had been his graduation present to her. The outer lid was decorated with a spray of diamond blossoms; on the back he had inscribed her name and the date she had received her medical degree. Yet in the past weeks his image, once static and familiar, once so beloved, had changed. His visage had become blurred, out of focus, as if she were no longer capable of seeing him clearly. His was the face that had once seemed a part of her own being—but a younger being, in many ways ignorant, in many ways naive, in many ways happier.

The rumble of a wagon interrupted her thoughts. She looked over at Therese. Her body was still twitching, but she was sleeping. The calomel hadn't yet worked, which was just as well; they needed to move her now. She rose and went to the door.

"Hello, Billy," she said as he was tying the draft horses to the hitch. "We've got a very sick woman here. I need you to help me move her."

"Sure, Dr. Mollie. Just tell me what to do."

"Put these blankets on the floor of the wagon. You and I can carry her out. We'll put her on the cot at my place."

Mollie rolled the groggy and shivering Therese into a blanket, and together she and Billy carried her onto the wagon. She put a pillow under the woman's head. Then she went back into the cabin and collected her coat and bag. As she came out, she saw Therese's oldest, Maria, coming along the road with the other children, a sleeping baby in her arms.

"I'm taking your mother over to my place," she said to the girl. "She seems to be much better, but I want to keep an eye on her through the night. Now, you and the children get some sleep. You can come by my office in the morning." She had spoken more positively to Maria than she felt.

She climbed up on the wagon with Billy. They drove back across the Grasshopper to Mollie's house—slowly, so as to not disturb their sleeping cargo.

Although she could scarcely keep her eyes open, Mollie only dozed on and off in the night. The door was open between her bedroom and the office where Therese lay on the cot. She still was not sure what she was dealing with. She assumed it was the Clark's pills that Therese had taken, but she couldn't be certain. Therese's body was still cold, which suggested that the poison was indeed ergot.

The calomel took effect in the night, and Mollie had to get up and clean her patient. And then in the early morning, she heard groaning. She hurried into the office. The stain on the bedsheets confirmed the ergot had achieved its purpose.

Mollie had just fallen into a deep sleep when May and Maria knocked at the door. She struggled out of bed and checked on Therese, who was finally sleeping calmly. She opened the door and, with her finger to her lips, motioned them to come through to the kitchen. Maria was holding some clothes and shoes for her mother. Her eyes were red and her face was blotched. Like Mollie, the girl hadn't slept all night.

"Therese is sleeping now," Mollie said. "I think she's going to be all right, but for a while there last night I wasn't sure. We won't know what happened until we can talk to her. I want her to stay here today. When her husband comes tonight, I'm sure she'll be able go home with him.

"And what about the little ones? Who is watching them?"

Maria spoke up. "Miss Coll says I should stay home today and watch them. We're stopping by the school, and I'm going to take my reader back home with me. Is it all right if I go in there and see my mother?"

"Of course, Maria," Mollie said, smiling at the girl. "Just be careful not to wake her. She's had a very hard night and she needs to sleep now."

"I think you've had a hard night, too," May said. "We'll leave you now so you can go back to bed."

Mollie did go back to bed after they left. She tried to sleep but she couldn't. The day had begun. As she lay there wide awake, she hoped that a day like yesterday wouldn't happen again. She didn't think she would have the energy. Dr. Pickman should be calling soon. Davey must have gotten to Dillon all right or Harry probably would have come to tell her. She hoped Harry could control Jeb; she didn't need a drunken maniac crashing in on her.

She heard Therese stirring in the office. She got up and went in. Therese was sitting on the edge of the cot, looking bewildered.

"Where am I? I have to go to the privy."

Mollie found a pair of slippers and a robe for her, and helped her outside. When they came back, the woman was hungry. Mollie fixed her some broth and crackers and sat down at the kitchen table with her while she ate. Relieved now that Therese was eating, she suddenly felt an anger she couldn't control.

"Why didn't you tell me you were pregnant when you came to see me?" she demanded. "What do you mean by taking pills when you don't know what's in them or how many to take? You almost died here last night! Your children were terrified they might lose their mother."

Therese dropped the spoon, splashing soup on the tablecloth. Tears started running down her cheeks. She made no attempt to answer, but got up from the table and stumbled into the office. Mollie could hear her sobbing.

In her exhaustion Mollie had lashed out at Therese for her irresponsibility; now, she was angry at herself for her own irresponsibility. She got up and followed her patient into the office. Therese was lying on the cot.

She had control of her voice again. "I'm sorry I spoke so harshly, Therese, but you had us all extremely worried. You go to sleep now, but I must talk to you later this afternoon. I'm going to need you to help me talk to other women in the camp, so that someone else won't do what you just did. Will you do that, Therese? Will you help?"

"Yes, Dr. Mollie," came the broken reply. "I'm so sorry. I'll try to help you."

CHAPTER SEVEN

Anthony Comstock, Post Office Prude

LATE THAT AFTERNOON there was a knock on Mollie's door. She opened to find a tall man with graying curly hair, rough in appearance, and clearly uncomfortable in her presence. Although he spoke English fairly well, Max Braunfels had a strong German accent. Not that he intended to speak any more than necessary. He made it clear he was there to pick up Therese and leave as quickly as possible. Maria had told him that her mother was sick, and that he should take the wagon. When he arrived, his wife was ready to leave. She was still pale, but she had managed to eat a little solid food in the afternoon.

Earlier in the day Therese had begged Mollie not to tell her husband what she had done. "He wouldn't understand. He thinks it's a sin to avoid having children. He doesn't realize how hard it is for me, especially now that I'm older."

"I won't tell him, but I won't lie, either, Therese. If he asks, I'll just say that you ate something that made you sick. That's the truth, of course, but he may be suspicious. And you'll have to deal with that. He's as much responsible for your pregnancy and its consequences as you are."

"He doesn't see it that way." Therese blushed and looked away from Mollie, embarrassed to talk about her sexual life even with a woman doctor. Mollie was used to this, but still it made her impatient.

"Therese, you've just risked your life to avoid having another child. There are far easier ways to do this. I want you to go home with Max when he comes for you this afternoon and rest. Perhaps Maria can stay home from school another day to help with the baby so you can sleep. But I want you to come to see me day after tomorrow. Will you promise me you will come?"

"Yes, Dr. Mollie. I'll come. I need your help."

After Therese and Max left, Mollie lay down and tried to rest. Dr. Pickman hadn't called over at Wright's about Davey. Athol always sent a boy down if there was a phone message for her. She wasn't sure if no news was good news. There was nothing for her to do but wait, and hope that Jeb had come to his senses.

She felt sure now that Therese would be all right. But she worried how she could approach the women who wanted help to prevent pregnancy, but were afraid to ask for it. As a physician, for Mollie to assist her patients with the information and materials to prevent conception was illegal. It had been for almost twenty years, since Anthony Comstock and his New York Committee for the Suppression of Vice had convinced Congress to pass an anti-obscenity law in 1873, a statute that criminalized reproductive control. To Comstock and his fanatics there was no difference between abortion, contraception, and obscenity. And he had managed to get himself appointed special agent of the Post Office with power to search, seize, and destroy illegal mail. He proudly boasted about the thousands of condoms and vaginal sponges and pamphlets and pills he had confiscated from the mail. To Mollie's amazement, the U.S. Supreme Court had ruled on the Comstock Law in 1877 and found that the right of the Post Office to search sealed mail was limited only by need of a warrant. Apparently Mr. Comstock felt he had a running warrant.

Mollie was disgusted by this "Comstockery," as she and her like-minded colleagues called it. And she was especially disgusted with the leadership of the all-male American Medical Association that supported the legislation. Some members even argued that contraception was not only criminal but medically dangerous as well, causing uterine disease. But then what should she expect from an organization that wouldn't allow certified women doctors to become members?

She had to admit, however, that some of the motivations of the AMA doctors were legitimate. There were far too many quacks performing abortions and advertising wares and nostrums that were potentially dangerous. She, too, as a doctor, had a stake in the suppression of disreputable abortionists and the unregulated drug companies that sent their questionable pills and worse through the mails. Yet Mollie knew that this was only one side of the AMA rationale. The other side was the desire to elevate the status of doctors as experts in gynecology and obstetrics. And this they did by denigrating the legitimate midwives along with the quacks, so as to set up the physician as the only competent professional, as well as the arbiter of social morality. Comstock and his fellow custodians of the public morals—that is, of other people's sex lives—as well as the AMA doctors, had created such a vituperative campaign that not only was the control of a woman's reproductive behavior now a matter of law, but even the subject of contraception had become unmentionable. In 1892 contraception was no longer covered in major medical textbooks.

Frank was a member of the AMA, but he, too, had been upset by the stance that the Comstock conservatives had forced the organization to take. He and Mollie had often discussed the fact that doctors who did not go along with the association's position on contraception and obscenity had no voice—or rather that their voice was drowned out by the clamor of the zealots.

Since the passage, almost twenty years before, of the federal statute making it a felony to send contraception articles and information through the mail, individual states had passed their own "little" Comstock Laws. And unfortunately for Mollie, Montana was one of these. Montana lawmakers sought to prohibit even private verbal transmission of information on abortion or contraception.

Underlying all this, Mollie was convinced, was the drive to disempower women. Perhaps the greatest fear of the more fervid of the bigots was the thought that if women could regulate their reproduction, they would have more free time to meddle in the affairs of men—why, they might even want to vote!

Mollie considered herself a fierce patriot. She was proud of her Revolutionary War ancestry, and as a child growing up in the Yankee North, she had experienced the viciousness of a civil war fought to hold the country together. But she felt no compunction about breaking a law that she considered illegal, discriminatory, and pernicious. Unwanted and possibly dangerous pregnancy was a matter of personal health. Not to be permitted to speak freely to her patients on such matters was, in her opinion, an infringement of her responsibilities as a physician to protect the health of her patients. And she believed the impact of the Comstock Laws was criminal. By banning information about contraception and contraceptive products, the laws were driving women to abortion, sometimes self-inflicted, sometimes by unlicensed practitioners—in both cases sometimes fatal. And it was the poor women who suffered the most. Middle- and upper-class women often had the means and sophistication to seek out private sources of contraceptive products or, if need be, to seek out those professionals who would discreetly assist them by removing their "menstrual obstruction" for a fee—usually a considerable one.

Nevertheless, Mollie was aware she had to be cautious. Doctors who defied the law, whether out of moral conviction or simple greed, faced the possibility of not only social and professional stigma, but also prison. She would have to be careful to determine the situation with the Bannack women on a one-to-one basis.

She had carefully sounded out Nate White, the Dillon pharmacist. He had assured her she could safely secure the needed materials from him. But he warned her never to order anything by telephone.

"Florence Brown, the telephone manager, is a very nice lady," Nate told Mollie, "but she's a terrible gossip. Never trust her with anything confidential. As for Postmaster Poindexter, he's a bit of a busybody, but harmless. He wouldn't go so far as to open your mail."

Mollie was able to order syringes and spermicides and vaginal sponges along with medicines she might need by sending Nate a note in the mail. In the 25 miles between Bannack and Dillon, there were no snoop postal agents interested in opening a physician's mail. The pharmacy would put the package on the stage as a personal delivery. There was always someone traveling to Bannack who could hand-deliver the doctor's supplies, and no one would be the wiser.

It wasn't until the next day that a boy delivered a message that Athol Wright had taken down. Dr. Pickman informed Mollie that Davey's fever had broken. The infection was draining out. The patient was extremely weak, but was beginning to take some broth. The doctor would be able to send him back in another week.

Mollie had been so concerned that Davey would not survive, she hadn't considered what would happen to him if he did. She would have to talk to Harry and find out if Davey had any relatives anywhere who might be able to take him away from his father. Yet she knew that she couldn't control Davey's life. Or Jeb's life. May had warned her.

Therese did return to Mollie's office as soon as she felt well enough. Since Mollie knew that Therese would be incapable of procuring commercial contraceptive goods on her own, she explained to the embarrassed woman how to make a contraceptive device out of an everyday kitchen sponge, attaching a thread to it for removal.

"Your husband won't know you're using this," Mollie told her in answer to Therese's fearful concern that Max would be angry. "Just leave it in place until he goes to work in the morning. Then you can douche with just water and vinegar or some alum and remove it and wash it out. It's as simple as that—just don't remove the sponge until at least six hours have passed."

Mollie took a glass tube with a rubber bulb on the end out of her medicine cabinet and handed it to Therese. "Keep this vaginal douche syringe out of sight in a drawer somewhere. If he finds it, just tell him it's for your personal cleanliness. I can't promise you that this process is 100 percent effective. But then nothing is outside of abstinence."

Over the next weeks she found that friends of both Therese and Janette were making appointments to discuss their female needs. She felt that if she could do something really important while she was in Bannack, it would be to teach the women how to take charge of their lives.

Late one evening toward the end of July, Mollie heard a rider reining in his horse at her gate. Looking out the window she saw J. Henry hurrying toward the house. She had seen Janette a few days earlier. The baby had turned head-down, so she knew that Janette was due anytime now.

"Please come right away, Mollie," J. Henry said, breathlessly, as she opened the door. "Her water broke a little while ago, and the pains are starting. Billy's already saddling your horse."

"Of course, J. Henry," she said. "I'm coming right now."

J. Henry had always presented himself to her as dignified, in command of every situation. Today, however, he was clearly distraught. His shirt was pulled out and his jacket disheveled. He was hatless and his hair was every-which-way from the ride. Mollie smiled. He would get used to it.

She saw Billy leading the mare along Main Street toward the house. "I'll be right there," she called to him as she took her shawl and picked up her saddlebags. She tied her things on the back of the saddle, mounted, and caught up with J. Henry, who was already heading up Main Street.

The two riders didn't speak much as they rode the mile or so down the Grasshopper to the old Marysville townsite near the Golden Leaf mill. J. Henry and Janette were living in a small two-room log house on the hill overlooking the mill.

Not only was J. Henry agitated, but Mollie, too, was concerned. This baby was special to her. The Longmaids had become her friends over the past months; moreover, the baby was the reason she had come to Bannack. She worried that Janette hadn't kept her weight down during her pregnancy, and this had begun to show on the veins of her legs. Part of the problem was the diet available in Bannack. There were plenty of tuber foods—potatoes, carrots, beets—as well as meats of all kinds, but very few fresh vegetables and fruits. She had concerns about the milk that was available from the few cows in the area. Some of May's pupils were sick, and Mollie suspected the milk. She had recommended that Janette not drink it.

When they arrived at the house, Janette was lying on the bed in the bedroom, comforted by a neighbor. The woman stood up as the two came in.

"The pains are coming about every fifteen minutes or so; you've probably got a long night ahead of you," the neighbor said to Mollie as she prepared to leave. "I'll look in on you in the morning."

The heat of the July day began to subside as the evening wore on. Mollie tried to get some rest on a bunk in the main room of the house, although Janette's groans kept her from sleeping. J. Henry sat in the bedroom with his wife, holding her hand while the pain washed over her. Sometime in the early-morning hours, the frequency of the moans and cries coming from the other room told her it was time to take over.

She went to the door and told J. Henry he would have to leave the room. "You'll need to keep the fire going and heat some water. I know you won't be able to sleep, but try to get some rest on the bunk. I'll take your place here." She went into the bedroom and sat down, taking Janette's hand. The pains were frequent now.

"I'm so glad you're here, Mollie," Janette murmured between groans, tears streaming down her face. "I'm so scared."

Mollie squeezed her hand. "You don't need to be scared. I know it hurts, but try to breathe deeply when the wave of pain starts. That will help you bear it better. I have to raise you just a bit now. The baby is coming soon and we need to put another rubber pad and a clean sheet under you."

Janette had had everything ready for the birth for several days. Two rubber pads and several clean sheets and towels were neatly folded on a table by the bed. Two new enamel basins waited next to the towels. Mollie removed the damp sheet from the bed and placed one of the pads and a clean sheet under her. Janette was covered with perspiration, her face flushed, her whole body in extreme agitation. Mollie took one of the basins and went into the other room to get some hot water to wash her hands. She was just returning to the bedroom when Janette let out a shriek. J. Henry looked at Mollie in alarm.

"It's coming now," she said with deliberate calm. "I know this is awful to hear, but it won't be long. Don't worry. Everything is all right." She took the basin of hot water and carried it into the bedroom.

Slowly, amid the agony of his mother's cries, Harold Esterbrook Longmaid poked his head out into life. Mollie felt around the baby's neck to make sure it was free of the cord. And then with a final push from his mother, the baby was fully of this world, demonstrating to all within earshot the power of his brand-new lungs.

J. Henry could contain himself no longer. At the sound of the baby's cry, he came rushing into the bedroom. Mollie was just wrapping the infant in a towel. Janette was lying back against the pillows, exhausted.

"You have a healthy little son, J. Henry, but we're not quite through here," Mollie said to him, firmly. "Go away and give us a few minutes. I need to cut off the cord in a minute or so, and take care of the afterbirth. I'll call you when we're ready."

J. Henry was banished again to the front room. After a few minutes Mollie unwrapped the towel from Harold Esterbrook and tied a piece of sterilized string 2 inches from his little belly. Then she tied another piece 2 inches farther along the cord, took the scissors from her bag, and cut between the two knots. She applied a few drops of antiseptic solution on the cut, and then dipped a towel into the basin of hot water and gently sponged the wiggling, gasping body. Taking a bottle from her medical bag, she put a drop of silver nitrate in each little eye and wrapped him tightly in a cotton blanket to keep him warm.

She set him in the basket bed that Janette had prepared for her baby, turning him on his side to prevent fluid or mucus from blocking his throat. Then she turned her attention to the mother.

Usually when she attended at childbirth, she would simply wait, and in a few minutes the placenta would move down into the vagina on its own. Experience had taught her over and over again that nature would do what needed to be done without interference from the doctor. But after some twenty-five minutes passed and the placenta had not descended, Mollie carefully, but firmly, pressed down on Janette's abdomen. This was the moment when Mollie knew she must be extremely careful. If she tugged on the afterbirth too hard, the cord could either break loose from the placenta—which would be a nuisance—or, worse, bring down the womb, which could be fatal. Most cases of an inverted uterus and possible fatal hemorrhage were caused by pulling improperly at the cord.

Gently tugging on the cord with one hand as she pressed with the other, she slowly worked the placenta down. She was relieved to see that it emerged broken free of the womb. She caught it in a basin. Then she removed the blood-soaked sheets and towels and gently bathed the new mother.

Mollie picked up the baby from the basket and laid him in Janette's arms. "I'll tell J. Henry to come in now," she said to the exhausted mother as she tucked a clean sheet around her. "I hope you can stay awake long enough to show your new son to his father. And I don't want you getting up for several hours. You've lost quite a bit of blood, and you need to keep quiet and let things heal. I'm going to go to sleep now in the next room. Have J. Henry wake me if you need anything."

Mollie's days that summer revolved around assisting at childbirths, treating snakebites, nursing fevers, and occasionally digging bullets out of gunshot wounds. Often she was called to perform surgical procedures, from lancing minor felons to appendectomies and setting compound fractures. She was not always successful. A childbirth could go wrong in ways that were beyond her control, and if a fever progressed to pneumonia, there was often little she could do but make the patient as comfortable as possible and wait. And always there was the abuse of alcohol, and its consequences, in the lives of the people.

Therese was not pregnant again, and Davey's leg had healed. She had called once at Spring Gulch after Davey was brought back. Jeb had greeted her civilly. He apparently had no memory of what had gone on that afternoon or how he had behaved toward her. May Coll reported that Davey's accident had jolted Jeb into realizing how important his son was to him. "I won't venture to say that Jeb has given up the bottle," May had told Mollie, "but Davey is learning to deal with his father's drinking, and Jeb at least has agreed that Davey can return to school in the fall."

From her successes, and perhaps from the way she handled her failures, Mollie had gradually established herself in the community not only as a person who could be trusted with the treatment of an illness, but also as one who would maintain a professional confidentiality. Even some of the miners, who at first had refused to allow Mollie to examine them, had succumbed to her authoritative, no-nonsense manner— in part, no doubt, because they were often too sick to put up a fuss.

As her life settled into a routine, Mollie began to feel restless. She was grateful to the Golden Leaf Company for her job, and she knew the practical experience she was gaining was invaluable. But she was ambitious. She could not advance in her career if she stayed in an isolated mining camp.

As it turned out, Mollie did not have the time to concern herself too greatly on this matter. J. Henry called on her in the early fall, a few weeks after his son was born. He sat down at Mollie's kitchen table while she brewed him a cup of tea. Then she sat down across from him and waited to hear the occasion for his visit.

"The Golden Leaf Company has decided that our operation here is well in hand and can be managed now by someone else," J. Henry began. "They want me to take over their Empire mine up near Marysville, just outside Helena. Also, our family owns the Penobscot mine near there, and I can help my brother Frank who's been managing it for some years now. Janette and the baby will be joining me as soon as I get settled. For a New York girl, moving to Bannack was something of a shock for her, but she's been a great sport about it. As you might imagine, she, especially, is looking forward to this move."

Mollie waited with trepidation for what might be coming next.

"If you wish to continue your practice here in Bannack," J. Henry said, "that is, of course, your choice. Certainly, you could stay on with the company here. But I want you to know, Mollie, that we're very satisfied with your work here. We would like you to come with us to Empire as the company doctor, and I would like you to work for our family mine as well."

She felt a rush of relief. She had been afraid J. Henry would say that her job was ended. Of course she was pleased that he had such confidence in her and wanted her to continue working with the company, but mining camp doctor was not the career she wished to pursue. Still, Marysville was a much larger town and was close to the capital at

Helena. She wouldn't be isolated as she was here in Bannack. The promise of secure employment, even if it was another mining camp, was exceedingly attractive—her experiences in Salt Lake City were still raw in her memory. The Golden Leaf Company paid well for her services. She had few expenses in Bannack, and was able to save a large part of her salary. She had opened an account at the bank and had already sent two checks for $100 each to Rita in Osage. When the company made its next payment to her, she would send Rita the last $100.

J. Henry finished his tea and stood up to leave. He held out his hand to Mollie.

"Take some time to think about it, but I do hope you'll decide to come with us."

Mollie did not take long to accept J. Henry's offer. The move made sense in many ways. Although she would be living in Empire—a town outside Marysville that was even smaller than Bannack—she could make contact with the medical community in Helena. The capital was only an hour or so from Marysville by train. She would be able to take her Montana certification examination and join the Montana Medical Association, which, unlike the AMA, accepted women. She had read of two women, Dr. Maria Dean and Dr. Katherine Holden, who were Helena members, and she longed for the company of women colleagues. May was the only woman in Bannack with whom she felt she could talk intimately, but May had left already to get married to her university professor in Kentucky. Her departure had left behind an emptiness in Mollie's life. Moving to Empire, small as the place was, seemed to Mollie a return to civilization.

Since J. Henry would not be relocating for several weeks, Mollie would have time to go back to Iowa. She had finally written Frank the letter she had been putting off. She had worked on it for several hours until she felt she had found the right tone. She told him her appreciation for the time they had spent together and her gratefulness for his help. She acknowledged how much she had learned from him and offered him her belief in the future of his work. She told him her sorrow for the hurt she knew she had caused him, her hope for his understanding and forgiveness. She had reread it again and again, changing a word here and there, slept on it, and sent it off.

She had heard nothing back for more than two months. Finally, in September, she had received a terse reply stating that he had started divorce proceedings at the Mitchell County Court on grounds of desertion. She could have the papers served on her in Bannack, or she could return to Iowa and complete the divorce process there. She should contact his lawyer immediately concerning her plans. He made no claims on her regarding property—she could have any household goods she wanted, and the wedding gifts they had received ten years earlier—and he expected her to make no demands on him. He was leaving Osage, returning to Louisiana to work, and had no interest in communicating with her again. Any concerns she might have should be directed to his attorney.

Mollie was angry and hurt at the abrupt cutoff. So much for her agonizing over that letter. It hadn't occurred to her that her sudden flight from Osage would be translated into legal terms as "desertion." Yet she had to admit that was precisely what it was. And she also had to admit that despite her annoyance, she was greatly relieved that Frank wouldn't be in Osage. He might be angry, but at least there wasn't going to be any trouble. She would go back home, take care of the divorce as quickly as possible, and come back to Montana. At least she knew there was a job waiting for her, and she even had some money set aside. She was eager to see her family—although she doubted they were overly eager to see her—and this time she could bring Willy back with her.

She missed the dog so much. He would have been so happy trotting along beside her when she rode out to answer calls. Now, anyway, she could have him with her in Empire. Clara had written her often about Osage news, always reporting Willy's adventures.

The only problem that stood in her way was what to do about her patients in Bannack. Because she was the only doctor, the town was dependent on her. There were two doctors in Dillon, but for an emergency, as she had experienced with Davey, Dillon was too far away.

She discussed the problem with J. Henry: "I do need to go back home for a short while before I go to Empire," she told him, "but I'm very concerned about leaving here before a replacement is found. We've been very lucky so far that there hasn't been a serious outbreak of anything this last year. There was typhoid in Butte, and Great Falls had a horrible bout of smallpox, but Bannack has managed to escape—at least for now."

"I've been thinking about this, too," J. Henry said. "The dredging companies are coming in, and it's their responsibility to bring in a physician. However, I talked with John Meade over at the hotel. You probably know that John actually has a medical degree, but he hasn't worked as a doctor for years. He came here as a prospector, and when the placers started to run out, he left for a while and then came back to take over the hotel and the pharmacy. He's willing to fill in until a new doctor arrives."

Mollie wasn't satisfied with this, but she was too discreet to discuss her concerns about the hotel owner with J. Henry. John's medical knowledge was certainly not current, and she couldn't imagine someone like Therese talking to him about her female problems. Still, there was nothing she could do. She couldn't stay on in Bannack. She hoped she had given the women the knowledge and tools to take control of their lives; it was time now for her to take charge of her own. No one in Bannack, not even J. Henry, knew about her failed marriage. She was impatient to put it legally behind her and move on with her career, with her life.

Mollie wrote to Frank's lawyer that she would be in Osage within the month; he could serve her the papers at that time. And to Edna, that she would like to see her for a day in Salt Lake. She wrote her mother that she was coming home for a visit, and she sent Rita the last of the money she owed her. Then she wrote Clara that she was coming for Willy.

Mollie made the rounds, taking leave of her patients, and making one last check on the babies she had brought into the world. She even stopped in to see the horse with the splayed neck they had brought her not long after her arrival. She had had no idea what to do for the poor animal but bind its neck tightly. Apparently that was all that was needed; the horse was doing fine.

For all her desire to move on, she felt a stab of sadness. Bannack had given her the chance to prove herself, and she was grateful. She was leaving behind an important piece of her life.

Then, early in October 1892, she packed up her dreams for a future and took the stage for the Utah & Northern station in Dillon.

CHAPTER EIGHT

Unwelcome Back Home

AS THE U&N CHUGGED SOUTH toward the Idaho border, the late-summer landscape presented a different world through the train window from the frozen land of Mollie's arrival. The cottonwoods along the Red Rock riverbed shimmered golden coins in the October sun. The ranch buildings and the fields along the tracks, which had looked almost destitute in the early-winter snow, now were alive: Horses were pulling balers; men were stacking the bales; neat packages of hay dotted the fields, waiting to be hauled off to the barn for the coming winter. The cattle, which last winter had huddled so seemingly miserably in the cold, were now indulging themselves on the abundant grasses of the foothills.

Perhaps it was not just the snow that had made the scene look so different almost a year ago. Yes, she had been grateful to J. Henry and eager to start her new job. But at the same time she had to admit she had also been afraid. She had known there would be no one to help her, and no hospital for miles. And there was her inability to find work in Salt Lake that had gnawed at her, and the break with Frank. She supposed all of those things, along with the cold and snow, had helped make the world look bleak.

She knew her return to Osage would be awkward, but she was relieved she would not to have to confront Frank. Bannack had given her back her self-confidence, and enough time had passed since their emotional parting in Salt Lake that she now felt sure of her decision. Clearly, he was angry. There was no point in either of them scraping those wounds raw again.

Mollie had changed trains in Ogden, and as the Utah Central pulled into the Salt Lake station she saw Edna through the window, standing in the midst of a crowd that was waiting to welcome the passengers. She had telegraphed ahead the time of her arrival.

She grabbed her purse and medical bag and stepped down to the platform. Edna rushed toward her and in a moment the two were wrapped around each other.

"Come, check your bags and we'll find a cabbie," Edna urged Mollie as they disentangled. "I'm so eager to hear your adventures! Let's get away from all this noise so we can talk."

Mollie checked her bags with the baggage master, taking only a small one with her.

In the cab Edna said, "I'm surprised you're back so soon. I was planning to visit you in the spring when I got your letter you were coming. I do hope the job wasn't too difficult. Your letters sounded as if you were quite satisfied, but then knowing you, you probably wouldn't let on if everything wasn't all violins and roses."

"Well, there certainly weren't any violins, although there was a band that played at dances. And nobody brought me roses in Bannack," Mollie said, laughing. "But don't worry, I wasn't run out of town. As it was, I was so busy that if you had come, I would have enlisted your services."

Mollie was grateful that Edna had rescheduled her patients as soon as she'd gotten Mollie's wire. She needed to talk, to compare stories with Edna. She especially wanted to ask how Edna was dealing with her patients' ignorance and inhibitions, as well as lack of access to information.

"I've run into the same problems in my practice here," Edna said, responding to Mollie's story about Therese. "These Comstock Laws are disgraceful. And of course, too often the result is to drive women to abortion, when that could have been prevented in the first place. I've had several experiences like the one you describe. Not with the Mormon women. The church has such a stranglehold on them, they wouldn't dare attempt an abortion. It's the poor women, the miners' wives, who suffer, here just as there in Montana."

"And what makes me especially angry," Mollie said, "is that there are so many women doctors caught up in this 'purity' attitude toward their own sex. I just can't understand it. But then they are unmarried, and have no idea what it must be like to go through ten or more pregnancies."

"That, or maybe unconsciously they advocate sexual abstinence and purity out of spite that they themselves don't have any fun," Edna said with a grin. Both she and Mollie had a sense of humor about those of their colleagues who were dubbed by certain philosopher-physicians of the day as "mannish maidens."

"Or maybe they just want to jump on the bandwagon and support the AMA," said Mollie in disgust. "As if that would do them any good. The AMA doesn't give a damn about women doctors. They think we're nothing more than nurses or—worse yet from their point of view—midwives. Some of them just assume that a woman doctor must be an abortionist."

Mollie was visiting Salt Lake in a far better mood than when she had been there before, especially because she didn't have to slush through streets oozing with winter's mud. And it was refreshing to talk to Edna, both as a woman and as a doctor. Isolated in Bannack, Mollie had missed the contact with her colleagues she needed for professional as well as personal reasons. The two women talked well into the night, and Mollie awoke still tired when the alarm on her bed table abruptly called her to consciousness.

Edna fixed a quick breakfast, and then insisted on accompanying Mollie in the cab to the station.

"This time you must come to visit me in Marysville," Mollie said, as she gave Edna a good-bye hug. "I have a feeling this is going to be a very important move for me. I'm going to take my certification test as soon as I get there, and Montana has a medical association that has the courtesy, as well as the common sense, to admit women. I'm hoping that after I've put in my time with the mining companies, I'll be in a position to start my own practice there."

"I'm so glad for you, Mollie. I know you'll have your own practice. You've already proved you can take on the Wild West and come out fighting. And of course I'll come."

Mollie sat in the coach of the transcontinental Union Pacific, staring out at the vast, monotonous fields of corn stubble—the near ones flashing past, the far ones seeming scarcely to move at all. She didn't really see them. Her mind was focused on her arrival in Osage. It was a little less than two years since she had run away from Frank. She felt she was staging the return of the prodigal daughter, although she doubted there would be feasting and celebration.

Nonetheless, she was pleased with herself. Perhaps Bannack was not the most elegant place to cut her teeth and go it alone, but she had done it, and she had survived without Frank's help. She knew she would be returning to a much better situation in Marysville. She would spend as little time as possible at home: see her mother and her sister, Sadie, sign the papers for her divorce, and get Willy. That would be all. And Rita. She must see Rita and thank her for her help. Still in all, it shouldn't take more than a week.

Mollie had missed her family, especially her mother. Yet it was so difficult to make Adelia Sophia and Sadie understand why she was getting a divorce. They both had thought it foolish and improper for Mollie to go to medical school, and then they both had been scandalized when she ran away from Frank.

Divorce on the frontier was almost a commonplace. Mollie had read that one in five Montana marriages ended in divorce, largely because a husband would abandon his family when his dreams of gold collapsed. He would be off to a new dig, to a new hope—maybe to a new wife. But there in America's heartland, divorce was viewed as a disgrace. It hurt Mollie that she had no support from her family. She knew they loved her, yet she had to stay away in order to live her life as she now knew she must. As for Jason, he didn't concern himself one way or another with his big sister. Adelia had written her that Jason was in Idaho looking around for a place to settle, and he wouldn't be home while Mollie was visiting. Jason was probably the only one who wasn't angry with her. She thought it was too bad he wouldn't be there. She could use his support, even if it was based more on indifference than on the conviction she should lead her life as she wished.

The days in Osage were indeed uncomfortable. The sense of scandal was a constant presence in her mother's house, and there seemed nothing Mollie could do about it.

"Divorce is simply not *done* in our family!" Adelia Sophia had angrily challenged Mollie the first night the errant daughter had returned. "Do you know what Sarah Moore has been saying about you all over town?"

"I don't care what that woman says," Mollie had exploded. "She's mean. She was impossible to live with. And she kicked my dog! No decent person would hurt an animal like that. All she cares about is her precious Frank. He at least had the good sense to get away from her and move to Louisiana."

"Well, you didn't marry Sarah, you married Frank."

"That's what you think," Mollie had rejoined angrily. "Any woman who marries Frank gets Sarah in the bargain. If you didn't care so much what people like that say, you'd be a much happier person."

That was a low blow, and Mollie was ashamed. The whole exchange was breaking her heart, and she knew her mother must feel the same way.

"I'm sorry, Mother. I know that my actions must be very embarrassing to you, but please understand that Frank and I no longer want to be married, and that I care very much about being a doctor. Women should be free to work in whatever way they wish. I hope that someday you will be proud of me."

Both women broke into tears. Mollie wondered if she and her mother would ever come to an understanding.

Mollie was anxious to get the unpleasant business with Fred Shelton, Frank's lawyer, over with. She was acquainted with Shelton; he had been a friend of Frank's for many years and had represented them once against one of their patients who had refused to pay for a medical procedure. When she entered the lawyer's office, there was, as she had expected, an awkwardness between them. There were a few embarrassed pleasantries, and then Shelton handed her the divorce papers to read.

She felt ashamed as she endorsed the accusation of "desertion" on the papers. It sounded so cold and ugly. And one-sided. There was of course nothing in the papers that said why she felt she had had to desert him. She signed them, feeling that they suggested she was some sort of tramp who had run away for a night on the town. No one seemed interested in her side of the story.

That wasn't really true. She knew Clara and Charles had understood all along that something had gone wrong in her marriage. And Rita. Rita was interested enough in her side of the story to help her get out of Osage and make a new life for herself.

After signing the divorce papers, she put up with a few minutes of strained utterances of condolence from Frank's friend. Finally, mustering a polite smile, she shook hands with the lawyer and escaped. On her way back to her mother's house, she stopped at the telegraph office and asked one of the delivery boys to take a message to Rita. Then she went home to wait for a response.

Rita invited her to meet for tea the next day at the tea shop on Main Street they had met in several times before. Mollie was already sitting at a table when Rita appeared, dramatically sweeping into the tea-room in her customary exotic getup: beaded shawl, multiple bangle bracelets, dangling earrings. Rita made no concessions to small-town decorum.

After a warm hug, Rita sat down and said, "Now talk. I want to hear all about it."

Mollie related how difficult her stay in Salt Lake had been. "I couldn't have held out without the money you loaned me. And I found the Bannack job at the last minute. I don't know what I would have done if I'd had to stay in Salt Lake—take another job nursing an invalid, I suppose. That would certainly have been a dead end. But I'm so fortunate to have such wonderful supportive friends, although I wish

I could say the same for my family. Without your help and the help of my friend Edna who found me the job in Bannack, I shudder to think what I might be doing right now."

Rita smiled. "I knew you'd be all right. I wouldn't have loaned you the money if I'd thought you were going to fail. I could see that you had to get away from your husband, and you needed the chance to prove you could be successful on your own. That's the best use of $300 I can think of."

The waitress came over to the table bringing a pot of tea, two teacups, and a plate of scones with jam. Mollie poured the tea and passed the scones to Rita.

"But Rita, I'm so rude talking only about myself. Tell me how are you and Michael?"

Rita's face clouded. "Mollie, Michael died a few months ago. I didn't write you . . . I guess I just didn't want to tell you. He seemed to be improving those last few months, and then suddenly he started to go down. He had a wonderful warm heart, but in the end it couldn't sustain him. I found him in his bed one morning."

"Oh, Rita, I am so sorry!" Mollie reached across the table and took hold of Rita's hand. "He did seem to be getting better right before I left." Actually Mollie was not surprised. She had seen dropsy cases where accumulation of the fluid seemed to subside for a while, and then suddenly the swelling would return. It was a sign of congestive heart failure, and there was nothing one could do. At the time she was treating Michael, she had said nothing about this to him since he seemed to be holding steady.

"Michael left me some stocks and the title to the building in which we were living. So I still have the apartment, and I've become the land-lady for the other two tenants. The only problem is, his daughter is contesting the will. She doesn't think she got enough out of him, although he left her a tidy sum. This is what I get for refusing to marry again." Rita smiled ruefully. "It hasn't come up for hearing yet, but my lawyer thinks I'll be all right. Michael and I were together for more than ten years."

"I'm so sorry. These things are ugly. I just left Frank's lawyer yesterday, and I don't want to see the inside of a lawyer's office ever again. I do hope it all comes out right for you."

"Now that Michael's gone," Rita continued, "I want to sell the apartments and go back to Chicago. Osage is no place for me, but I can't do that until the lawsuit with his daughter is decided."

Mollie and Rita finished their tea. As they rose to leave, Rita picked up the check and insisted on paying the bill. On the street they embraced again, promising to keep in touch.

Although Mollie had enjoyed meeting Rita again, a cloud of depression settled over her as she walked back to her mother's house. The divorce papers had unnerved her; it was all so cold and uncaring. Ten years of her life erased in a scribble of legalities. She didn't want the marriage any longer, but she had indeed once loved Frank. She was stung with the sadness of the death of love. And Michael O'Brian, whose love for Rita had been so warm, so alive, was dead. Poor Rita had to contend with his daughter's greed, as if losing Michael's love wasn't bad enough.

After the fight with her mother, a reconciliation had warmed the house somewhat. Mollie appreciated that the warmth was based on caring and goodwill on both their parts, but it was not based on the understanding she would have wished for. She was aware that her mother had not invited anyone to the house to visit. Apparently, she was still the town pariah.

The one truly happy event of Mollie's return home was her reunion with Willy. When Clara answered the door, Willy was by her side as he always was when the doorbell ringer was turned. Mollie was aghast for the first few seconds when Willy didn't react to her presence. Then suddenly he flung himself at her with such joyous abandon he almost knocked her over.

"Down, Willy!" Clara ordered the dog, to no avail.

"Never mind, Clara," Mollie protested, laughing. "You can't imagine how wonderful it feels to be greeted with such love."

"Shame on you, Mollie! You know that you will always be welcomed here with love, although perhaps not quite in the same manner as Willy's."

"Thanks, Clara. I need someone to say that." Mollie entered the house and gave her coat to Clara, who hung it on the hall coatrack. "This trip back home has not been pleasant. I've been dealing with a divorce lawyer and an angry mother and sister. I've been praying that if I see Sarah Moore, I'll get out of the way before she spots me. And Jason isn't even here."

"Well, we are! Charles and I are delighted to see you. Come in and sit down and tell us everything."

Mollie followed Clara into the drawing room. Charles Bennet, on seeing Mollie enter, stood up and held out his hand.

"How wonderful to see you, Mollie. Clara has kept me abreast of your adventures in Montana from your letters. Please, come and sit down, and let me offer you a glass of sherry."

"You've been wonderful to keep Willy for me," Mollie said as she took the seat Charles offered her and accepted the sherry. "I've missed him so much. He would have loved to be with me in Bannack, but of course when I left here, I had no idea what would happen. But now I'm going to another mining camp, near a 'real' town this time, and Willy can accompany me on calls out in the wilds."

From Clara's letters, Mollie knew that she and Charles had grown to love Willy, and would want to keep him. She felt guilty asking for him back after they had cared for him for so long. Still, guilty or not, she had to have him.

Mollie's love of dogs had almost a religious quality. She had been a doctor too long to have faith in any church's version of religion, yet she believed in a divine presence, in divine intervention. That evening she told Clara and Charles of an experience she had had as a medical student in Chicago. She hoped that her story would explain how important it was for her to take Willy back.

"I had to work late at the school library," she began. "Usually I would get back to our apartment by seven or eight at the latest. But the class was having an anatomy exam the next day, and I needed to study. The library closed at eleven o'clock, and it must have been close to midnight when I was walking alone along a rather dark street. Willy was home with Frank. The only streetlight was at the far end of the block, and in the dim light I saw a gang of young toughs coming toward me along the street. I could see that they were pointing at me and laughing. I was terribly frightened. Just a few days before, the anarchists had bombed Haymarket Square, killing and wounding so many. Everyone in Chicago was frightened, not knowing what might happen next. There was no one else around that late. Suddenly out of the night two huge German shepherds appeared. Each positioned himself on either side of me and guarded me as I walked down the block past the toughs, who swerved to the side without a word. I could see that the men were afraid. The dogs walked beside me for another block or so until the gang was out of sight and I was almost home. Then they disappeared back into the night from wherever they had come."

When Mollie finished speaking, Clara and Charles were silent for a moment. Then Charles smiled and said, "I always suspected that dogs are really angels in disguise. Or is it that angels are really dogs in disguise? Well, either way. I'm sure Willy will be very happy in Montana." He reached down and patted the dog on the head. "Sure beats getting walked on a leash here in town, eh, Willy?"

Charles turned back to Mollie. "Leave him here until you're ready to go. We'll need to get a cage to put him in the baggage car. I hope they'll let you check on him on the train."

"I've already talked to the UP office. They said I could see him during stops of an hour or more. There are several along the way."

It wasn't a pleasant train ride for Willy. Nor was it for Mollie, who was worried about him. The dog refused to eat the food she had brought. And he wasn't let out of his cage until they got to Saint Louis, and then again at Ogden, where there was a wait of several hours before they transferred to the Utah & Northern and Willy was dragged back into the boxcar. At least the Utah & Northern stopped occasionally to take on water and coal, and during those breaks the conductor let Mollie walk Willie for a few minutes. It nearly broke her heart to put him back into his cage each time. It was the way he looked at her, his eyes full of her betrayal.

When the train pulled away from the familiar station at Dillon, Mollie grew excited. Back in the flatland of Iowa, she had realized how much she missed Montana. Not only was the land spectacular in its stark ruggedness, she had found the people much more open than in the more formal society she was used to back home. Everyone she knew in Montana was coming to the new state from somewhere else: to search for wealth and excitement, or to escape the mistakes they had made and to hope for a new life. Just as she was.

North of Dillon was all new country for her. The cottonwoods she had admired just a couple of weeks before were losing their golden crowns. A few hardy leaves still clung to the branches. She was struck by the sweep of the jagged peaks in the distance and the abundance of water in the rivers even this late in the fall. At Deer Lodge Pass the train crossed the Continental Divide for the second time, then descended to Silver Bow and followed the Clark Fork past the town of Deer Lodge to Garrison Junction. Once again Willy had some time to walk free of his cage while Mollie waited for the Northern Pacific's Helena line to take her the last leg of her trip. It was midafternoon when the train chugged over MacDonald Pass, descended into the Prickly Pear Valley, and pulled into the Helena station. After Willy and her baggage were unloaded, she was just in time to catch the four o'clock NP to Marysville.

The Marysville train chugged the 25 miles from Helena daily, arriving at the mining town at five in the evening. She had wired J. Henry her arrival from the Western Union office at Garrison Junction, and he was at the station with a wagon to meet her. Mollie let Willy out of his cage. The dog watched the baggage master shoving Mollie's cases onto the wagon and jumped in afterward. He wasn't going to let anyone put him back in that cage.

J. Henry had a large home at the top of Grand Street. He assured Mollie that he and Janette were expecting her—and of course Willy—to stay with them for a few days until she could set up her office in Empire. Mollie was so tired from the trains, the transfers, the worry about Willy—he hadn't eaten anything for more than three days and had barely touched his water—that she could hardly stay awake through dinner. When they had finished eating, Janette went upstairs to nurse little Harold, and Mollie scraped the leftovers into a pan and put it down on the kitchen floor. Willy's fast was over. He pounced on the pan, voraciously guttling his dinner. As soon as she could politely get away from her host, she climbed the stairs to the guest room. On the way she looked in on Janette and Harold to say good night, and then fell exhausted into bed, Willy on the floor by her side.

CHAPTER NINE

Dr. Mary B. Moore Has Arrived

THE TOWN OF MARYSVILLE, MONTANA, sits on top of a gigantic subterranean granite intrusion into the Rocky Mountains known to geologists as the Boulder Batholith. From Butte westerly and northerly to Helena and the Marysville area, the formation hides what was, arguably, the richest trove of valuable metals in the United States. When Mollie arrived at Marysville in the fall of 1892, there were hundreds of tunnels worming into this subterranean granite mountain. Enormous buckets hoisted the riches out of the depths and up to the mills, where, to release their treasure, the ores were pounded night and day by huge, 1,000-pound weights that dropped a hundred times in a minute. The thumping of the stamp mills was such a part of Marysville life that after a while people seemed to get used to it and no longer hear it.

Mollie, however, wasn't used to it. The stamp mill in Bannack had been far enough from the town that she could hear it only if the wind was blowing up the Grasshopper canyon. When she awoke in the Longmaids' guest room early the next morning to the sound of Willy scratching at the door to get out, immediately the thumping took over her consciousness. She wondered if the pounding ever stopped.

Grateful that the Longmaids' house was hooked up to Marysville's new electricity system, she switched on the light by her bed and picked up her watch: four thirty. She searched her trunk for a robe and slippers and, moving as quietly as possible so as to not waken the sleeping household, started for the stairs. Her efforts at silence were in vain. Willy descended in great noisy gallumpfs. She opened the front door, and the dog raced out into the dark road to relieve himself. She would have to figure out a routine with him so he wouldn't upset the whole town at that ungodly hour. Willy was happy to be running free and paid no attention to his owner's loudly whispered calls. Furious at him, Mollie chased him till she finally caught him by the collar just as he discovered a dead chicken at the edge of the road. As she dragged Willy back into the Longmaids' house, she was relieved that nobody would be up that early to see her prowling around town in her nightclothes.

In this she was mistaken. A light drew her to the kitchen, where she found J. Henry already dressed and sitting at the table drinking coffee, a stack of papers in front of him.

"I'm sorry I woke you up so early," she apologized. "Willy had to go out and I just couldn't keep him quiet."

"Not at all," said J. Henry. "I'm always up this early. I was about to come down and fix coffee when I heard you go out. The three hours between four and seven every morning I spend doing the paperwork for the mines. Then Janette joins me with the baby and we have breakfast together. The maid comes in about nine, and I leave for Empire."

For a moment Mollie felt a surge of envy. The life of this little family seemed so ordered, so loving, so happy with their new baby. And she had chosen the childless life of the woman professional. The thought of her brand-new divorce underlined her sense of aloneness. She pushed the thoughts away.

"I don't mean to disturb your work. I'll take Willy up to my room now."

"Please don't go yet. Come and have some coffee with me," J. Henry said, pushing the stack of papers to one side. "These can wait. It's a good time for us to talk. You'll probably want to spend a day or two exploring Marysville. I think you'll like it here. It's not at all like Bannack."

Mollie sat down at the table while J. Henry poured her a cup of coffee from the kettle on the stove. Willy curled up on the floor. "I must admit," she said as J. Henry handed her the cup, "I was beginning to feel constricted in Bannack, although it was an invaluable experience working in the backwoods of the world. I learned some survival skills in Bannack that most doctors never have to deal with. And I'm very grateful for that. But I'm ready for the big-city life now," she said, laughing.

In the background of their talk, the incessant thumping of a stamp mill pulsed through the town like a giant hammering heartbeat. "Tell me," she asked, "does the pounding ever stop?"

"Frankly, no—except on Sundays. There are mines and mills all over these hills. But you'll get so used to the thumping that after a while you'll only notice it when it stops. And at night the rhythm lulls one to sleep. That's the Drumlummon mill you hear. They've got 110 stamps going day and night and 450 men working there. It's the richest mine in Marysville. In fact, it's the reason there's a town here at all. Marysville was just another little mining camp back in the '70s."

Mollie stirred a spoonful of sugar into her coffee. "I heard talk of the Drumlummon back in Bannack. It must be an incredibly rich mine."

"The Drumlummon was discovered by Tommy Cruse back in '76. Tommy's an illiterate but determined Irishman, and he has indeed pulled a fortune out of that mine. He sold it to an English consortium that developed it much further than Tommy could, but he's smart enough to keep a financial interest in it. This year's been a bad one for the Drumlummon, though. They had a fire last May in one of the shafts, and it took out about 800 feet of timbering. Then there was a flood and a cave-in, but, as you can hear, they're making up for it. The mill's right at the edge of town. You should walk down and see it."

"Oh, Willy and I are going exploring this morning. And now that you mention it, I think last night the pounding did put me to sleep."

Mollie was concerned she was keeping J. Henry from his work. She finished her coffee and stood up from the table. "I'm going to leave you to your papers and go get dressed. Thanks for the coffee. I'll be down to join you at seven when Janette comes."

After the Longmaids and Mollie had finished breakfast, J. Henry left to ride out to Empire, and Mollie put Willy on a leash and set out with him to explore the town. Inside the house, the drumbeat of the stamp mills was somewhat muted, but outside the sound was a pervasive staccato. Not that it was so loud, she decided, rather it was simply there— a presence syncopating the rhythms of one's body. Less than a year before, Mollie had walked down the main street of Bannack, exploring her new home. Now as she walked down Marysville's Grand Street, Bannack receded into the past as if the events of that period of her life had taken place years ago.

Marysville, that fall of 1892, was perhaps the richest little town in the United States. There was a pulse of excitement in the air. The sense of its own prosperity pervaded the town. And expectation— expectation of the fortune to be made in the mines, or at least of the good living to be made servicing those who dug for that fortune.

Along her walk Mollie passed several well-appointed houses, some with expensive landscaping. They would be the homes of the company officers J. Henry had told her about at dinner last night. The town was full of young administrators who enjoyed a sinecure with the English mining companies. In addition to their extravagant salaries, they were provided fancy housing with electricity, steam heat, hot and cold running water, and expensive furnishings. J. Henry's house was one of those, too.

Much of the town, however, was not fancy houses. There were an inordinate number of saloons, and here and there were piles of garbage along the road and in the side alleys. For all the town's riches, the practical aspects of urban life left a lot to be desired. In some of the alleys the flies were buzzing in droves. She held tight to Willy's leash to keep his nose out of the garbage.

She turned at the train depot where she and Willy had arrived the night before, and walked over to Main Street. Ahead of her she saw a sign above a doorway that read:

THE MOUNTAINEER, *"THE GREAT ADVERTISING MEDIUM OF MONTANA."*
WM. C. MAHURIN, PROPR.

Mollie smiled at the blatant self-importance; yet it did seem appropriate to the town's sense of itself. And what better place to find out what was going on than the local newspaper? She tied Willy to a drainpipe along the wall of the building. As she opened the office door, a man looked up from his desk behind a long counter.

"Are you Mr. Mahurin?" she asked. "I would like to buy a paper. And perhaps you could tell me where I can find the doctors in town?"

The man came over to the counter and handed Mollie the weekly edition from the previous Thursday. "I'm Bill Mahurin, owner, publisher, editor, beat reporter. We've got only one doctor in town. That's George King. Here's his ad." He opened the paper for Mollie and showed her: *"G. W. King, MD. Physician and Surgeon, Marysville."*

"George is also the public health officer here. We've been running some stories for him lately about the garbage problem in Marysville. Here's an ad for Dr. Liebig, but he's in Helena. You can make an appointment with him on the days he comes to town. I hear the Golden Leaf people are hiring a doctor to cover Empire and Penobscot, but he's not here yet far as I know."

"Yes he is," Mollie said with a smile. "I am he."

"Excuse me, ma'am, I just assumed—"

"I know, Mr. Mahurin," she said. "You just assumed that a doctor would naturally be a man."

"No offense, ma'am. But hey, this will make a great story! A lady doctor for the miners. Can I interview you for next Thursday's paper, Dr. . . . uh?"

"Dr. Moore. Perhaps later—in a few days. I'll be back to run my own ad in the *Mountaineer* as soon as I get settled out in Empire. Right now I'd like to meet Dr. King. Could you tell me where I can find his office?"

"Sure, Doctor. George is up in the next block of Main, across the street. You can see the building from here." The editor ducked through an opening under the counter and opened the door for her.

"It's that brick building next to the saloon," he said, pointing up the street.

"Thank you, Mr. Mahurin, I'll be in to see you soon."

Mollie untied Willy from the drainpipe and led him across Main Street. She found a hitching post to tie him to at the edge of the board sidewalk, and entered Dr. King's office. There were several empty chairs set around the room. A receptionist looked up from her work.

"May I help you?"

"Yes," said Mollie. "I'm Dr. Moore, physician for the Golden Leaf Company. I am wondering if Dr. King might have a few minutes to talk with me."

The receptionist gave her the same surprised look that Mahurin had just given her, a look to which she had grown accustomed whenever she introduced herself, a look that never ceased to annoy her. "He's with a patient right now. I'll see if he has time when he's finished. Please sit down. I'll be right back."

The receptionist disappeared through a door and Mollie took one of the chairs. Looking around, she immediately compared the office to the one she had decorated for Frank and herself. Somewhat to her surprise, she found that it no longer hurt. Not at all. In fact, she felt a quiet relief. She picked up the newspaper she'd just bought.

In a moment the receptionist came back and informed Mollie the doctor would be free in a few minutes. Shortly, an attractive young woman emerged from the same door, followed by a young man. He was the first man Mollie had seen that day who was wearing a suit and a cravat. The clothes signified to her that he must be the doctor. The woman said good-bye, nodded to Mollie, and left.

The man turned to Mollie: "Dr. Moore. So glad you stopped by. I'm George King." The doctor held out his hand to her. "Please come into my office where we can talk. I don't have any patients till after lunch."

George King ushered her into a small room with a desk and chairs in one corner opposite a white enameled-metal medicine cabinet. A raised examination table extended out from the wall. He took his seat behind the desk and motioned Mollie to take one of the chairs. Facing the doctor across his desk, she had the uncomfortable feeling that she was a patient there for an examination.

"I understand from Mr. Longmaid that you have been practicing in Bannack," the doctor began. "I imagine that must have been very difficult for a woman."

Mollie inwardly bristled. Was she going to be dealing with another one of those arrogant, anti-female doctors? She was careful not to show any reaction to his words, only to answer calmly, "No, I didn't find the work particularly difficult. At first, some of the miners were surprised to be dealing with a woman doctor, I'm sure. But they soon got used to it. I certainly had no problems there." This was not entirely true, but she wasn't going to rise to his bait.

"And may I ask where you earned your medical degree?"

Mollie knew she was on trial, but she was ready for him. "At the Woman's Hospital Medical College in Chicago," she answered. "I presume you've heard of it?" She smiled her most patronizing. She knew hers was an excellent degree. Even if it was from a "woman-only" college, it was well known in the profession that the college boasted an outstanding faculty. "And if I may ask, where did you receive your degree?" It was a return dig. Dr. King smiled for the first time.

"The Chicago Woman's College has an excellent reputation," he said. "And I presume you'll be seeking certification here in Montana?"

"Of course," said Mollie. "I never had time to come up here to take the Montana certification examination while I was working in Bannack. However, Mr. Longmaid was satisfied with my certifications from Illinois, Louisiana, and Iowa. But of course I'll be taking the examination as soon as I have a chance to get to Helena." She knew her list of state certifications would shut him up. It did. If she was reading his expression correctly, Dr. King was impressed.

"Well, I'm very glad you're here, Dr. Moore. Marysville needs more doctors. I can hardly take care of the business I've got. Last year Dr.

McNiven was here, but he became ill and has left town. I've been holding the fort alone for the last several months. I'm sure we'll be working together quite a bit."

"I'm certainly looking forward to working with you, too, Dr. King," Mollie said with her sweetest, if secretly somewhat ingenuous smile. "And I'm wondering if you could give me some idea about the medical situation in Marysville?"

"Well, we've got some bad public health problems here," King answered. "Marysville doesn't have an adequate water system. And given that the town is growing like crazy with new people coming in here every day, we have to do something about the water. We've got outhouses next to wells all over town." The doctor seemed to be warming up to Mollie as he listed his concerns. "Jim Hendricks has a good spring above town. If the town could establish a water company that would build a reservoir, there's enough water there to serve us for some time. And along with a water system, we'll soon need to put in sewers as well. Just about every week Bill Mahurin and I make an issue in the *Mountaineer* of getting that water source developed. And there's a garbage problem. We're only a mile or so below the divide; we need to haul the garbage over to the other side and let it float down to California." Dr. King laughed. "But seriously, we can't just keep dumping it in the creek canyons."

"Yes," said Mollie, "just walking around the downtown today, I could see the haphazard growth crowding in everywhere. And I could see what you mean about the garbage. That's going to cause trouble."

"Especially when the epidemics hit. We had a bad run of scarlet fever here this spring. And typhoid the year before. I really worry about another typhoid occurrence. It's only going to get worse."

"What about the miners?" Mollie asked. "Do you have a lot of silicosis and TB problems?"

"Maybe not as bad as in Butte," King replied, "but we've sure got them. It's hard to convince people here that TB doesn't have to be fatal. And of course the mine owners are balking at including TB in their medical contracts. They're still claiming that TB has nothing to do with the mining, that it's a hereditary disease. They don't want to take any responsibility. I'm afraid you're going to run into a lot of this."

"I was already aware of that in Bannack. And of course in Salt Lake City it's a hazard to breathe the air even above the ground, let alone what it must be doing to the workers' lungs down in the mines."

"This is a major public health problem that we've got to deal with here in Montana, but so far not even our own Montana Medical Association is very interested. Along with the miners, most of the doctors seem to still believe that TB is hereditary."

"Well, Dr. King, maybe you and I will just have to change that: Start a campaign with the doctors; organize a state health department; arrange a public education campaign; go after the legislature. But not today," she said, smiling. "I promised Janette Longmaid that I'd be back at the house for lunch, and it's almost noon." She stood up to leave. "I'm sure we'll be seeing each other soon, Doctor. I think you and I already see eye to eye on a number of things."

Dr. King rose from his chair and held out his hand to his visitor. "I'm so glad to meet you, Dr. Moore, and I do look forward to working with you. Please stop by again as soon as you're settled in Empire, and we'll continue this conversation."

Mollie said good-bye to the doctor and his receptionist and went out to get Willy. While she'd been gone, Willy had attracted a group of schoolgirls, who were standing around him. Some had gotten up the nerve to pet him, and of course he loved nothing better. He tried to reciprocate by licking the girls' hands, which caused them to squeal and jerk their hands back.

146

"Don't be afraid," Mollie said to the group. "By licking your hands, he's just trying to show you that he likes you to pet him. His name is Willy, and he's very friendly."

Gingerly, a few of the girls reached out again and patted Willy on the head. Then they all ran up the street together, squealing as if they had just braved a hand in a lion cage. Mollie was amused, but at the same time sorry that the girls were afraid of the dog. She felt it was too bad they had never learned to live with an animal. If it was all right with Janette, she would teach little Harold to play with Willy so that he would grow up unafraid.

As she untied Willy's leash from the hitching post and started to walk up the hill to the Longmaids, it occurred to her that George King had not answered her question as to where he had received his medical degree. Yes, this was his territory, but she knew she had passed at least the first round of his interrogations with flying colors. Clearly, he knew it—and he knew that she knew it. But he certainly needed help, so he had better stop trying to intimidate her. But she knew, too, that she must get to Helena as soon as possible and take the certification examination.

The entrance to the Empire Mine was high on the side of Mount Belmont above Lost Horse Gulch. Three shafts burrowed into the batholith, the longest of which stretched a half mile, 400 feet down. Enormously profitable since being taken over by the Golden Leaf Company six years earlier, and now with the appointment of J. Henry as manager, the mine produced millions for the company and its investors. Each month 4,000 tons of gold ore, carried in buckets on a tramway pulled by gravity, were fed into the sixty-stamp mill that hugged the hillside at the edge of Lost Horse Creek. The mine employed sixty men, all Dr. Mollie's potential patients.

Eager to get established in Empire, Mollie took Willy early the next day and rode the 2 miles out to the mine camp in the buckboard with J. Henry. Empire boasted a post office, located in the Golden Leaf general store, a blacksmith shop and livery, two saloons, and a changing house with showers near the mine entrance. Some of the miners lived in a boardinghouse, and some in shacks scattered along the gulch. A few lived in Marysville. The main event of Empire, however, was the stamp mill. It was a magnificent structure, built into the side of the mountain against three tiers of masonry retaining walls, the building's wooden walls of Pacific Coast Douglas fir. The stamps, falling faster than one a second, boomed against the surrounding mountains.

"My men are still working on your cabin," J. Henry said as he reined in the horse in front of the mill. "Give me a few minutes in the office, and then I'll show you where it is."

J. Henry disappeared into the mill. Mollie climbed down from the buckboard and surveyed her new "town" with amusement. If Bannack had seemed primitive, it was a metropolis compared with Empire. On the other hand, Empire was only a couple of miles from civilization. Marysville had a population of 2,500 and the usual assortment of commercial establishments to serve that population. In addition, town pride celebrated two theaters and an opera house, beer gardens and dance halls, as well as apparently countless saloons. And most important of all, Marysville was an hour's train ride from Helena.

In a few minutes J. Henry returned, accompanied by another man. "Mollie, I'd like you to meet my brother, Frank. Frank manages the Penobscot mine for the family, and is taking over the Bell Boy for us, too. Our men, as well as the Golden Leaf men, will be contracted with you."

Mollie exchanged a few pleasantries with Frank Longmaid. She was, however, feeling suddenly overwhelmed by the number of prospective patients. So far there were only two doctors in the vicinity, herself and George King. If they were hit with a plague, she hoped the two of them could manage. Surely they were going to have to get some more help soon.

Frank took his leave of them and went back into the mill office. J. Henry drove Mollie a few hundred yards along the gulch to where some men were working on a small cabin. She was taken with the site immediately. The cabin sat in a sunny glen at the edge of Lost Horse Creek. To one side was a small corral. Above, in a grove of box elders, a spring dripped from a pipe into a half whiskey barrel, then ran on down a narrow gully to the creek. The men were stringing an electric wire from the mill to the cabin. Willy expressed his approval by jumping out of the wagon and splashing in the creek. Except for the incessant pounding from the mill, the setting was idyllic.

J. Henry walked over to one of the workmen and spoke to him for a moment, then came back to Mollie. "The cabin will be ready for you day after tomorrow. I've already ordered the furniture. We got you a regular examination table this time, not like that cot you had to use in Bannack. It should be at the depot tomorrow."

"I'm glad to hear that," said Mollie. "It wasn't easy performing surgery on that cot."

J. Henry smiled. "I think you'll find that in Marysville, you're back in civilization. But you must excuse me, I have to get back to the mill. Why don't you take the buckboard back to town, and I'll catch a ride or come on the stage later. Perhaps this afternoon you can go down to Dudley's drugstore and order what you'll need. Charlie's pretty well stocked, and he can order things from Helena if need be. Put the bill on the Golden Leaf account."

Mollie climbed back into the wagon with J. Henry, and Willy, dripping wet from his frolic in the creek, jumped into the rear. She took the reins and drove back to the mill.

J. Henry jumped down. "I'll see you tonight," he called as she turned the wagon toward Marysville.

There was considerable traffic on the narrow road. Every few minutes a wagon or lone rider would pass her. In places, the forest had been decimated; freshly cut stumps hid the shame of their amputation among the tall grasses and wildflowers that were taking over the cleared areas. The need for wood to feed the steam engines in the mills was devouring the hillsides. The road wound upward to a high meadow at the top of the Continental Divide. Groups of Black Angus cows were lolling in the grass. Mollie pulled the wagon off the road and stopped. From the ridgetop she could look out over the entire Prickly Pear Valley, from Helena on the south almost as far as Great Falls to the north. There was a strong breeze that cleared the air around her, although in the distance the smoke from mill operations hung in the valleys. The wind made her grab at her hat. She breathed the expanse into her body. For the first time in years she realized she was happy. The burden of her marriage had oppressed her for so long, and the fear that she might not succeed as a doctor, that she had forgotten what happiness could feel like—that happiness was, indeed, the fresh air of freedom. Now her life felt full of promise. She had earned the respect of the community in Bannack and the respect of her employers. What's more, she had made George King sit up and pay attention. And she had done it without Frank; she had done it on her own. Here in Marysville and Helena, she could now become part of the established medical community. In a year or two, she would have her own independent practice—she was sure of it.

Willy must have sensed her happiness; he jumped from the bed of the wagon into the seat beside her and nuzzled his wet nose under her arm.

Mollie slapped the reins against the horse's flank, and the wagon moved back onto the road. She began a steep descent, passing the old Belmont mine and forty-stamp mill on the side of the mountain. The mine was idle now, although she had read in the paper of plans to reopen it. Across the road was a creek with small miners' cabins sprinkled along its banks. In a few minutes she was at the edge of town.

Before returning the wagon to the livery and stopping at Dudley's, she reined up in front of the *Mountaineer* office. She told Willy firmly to wait in the wagon, climbed down, fastened the reins to the hitching post, and entered the office.

"Mr. Mahurin," she said brightly as the man stood up at her entrance, "I've come to buy that ad space from you. Starting next Thursday, I want you to run the ad every week."

"Excellent, Dr. Moore," Bill Mahurin answered. "Just fill out what you want to say on this paper. We charge $1.00 per month." He handed Mollie a sheet of paper and a pencil. She wrote:

> *Dr. Mary B. Moore, Physician and Surgeon*
> *Golden Leaf Mining Co., Empire, Montana*

Mollie paid him for the ad and went back to the wagon. As she and Willy drove up Main Street, she smiled with excitement. Next Thursday when the ad came out, everyone within range of "the great advertising medium of Montana" would know that Dr. Mary B. Moore had arrived.

Dr. Mary Moore in 1885
FROM THE AUTHOR'S COLLECTION

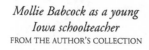

*Mollie Babcock as a young
Iowa schoolteacher*
FROM THE AUTHOR'S COLLECTION

The Hotel Meade in Bannack
FROM THE AUTHOR'S COLLECTION

A.F. Wright's General Store and the Bannack Hotel
MONTANA HISTORICAL SOCIETY, HELENA

A typical miner's cabin near the Empire Mine, above Marysville
MONTANA HISTORICAL SOCIETY, HELENA

The Marysville train
HAYNES FOUNDATION COLLECTION,
MONTANA HISTORICAL SOCIETY,
HELENA

*Marysville, Montana, now a
virtual ghost town, was a bustling
city in the late 1890s.*
MONTANA HISTORICAL SOCIETY, HELENA

The Empire stamp mill
MONTANA HISTORICAL SOCIETY, HELENA

Ben Atwater, circa 1920
FROM THE AUTHOR'S COLLECTION

The Drumlummon Hotel in Marysville, Montana
MONTANA HISTORICAL SOCIETY, HELENA

Dr. Mollie and Dorothy in 1902
FROM THE AUTHOR'S COLLECTION

Dorothy Atwater, age 17
FROM THE AUTHOR'S COLLECTION

GOLDEN LEAF, LIMITED.

Cavendish,
Beaverhead County,
Montana, _Aug 17_ 189 _2_

To whom it may concern:

From my own observation and experience
I feel justified in recommending Doctor
Mary E. Moore as a physician and surgeon
of more than ordinary skill and ability.

Since I have known her she has been my
family physician and has prescribed for my
own and other children with great success.

As a physician for childrens complaints
I unreservedly state that I have the utmost
confidence in her

Respectfully
J C Hanrahan

A glowing letter of recommendation for Dr. Moore
FROM THE AUTHOR'S COLLECTION

Mary Atwater fought for woman suffrage alongside Jeannette Rankin, the first woman to serve in the U.S. House of Representatives.
MONTANA HISTORICAL SOCIETY, HELENA

The normally serious Dr. Atwater kept this photo because it amused her so much.
FROM THE AUTHOR'S COLLECTION

This photo of Dr. Mary B. Atwater was probably taken in Bannack, Montana, circa 1922.
MONTANA HISTORICAL SOCIETY, HELENA

Pioneer Woman Leaves

DR. MARY B. ATWATER
Who left last week for California.

A fond farewell for Dr. Mollie
FROM THE AUTHOR'S COLLECTION

Dr. Mary Atwater in Berkeley, California, 1940
FROM THE AUTHOR'S COLLECTION

CHAPTER TEN

The Marysville Strangler

MOLLIE AND WILLY SETTLED INTO their Empire cabin at the end of November. Already the air had the bite of approaching winter. The leaves of the box elders had turned to gold, to brown, and then dropped, and the forest floor crunched when Mollie walked up to the spring for water. The nights were cold, but the miners made sure that plenty of stove wood was chopped and stacked outside on the woodpile.

Mollie needed a horse always ready for when she was called out, so the workmen had built a small shack at the edge of the corral, just big enough to winter one horse. For the first few weeks, aside from lancing a few minor felons and a broken wrist that needed attention, business was mercifully slow. There had been only one childbirth, and it had gone well. Dr. King had climbed down from the superior attitude he had taken with her when they first met, and they had become friends. She had passed his test, and he had realized she could be the help he so obviously needed. And she knew she was going to need his help as well.

While Mollie was in Osage dealing with the legal closure of her marriage, she had collected her medical school books. She'd left in such a hurry two years before, she hadn't been able to pack them. The small library that she had shared with Frank, he'd taken with him to Louisiana, but he had delivered her textbooks to Adelia Sophia's house. These, along with some recent journals she was able to borrow from Dr. King, were her companions on many a cold night that first winter in Empire. She had applied to the Montana Board of Medical Examiners for certification, and received a reply that the exam would be given in Helena the next April.

Mollie did not languish through the winter absorbed only in studying medical texts. She soon discovered that as a friend of the Longmaids, she was quickly drawn into the social whirl of the elite of Marysville. There were whist parties and anniversary parties and engagement parties. There were weddings and church socials and sleigh rides. The Patriotic Sons and the Patriotic Daughters of America held dances at McKendrick's dance hall, as did the Odd Fellows and the Masons. There were opera parties and theater parties and train-ride parties to Helena. As a single, "mature" woman, Mollie was often asked to chaperone the young ladies of Marysville to these affairs. And always the following Thursday there would be a column on these events in the *Mountaineer:* a listing of who had attended, who had won prizes, the gifts people had brought, even what the ladies were wearing. Mollie was amused to read about herself one Thursday after a grand ball at McKendrick's: "Dr. Moore wore gray silk crepe trimmed with steel beads, gloves and slippers to match, and a carnation bouquet." The bouquet was a gift from Ben Atwater, a young accountant and the secretary of the Marysville Agnostic Club. Ben was seen more and more frequently escorting Mollie to these affairs.

"That newspaper has its nose into everything!" Mollie had exclaimed to her new friend. "It's embarrassing having one's clothes described as if the event were a fashion show, let alone listing everyone's gift at a wedding so the whole town can compare them. I wish Bill Mahurin would spend more time telling us what's going on in the world, rather than who's who at every Marysville dance and card party."

"Yes, Bill seems to think that the world revolves around Marysville society." Ben laughed with her. "You'd think there was nothing more important to write about."

Mollie found herself in such social demand, she soon realized that living in Empire was a great disadvantage, especially when the temperature was well below zero—as it often was those winter nights.

"Why don't you move to Marysville?" Ben asked her one evening when they were on their way to a whist party at the home of one of his friends. "You can go out to Empire when you're needed. Then I could see you more often in the evenings."

"I can't do that, at least not now," Mollie had replied. "J. Henry expects me to live in Empire, and after all, he does pay my salary. Besides, I've got to study for the April exam, and unless there's an emergency, I have plenty of time to read out there. But I did talk to Charlie Martinson over at the Peterson House. I've made arrangements with him to stay over at the hotel on nights that I want to be in Marysville."

Mollie was surprised that Marysville society had so warmly embraced her. And surprised, too, that she found herself accepting Ben Atwater's attentions. She couldn't help but notice that her new friend had an attractive twinkle in his eye. He was tall and slender, and his slightly receding hairline was countered by a full and most elegant mustache. She had been so caught up in the misery of her failed marriage, as well as in her compulsion to succeed in a man's world of medicine, that she had not been able to foresee a life other than one of complete dedication to her work. She had not stopped to think that the world might consider her an interesting, attractive, and still relatively young woman.

As the year moved into the early months of 1893, the sense of excitement, of euphoric expectation that had struck Mollie when she had come to Marysville just a few months before, suddenly dampened. The entire country was sliding into a depression, and Montana was not spared. The "Panic of 1893" closed down businesses and sent railroads and banks into receivership across the country. In addition to gold and other metals, a large part of Montana's economy was based on silver. President Cleveland had determined that the Sherman Silver Purchase Act of 1890, which mandated that the government purchase all of the country's silver output, was the cause of the depression.

"Cleveland's convinced Congress to repeal the Sherman Act," Ben said to Mollie as the two were sitting in the lobby of the Peterson House, reading the *Helena Independent*. He pointed out the article to Mollie.

"Doesn't he realize what a disaster this is for us—for the entire mining industry of the West?" she said, when she had finished reading the piece. "Not only has the price of silver fallen to half its previous value, but copper and other metals are also down."

While much of Marysville mining was for gold, around this time the veins of some of the mines were beginning to wear thin, and the mines that were silver were badly hit by the drop in value. To make matters worse, there was a severe drought across the Great Plains, including the wheat fields and cattle ranges of eastern Montana. Two of Helena's six banks had folded, and to feed the depleted municipal coffers, the city council voted to cut teachers' salaries—they were only women anyway and wouldn't put up a fight—and to fine all the prostitutes and pimps the police could round up.

"Look, Ben," Mollie said, handing him back the newspaper. "Helena must be in a very sorry state. The city is reduced to squeezing its prostitutes to keep itself in business."

"Yes, I read that," Ben said. "And it looks like the women, be they teachers or prostitutes, are going to be made to pay for it."

In addition to the state's economic woes, the late winter brought waves of sickness to the mining camps. The *Mountaineer* reported there were several cases of diphtheria in Helena, and in Marysville several children had come down with scarlet fever. Mollie was called out again and again to the families of her contract employees to care for feverish children.

Scarlet fever was a serious public health problem, and Mollie was concerned that the community be alerted to the need to contain it. She stopped by Dr. King's office one morning to discuss what they could do.

"George, we've got an education problem here. That school's the worst crucible for these germs. And did you read there's diphtheria again in Helena? Maybe we can put out a letter to all the parents and teachers, explaining the highly contagious nature of these diseases, and how necessary it is to keep sick children isolated."

"Good idea, Mollie," Dr. King said. "I did read about the diphtheria in Helena, and I've been worrying about those children in the schoolhouse, too. About a fourth of them are out sick with scarlet fever, and God knows how many more will come down with it. So far at least, we haven't had any fatalities."

"Yes," Mollie said, "but little Jenny Slotski has lost her hearing, and I'm afraid we may have more of this before the fever runs its course."

"I didn't hear about the Slotski girl," he said. "I'm so sorry. Marek Slotski's a good man. If we can get people's attention now about scarlet fever, explain to them the consequences and how to prevent contagion, maybe they'll start paying attention when something even more deadly hits, like smallpox or diphtheria. I'll get Bill Mahurin on this. I'll have him publish the early signs to look for, and the importance of keeping the children separate. Why don't you contact the school and get a list of names. We can put together a letter."

Mollie's concern was prompted by her growing conviction that the prevalence of contagious diseases assaulting Montanans was the result of unsanitary living conditions and ignorance. Four years before, an epidemic of smallpox had broken out in Great Falls. No quarantine had been required, and the disease had spread all over town. And now smallpox was raging in Deer Lodge and Silver Bow Counties. It had not yet come to Marysville, but it might just be a matter of time.

"When I was working in Bannack last year," Mollie said, putting on her coat and scarf to leave, "the U&N pulled into the Dillon station with a trainload of Chinese workers suffering from smallpox. Dr. Bond found out about it in time and convinced the railroad not to let them off the train. The people of Dillon were lucky. But now with diphtheria in Helena, one of these days someone who maybe doesn't even know he's infected is going to get off the Helena train, and we'll have a roaring diphtheria epidemic here in Marysville. What Montana needs is a statewide board of health with some muscle. We need public education and the legal authorization from the legislature to impose quarantine."

"I certainly agree with you there," King said, opening the office door for her, "and I hope the medical association will take the lead on this. I'm going to bring it up next meeting. Meanwhile, maybe we can do something now to help Marysville."

A few days after her conversation with Dr. King, Mollie had just lit the woodstove and was settling down for the evening to study her medical books when she heard the sound of a horse stopping outside. Soon there was a knock. Willy bounded to the door as he always did, ready to welcome a visitor—at least to welcome one his nose told him meant no harm to Mollie. She got up and opened the door. A young man stood on the threshold, his face drawn with worry.

"Please, Dr. Moore, you must come right away. I'm George Coombs. My friend Jerry McCullaugh is so sick, he can hardly breathe, and he's got a terrible bad sore throat. Jerry works at the Penobscot, our cabin's in Towsley Gulch."

Mollie gathered her coat and the saddlebags that contained her mobile medicine chest. "I'll saddle my horse and follow you."

"Better leave your dog, Doctor. We've got a little bitch over there that's about to go into heat." Much to his disappointment, Willy was told to stay and watch the cabin.

It wasn't far from Empire to Towsley Gulch, but it took some time for the riders to cross a low range of hills to get down to the gulch. The evening was dark. The moon hadn't risen high enough to light the trail. Mollie was glad that she could let her horse follow the one ahead. She was worried. George Coombs had said his friend could hardly breathe. That could mean any number of things, all of them serious. But with a sore throat, too . . . she hoped it wasn't diphtheria.

Jerry McCullaugh was one of the Cornish miners who had been hired by the Montana Company to work at the Drumlummon. In the past year Frank Longmaid had lured him away to work for him at the Penobscot. Jerry and George Coombs shared the cabin in Towsley Gulch. Mollie was acquainted with Jerry; she had treated him for an infected finger some weeks back.

The two riders arrived at the cabin. George dismounted and opened the door. A small mutt of indeterminate heritage rushed out to meet them.

"That's Minnie," George said, patting the dog affectionately. "She just showed up here one day and moved in with us. Nobody knew who she belonged to, so we just kept her. She's been pretty upset about Jerry being sick and all. She's been lying on the floor by his bed. I have to pry her away to make her go outside now and then."

George took the horses, and Mollie took her saddlebags and hurried into the cabin. The sound of strangled breathing punctuated by explosive gasps came from a cot in the main room. The fire in the stove was almost out, and the cabin was cold. George came in with the dog, and Mollie told him to see to the fire immediately and to put a kettle of water on to boil.

She took off her coat and washed her hands at the washstand with antiseptic soap. Then she took a sterile mask from one of her bags and slipped it over her nose and mouth. As she approached the man struggling on the cot, she could see by the lamp hanging from the center of the ceiling that the lymph glands in his neck were swollen and his face looked feverish.

"Hello, Jerry," Mollie said as she bent over him. "I've come to help you. I need you to open your mouth so I can take a look at your throat."

"It hurts bad, Dr. Mollie," Jerry's voice croaked. "It feels . . . like somebody's . . . strangling me."

Mollie took a sterile probe and pressed down on Jerry's tongue. His mouth confirmed what she had feared. The tonsils and pharynx were covered with whitish gray spots. The diphtheritic membrane was forming, causing him to struggle for air. She would have to act quickly. She took a bottle of carbolic acid solution and a piece of cotton from her bag and swabbed the solution on the lesions in Jerry's throat. She knew the membrane would form again immediately if she just removed it. She would have to insert a tube in the trachea to provide a bypass to get him some air. She couldn't imagine a worse time or place to perform a tracheotomy.

160

"You're going to have to help me, George," she said. "First, put Minnie outside. I can't be distracted by the dog. Then find me a clean sheet we can put under Jerry. I'm going to have to operate." She took the package of sterilized surgical tools from her saddlebag, along with a bottle of chloroform and a mask.

George shooed Minnie outside; the dog immediately started whining and scratching at the cabin door. Then he produced a sheet from a trunk in the back room.

"Bring that light over here." George unhooked the lamp from the ceiling chain and brought it over to Mollie. "Set it on that shelf above Jerry's head. I'll need you to help me in a few minutes."

Mollie turned to Jerry. "I'm going to put you under for a short time while I work on your neck. You won't feel anything, and it won't take long." She smiled at him reassuringly as she lifted him to put the sheet under his shoulders and then adjusted the chloroform mask over his face. When Jerry was unconscious, she pulled on the operating gown she carried in her saddlebag and again washed her hands with antiseptic soap.

"George, you have to help me. I need you to hold this syringe and draw the saliva from Jerry's throat while I work on his neck." She forced Jerry's jaws apart and braced them open with a sterile cloth pad. Then she took the syringe and demonstrated to George how to keep the throat clear of saliva, emptying the syringe into in an enamel dish.

"Now watch carefully that no saliva forms or Jerry will choke." She handed the syringe to George.

She laid her surgical instruments on a clean towel next to her patient. Taking her scalpel, she cut into Jerry's neck. Praying that George would keep the saliva out of Jerry's mouth, she inserted a small rubber tube into the opening she made, and heard Jerry's breathing return to normal.

161

When she had finished the operation and cleaned Jerry's throat with antiseptic, she glanced up at George. For a moment she had to laugh—both to relieve her own tension and at the spectacle of George. He had indeed managed to keep the saliva out of Jerry's throat, but he had observed as much of the operation as he could take.

"Why, George," Mollie teased. "You're the color of a frog!" At that, George bounded for the door, crashing into Minnie, who had dashed into the cabin.

Mollie washed up, waiting with amused patience while George relieved himself of his dinner. After a few minutes, he came back into the room.

"Well, you do look a little better now." Mollie grinned at him. Then her expression became serious. "We'll let Jerry lie here till morning and let the wound rest. He'll be able to breathe freely now through the tube in his neck, but we've got to get him to the hospital in Helena in the morning. Diphtheria is systemic as well as localized in the throat. He's going to need extended treatment. You've got to have some of the men help you take him in a wagon to the train tomorrow morning. And you'll need to stay with him to Helena. I'll call over to Saint Peter's and have them send the ambulance wagon to meet the train."

"I'll round up some of the men at Penobscot," George assured her. "We'll get him to the train all right."

Mollie gathered up her instruments and took off her gown. "George, I don't want to alarm you, but diphtheria is highly contagious. I want you to wash with carbolic soap everything that Jerry may have touched in the last few days. Here," she said, handing him a clean gauze face mask from her bag. "Wear this while you're around Jerry. And tomorrow when you get back from Helena, wash Minnie as well. If Jerry has breathed on her and touched her, and he probably has, she may have the bacillus on her fur. If you feel the least bit sore in the throat in the next few days, come and see me immediately. And you should take off next week from the mine; you may be contagious even if you don't get sick. I'll talk to Frank Longmaid about that. Let's hope we can keep this from spreading."

As Mollie rode back to Empire in the moon of the early morning, she was worried. Not so much for herself, although she was aware that few diseases prove more fatal to physicians and nurses. She had been careful around Jerry; her worry was about George. He was bound to have come into close contact with things Jerry had touched. Of course not everyone exposed caught the disease. Yet she knew the appalling statistics: a 35 percent mortality rate, and if the disease spread to the larynx, it could be as high as 90 percent. Diphtheria was primarily a disease of children. If it attacked an infant, there would be little she could do. What was also worrisome was that the bacillus could persist in the throat or nose for weeks—sometimes months—after a patient had contracted the disease and recovered, even if the patient was exposed but never developed the symptoms. That was why it was so difficult to control the contagion.

Mollie's concerns proved well founded. Within days, several more miners and a number of children came down with diphtheria. In most cases the diphtheritic membrane did not form, and with the help of disinfectants swabbed on the throat and through the nose, the patients gradually recovered. Still, the delicate tracheotomy she had performed on Jerry had to be repeated more than once, often under circumstances worse than those at the cabin in Towsley Gulch.

The work was discouraging; there seemed no way to stop the spread. She had read in one of Dr. King's medical journals that researchers in Germany had developed a modified toxin suitable for immunizing animals to obtain an antitoxin. But it was found to cause severe local reactions in humans and couldn't be used as a vaccine.

"They seem so close to finding an antitoxin for this," Mollie said to Ben Atwater one afternoon when he had stopped in to see her at her office. "But it won't be in time for our people. I've already had three deaths."

Mollie was so busy that Ben had not seen her for several days. He had ridden over to Empire hoping to catch her. She was glad to see him, and had invited him in for a cup of tea. She was telling him about her patients, many of whom Ben knew.

"What about Jerry McCullaugh?" Ben asked. "Have you heard from the hospital?"

"I'm so relieved," Mollie answered. "Saint Peter's called yesterday and reported that he's getting better. Jerry's a very lucky man. I must confess I had my doubts he would survive."

A few days after Mollie had operated on Jerry, George Coombs arrived at her cabin, complaining of a bad sore throat. When she examined him, the telltale grayish white exudate of bacteria was attacking his nose and throat, but she was relieved that no membrane had formed. Mollie swabbed out his throat with carbolic acid solution, sent him home, and promised to come in the morning.

She was late getting to Towsley Gulch the next day. She had stopped at a cabin along the way to check on one of her young patients. The little boy had taken a turn for the worse, and Mollie had spent a good part of the morning trying to get his fever down and advising his mother how to care for him. As she rode down into the gulch early in the afternoon, she heard what sounded like a child wailing. The sound grew louder as she approached the cabin. She dismounted and knocked on the door, but there was no answer. She pushed open the door and entered. Minnie was on the floor by the bunk, howling. The stench of diphtheria pervaded the cabin. George lay on the bunk, his knees drawn up, his hands still clutching at his neck, his eyes bulged in his blue, oxygen-starved face. The bacillus had been more virulent than she had anticipated. The membrane had grown across his throat, closing off his life.

CHAPTER ELEVEN

A Visit to a Brothel

MOLLIE WAS, OF COURSE, ACCUSTOMED TO DEATH. Not that she was ever comfortable with it, but as a physician she could accept the circumstances that brought it on without allowing the loss of patients to unsettle her. Yet even though she barely knew him, the death of George Coombs grabbed at her heart. He had managed to save his friend by coming to fetch her to the cabin in Towsley Gulch that night. But the exposure to his friend had cost him his life. She berated herself: She should have gone sooner. She shouldn't have let him go back there alone. She should have let him stay in the back room of her office. She went around and around with these thoughts. It was a small gesture, but the only thing she could do for him now: She took Minnie to stay with her, heat and all, until Jerry recuperated and could take the dog back. Willy was delighted.

Ben tried to console her. "Mollie, you know you're not responsible for George's death any more than you are for the others who died. You did your best. You saved the lives of those miners and those children who would have died if you hadn't been there to help them through this."

"I know, Ben. I guess it's the irony of exchanging one life for another. And Minnie's grief that afternoon cut right through me. I wish I could grieve like Minnie. No thoughts to interfere with my feelings. Just howl—pure and uncomplicated."

The Marysville diphtheria scourge finally passed. "As these things do," sighed Mollie as she sat talking to George King in his office. "But what will come next? Smallpox? Cholera? Typhoid?"

"We could better control these attacks if we could get some assurance from the mine owners that the sick men won't lose their jobs if they stay away for several days," George said. "The men go back to work before they're fully recovered and spread the germs to their co-workers. I've talked to the owners, but aside from J. Henry, they aren't listening."

Although the crisis was over, Mollie and George King were still shaken from the experience. They had been called out day and night, often unable to save the victims. They were both exhausted.

Drought and disease were not the only problems assaulting the state that year; the Panic of 1893 had major political repercussions in Montana. Dissatisfied with the platforms of traditional Republicans and Democrats, the Populist Party had gained a stronghold among the farmers on the eastern plains, and particularly among the miners in the West. There was widespread unemployment in Butte, in Anaconda, in Great Falls. Workers were abandoning Helena. In Marysville the Golden Leaf's Empire mine closed. This did not mean Mollie was unemployed; she was still the contract physician for the family-owned mines of the Longmaids. But with the Empire closed, she was now free to move to Marysville. She had passed her certification examination in April. Of the 361 Montana physicians licensed before her, she was the third woman. Her certification meant she could now set up her independent practice. She wouldn't be able to join the Montana Medical Association for another year, however, since the association considered applications only at its annual meeting.

Ben Atwater was delighted that Mollie was moving to Marysville. "Where are you going to set up shop?" Ben asked her when they met at a whist party one evening in the home of some friends.

"Bill Mahurin said he would rent me rooms upstairs from the *Mountaineer* office. I've put an ad in next Thursday's paper. My office hours will be one to four, in case you need my services," she said with a smile.

Mollie was tremendously excited. Although the economic situation was bad in Marysville, as it was everywhere in Montana, setting up her own practice was her dream. And she had the Longmaid family contract to carry her. Since the mine had closed, there was only a skeleton crew at Empire, so she was still the physician for a handful of Golden Leaf miners. But J. Henry was looking for a buyer for the mine, and that contract would come to an end. The few miners left in the tiny town would, like Mollie, soon be leaving. The Longmaids' store manager, Jim Hanrahan, was liquidating the Empire store, consolidating the goods with the Golden Leaf store in Marysville.

"I finally have a chance to achieve my dream," she said to Ben, as they were riding together one late afternoon, "and here I am in the middle of an economic disaster. Most of the people who need my services are out of a job and can't afford to pay me."

"I know, Mollie," he answered. "George King was lamenting the same to me the other day. And I've lost some clients, too. Who needs an accountant in the midst of a depression?"

As Mollie was packing her belongings for the move one evening, she thought she heard a faint scratching at the cabin door. She was surprised; she hadn't heard a horse pull up. Willy sat up alert, and then bounded to the door, his nose to the crack at the threshold. She opened the door to find a young woman hunched against the doorjamb. Her face was cut and bruised, and one eye was severely blackened. The sleeves and bodice of her dress were torn. The woman tried to step through the door and stumbled with a whimper into Mollie's arms. Half carrying her, half dragging her, Mollie maneuvered the woman over to the bed and laid her out. Mollie realized she was not much more than a girl, maybe seventeen, eighteen, if that.

"Who are you? What happened!" the doctor asked in alarm. The response was only a breathless sobbing emanating in gulps from the back of the girl's throat.

Mollie had never seen her before. She was sure she wasn't one of the miners' wives; as far as she knew, she had, over the past months, met all the contract families. Mollie helped her to the bed and unbuttoned the girl's blouse. She was shocked to see that the breasts had been battered. Large splotches of purple showed on the soft tissue, and one nipple was smeared with dried blood. She felt along the girl's ribs. They weren't broken, although they, too, showed bruising. She felt along the arms. There were some minor cuts but nothing seemed to be broken.

"Who has done this to you!" Mollie demanded. There was no answer, only the quiet breathless sobbing.

Realizing the girl was too traumatized to talk, Mollie held her around the shoulders and gently removed her clothing. She cleaned the cuts with hydrogen peroxide and washed the blackened eye with warm water. Then she put a few drops of tincture of laudanum in a cup of water. Supporting the girl with one arm, she held the cup to her lips.

"This will help the pain," she said, gently, "and will help you sleep." The girl sipped the solution and lay back without speaking. "You rest now. You must tell me about this in the morning." The girl had stopped her quiet sobbing, but she was shivering. Mollie covered her with blankets. She closed her eyes, and in a few minutes Mollie saw that she was asleep.

Mollie paced the floor in a rage. *What kind of beast would do this?* she stormed. *And however did she get here? Surely she couldn't have walked here.* She opened the door and looked out into the night. There was no horse tied in front of the cabin. She would just have to wait for morning to find out what this was about. She hoped the girl would be able to speak by then. She determined to talk to Constable Dillon about this.

A whimper drew Mollie's attention. Willy was cowering in the corner, shaking. She went over to him and ran her hand down his back.

"Poor Willy," she said gently to the dog, reassuring him. "You're afraid of me because of my anger, aren't you? It's all right, my friend. I'm not mad at you." As she stroked his ears, she suddenly remembered the scene in Sarah Moore's house when Sarah had kicked him. It had been the last straw of her marriage. How long ago that seemed now, she mused, as she comforted the dog.

Since the girl was sleeping on Mollie's bed, Mollie lay down on the patients' bed in the back room. She was still so angry she couldn't relax. It was several hours before she could fall asleep.

The sun woke her early. She pulled on her robe and went into the main room of the cabin. The girl was sleeping soundly. Mollie could see that her body was well formed, but her face was very plain. Not ugly, but certainly not beautiful. She built a fire in the stove and put on some water for tea. Then she washed and dressed and started to fix some breakfast.

Suddenly there was a cry from the bed: "No! Please don't. Don't hurt me!" The girl awoke with a start.

Mollie went over to the bed. "You're safe now. I'm a doctor. You're going to be all right." She laid her hand gently on the girl's forehead. The girl flinched at her touch.

"You have to tell me who did this to you," Mollie said. "This is a matter for the law."

"No!" the girl cried. "You mustn't tell them. He'll hurt me again if he finds out."

"Who will hurt you? You must tell me." Mollie put her hand back on the girl's forehead, gently stroking her. "Was it your husband who did this?"

"No, I don't have a husband."

"Then tell me what happened," Mollie insisted. "Someone beat you so badly last night you could hardly stand up. Whoever did this should be brought to justice."

The girl gave a bitter laugh. "Justice? You think there's any justice for us? They can do whatever they want with us."

"What do you mean 'they'? Who are you talking about?"

The girl didn't answer. Tears formed in her eyes; she turned away from Mollie.

Suddenly Mollie understood. The girl was from a house. Marysville had an undersociety of girls who made their living in the brothels. From time to time, both in Bannack and now in Marysville, Mollie had been called upon to treat one of the prostitutes. She could never approve of their behavior, but she had heard enough of their stories to know many of them had no options for survival but to sell their bodies for whatever they would bring. If the girls worked out of a saloon or belonged to a house, there might be some protection. At least they were better off than the women whose shanty "cribs" lined certain streets in the camps. Most of those women were old and sick, often addicted to drugs or alcohol. There was nothing Mollie could do to help them. The occasion rarely arose to treat their mishaps and illnesses, which, often as not, were syphilis or other sexual diseases. Half the prostitutes in the mining camps had syphilis. The most she could do was try to convince them, with little efficacy, to refrain from spreading their diseases. She urged them to douche with carbolic acid solution between customers. And she was well aware of the high suicide rate, especially among the women in the cribs. The deliberate ingestion of the acid was a frequent cause of their intentional demise.

Still, for all she had witnessed of the ladies of the night, Mollie had never seen a girl battered like this before. Her outrage returned.

"No one has the right to treat you like this!" Mollie was so angry, she realized she was yelling at the girl. A bitterness had swelled in her that surprised her with its intensity. She recognized that at some level she could indeed identify with this poor little battered whore. How dare they treat women like this? Of course, Mollie knew that because of her background, her education, her privilege, no man would get away with abusing her as someone had abused this girl. She, at least, would have the means to get away from him. Yet it was all a matter of degree. There but for the grace of God . . . Indeed, Mollie had had the money to go to school, to buy herself a profession. Yet what rights did she really have as a woman? She thought about the maid who had worked for Frank's parents. Seventy-five cents a week. Seventy-five cents was the line between employment and slavery. Even Frank couldn't consider her his professional equal after she had received her degree. And he had helped her get it. Yet she had had to accept his humiliating statements on the divorce papers. No one was interested in how *he* had behaved.

Would there ever be any way to change these attitudes, these prejudices? Maybe, she thought, if women had the power to vote for their own rights. But women would never vote until men permitted them to. So she, as well as every other woman, was a second-class citizen. Some were better off than the girl lying on her bed, but still second class. And unless one had money and family or at least education, a girl who was not protected by a man might end up just like this one.

Mollie stood up from the girl's side and started to pace back and forth across the cabin floor. She should talk to Pat Dillon. The man must be caught—and hanged for all she cared.

But there were still too many questions. She sat back down on the edge of the bed and took the girl's limp hand in hers.

"What's your name?" she asked gently.

There was no answer for a few moments. The girl seemed to be considering if she would answer at all.

Finally she turned back to Mollie: "Isabel."

"Isabel," Mollie said to her, smiling. "That's a beautiful name. I knew someone named Isabel when I was in school."

Isabel turned her face again to the wall. She was not going to be drawn into any chitchat with Mollie.

"Tell me, Isabel, how did you get here last night?"

There was no response. Mollie heard again the deep, quiet sobbing from the night before. She was not going to get an answer out of the girl, at least not for now.

She got up from the bed and went outside to the cold box and brought in a tin of bacon. She opened the tin and put the bacon to cook on the woodstove. She poured some hot water into a pot, added some salt, and stirred in a scoopful of oatmeal from a sack in the pantry. She went back to Isabel.

"Isabel, let me help you to the privy. I know your wounds hurt, but they're not serious. You can walk now."

Slowly, Isabel rolled over on her side. She moved her legs around to the floor and gradually, using her hands as support behind her, pushed herself up. She was shaking slightly, and Mollie took her arm.

"There now," she said to the girl. "See, I knew you could stand all right. I'll help you. We'll go together to the privy."

Mollie was in a dilemma. When Isabel had started to talk, she had pleaded with her not to go to the constable. The girl was afraid of the reprisal she was sure would come, possibly from the man who had hurt her, but assuredly from the madam who didn't want her girls making trouble for her with the law. On the other hand, there was a beast out there who next time might go farther than just beating a girl. Isabel had finally told her the location of the house where she worked. Mollie mentally noted the name of the madam.

The girl swore she didn't know the man who had beaten her. "He was just another customer," she said. "I had no idea what he was planning to do to me. I thought he just wanted the usual." She started to cry again. Mollie sat quietly and waited for her to go on. "But then, after he'd finished, he said he wanted to take me for a ride in his wagon. I didn't want to go. There was something strange about him, but he insisted. There wasn't anyone around. I guess the others were all busy with customers and the madam wasn't in her chair in the parlor. Joe was outside on the porch, but he just looked the other way when we went past.

"He pulled me up into his wagon, and we started up the road here to Empire. He seemed to be in a good mood, talking to me real nice. When we got to the top of the Divide, he pulled a ways off the road and stopped. Then he yanked me down from the wagon and pushed me onto the ground. He did it to me again, and then started beating me all over, on my face and chest and arms, and calling me horrible dirty names. I pleaded with him to stop, but he wouldn't. He was laughing the whole time, crazy-like. Finally he dragged me back to the wagon and drove me down here close to your cabin. He threw me out on the ground and said, 'Let that bitch doctor take care of you,' and drove off."

Mollie was appalled. Of the many stories she had heard from the soiled doves she had treated, this was the most horrifying. The man was a potential murderer. Obviously a woman-hater, he could strike again anytime. Anyone, not necessarily a prostitute, but certainly they would be his easiest prey.

It occurred to Mollie that whoever had beaten Isabel and driven the poor girl to her cabin knew she was a doctor. She herself might be in danger if she told Pat Dillon what had happened. Not that this would deter her. Nevertheless, she was glad to be moving out of her isolated cabin and into town.

She was torn. If she talked to the constable, there was the possibility she might cause more harm for Isabel. Maybe even for herself. If she said nothing, the scoundrel would likely hurt another woman. And creeping into the back of her mind, there was something about Isabel's story—she couldn't quite say what it was—that made her wonder if the girl might not be telling her everything.

Before doing anything, she decided she would discuss the situation with Ben. She needed advice, and she had come to value Ben's thoughtful consideration.

"I can't answer this for you," Ben said, as they rode along the crest of the Continental Divide later that day. Isabel was still at the cabin. Mollie had rung up from the mill office and asked Ben to meet her. They had ridden up to the crest from each side and met at the top. "But if I know you, Mollie, you will do whatever you determine in your own mind is right. My advice won't make any difference."

"Am I really that bad?" she asked, smiling at him.

"Yes you are, Mollie, and I love you for it."

Ben's remark startled her. She didn't know what to say to him. Quickly she brought the subject back to Isabel. "She's really afraid I'll go to the constable. She pleaded with me not to. The brute thinks that just because she's a prostitute, he can beat her and nobody will care. Well, damn it, *I* care!" Mollie was surprised at her own vehemence. "The only reason this poor girl is in that whore house is because our society doesn't give a damn about its women unless they have enough money to buy their civil rights—such as they are. Or marry them," she added. "But then they're a matter for the husband to decide."

Ben seemed taken aback at Mollie's passion. He looked away, silent for a few moments. Finally, he turned to her. "Why don't you see if you can talk to the madam? She probably won't see you, but it's worth a try. Surely she would want to know if her girls are being hurt. Perhaps she can give you some information about the man—if he's local, whether he's caused any trouble before."

"That's an excellent idea, Ben, I'll do that." Mollie offered him a smile in apology for her outburst. She determined to talk to the woman right away.

Isabel was upset when Mollie returned to the cabin to tell her she was going to talk to the madam. "She'll be mad at me. At least promise me you won't go to the law."

"I promise not to go for now," Mollie assured her, "at least not until I talk to you again after I've seen her."

She rode into town the next morning, leaving Isabel again in the Empire cabin. She found the house as Isabel had described it, located slightly up on the hill above Silver Creek, not far from the Drumlummon. The location was certainly advantageous.

Mollie twisted the bell ringer in the door. There was no answer. She twisted it again. Of course, she realized. Ladies of the night slept during the day. Finally she heard a shuffling step moving toward the door. A little window in the door opened.

"Yeah, what do you want?" said a woman's gruff, sleepy voice. "Everyone's asleep."

"I want to talk to you about Isabel."

"She ain't here. Haven't seen her for a couple of days. Don't know where she is." The woman started to close the window.

"Wait!" Mollie said. "I know where she is, and she's hurt." The woman opened the tiny window again.

"Look here. I don't know who you are, but go away. I don't want no trouble."

"If you don't want trouble," Mollie said angrily, "then you'd better open this door and talk to me. Otherwise I'm going to the law." The little window closed, and there was the sound of a bolt sliding back.

The door swung open and Mollie stepped into a large parlor—a little shabby, but with a pretense to elegance. Four large velvet-covered sofas were placed around the sides of the room, and on the wall was a long, gilt-framed mirror. Several small tables were each set with two chairs; half-empty glasses and ashtrays stood on many of them. The room was dark and smelled of stale tobacco smoke. To keep out the day, heavy drapes had been pulled across the windows. The middle-aged woman who had opened the door was wearing a Chinese silk robe and slippers. Her slightly graying hair was in a net cap. Mollie's ring had obviously dragged her out of bed.

"I'm a doctor," Mollie said. "Isabel came to my office two nights ago, severely beaten. I want to know who her client was. He should be arrested."

"The names of our clients are confidential. We don't give out that information." The woman spoke in an aloof, condescending manner, apparently amused that Mollie would be so naive as to think she would answer such a question.

"What do you mean? He's beaten Isabel and very likely he'll hurt someone else. He has to be stopped."

"Look, miss, or Doctor, or whatever you are. Some of our clients have special needs, do you understand? And they pay very well for our services." She stressed the "very well" and glared at Mollie. "They expect privacy and they pay for it. You must be that lady doctor Long-maid hired. Well, you just keep your nose out of our business. And I don't advise your going to the law. You won't get anywhere with them if you do. And you won't get any information out of me or any of my girls. Isabel knows perfectly well who her client was, but she won't tell you 'cause she knows what will happen to her if she does. Now please get out of here so I can go back to sleep." She opened the door. "And let me tell you," she said with a leering smile as she ushered Mollie out of the house, "you *don't want* to know who he is."

Mollie was shaken. There was something very ugly going on. Isabel had lied to her about not knowing who had beat her. Mollie had had a hunch about that. But why? Was she just protecting herself, or was she protecting the man, too? Certainly she was protecting the house.

Once again, she felt she needed to talk to Ben. She mounted her horse and rode over to his rooms on Grand Street. She found him in his upstairs office, working on a client's account books.

"I'm sorry to interrupt you, Ben, but I need to talk to you."

"Of course, Mollie. Please sit down. You look upset. What's happened?"

Mollie sat down on the sofa facing Ben's desk. "I took your suggestion and went to see the madam of Isabel's house just now. I had the naive thought she would be concerned that someone had beaten up one of her girls. On the contrary, she acted as if she'd expected it. She implied that beating was a 'service' of the house." Mollie snorted in disgust. "What's more, she strongly gave me to believe that not only does she have an understanding with the law, but that whoever it was who beat up Isabel would be protected."

"My God," said Ben. "It must be someone important in Marysville, someone with enough money to buy silence. But who?"

"It could even be someone from Helena who comes here because people won't recognize him," Mollie said. "I can't imagine Pat Dillon is mixed up in this. Pat's as honest as Abe. But I'm sure that Pat as well as the mine owners probably consider the whole brothel business a necessary community service."

"I agree about Pat," said Ben, "although I've been fooled before. Keeping the miners happy is one thing, beating up a girl is another matter." Ben stood up from his desk and went over to sit with Mollie on the sofa. He took hold of her hand and looked directly into her eyes. "Yesterday," he said, "I told you I thought you would do whatever you thought was right, no matter what my advice would be. But after what you've just told me, I'm going to give you my advice anyway, and hope that you will follow it. Mollie, I don't want you to go to the law. You don't know what you may be getting into. You said yourself the girl pleaded with you not to talk to Pat. I know this assaults your sense of justice, but you can't take the sins of the world on your shoulders. You might cause Isabel far more harm than you know if you do this. She undoubtedly lied to you out of fear of what would happen to her."

Mollie pulled her hand away and stood up. She walked over to the window and looked down on Grand Street. The two saloons she could see from the window were already doing a booming business although it wasn't yet noon. She felt a strong repugnance, and a sadness. What Ben was saying made sense. By meddling in this, she might be putting Isabel in jeopardy, maybe others as well.

"I'm going back to Empire now," she said, turning to Ben. "I need to talk to Isabel about what I've found out. I promised her I wouldn't go to Pat Dillon until I talked to her again. I don't know yet what I should do."

Mollie mounted her horse and walked her slowly up the road toward Empire. There was little traffic now that the mine was closed. At the top of the Divide she stopped and turned back to look out over the Prickly Pear Valley. This was where Isabel was raped and beaten. She shuddered to think about it. She felt pity for the girl, but she had to admit she also had developed a fondness for her. Isabel had told her that both her parents had been killed in accidents: her father in a mine cave-in, her mother drowned while fishing from a boat on the Missouri. The boat had been caught in the current and capsized. The girl had no one to look out for her, to care for her. She seemed so vulnerable, fragile almost—not like the hard, embittered women Mollie had met before. She supposed it would be just a matter of time—if the poor girl lived so long.

It was a half year ago that Mollie, for the first time, had stood looking out from this same spot, determined to make a life for herself in Marysville. And indeed things had gone her way: She was successful as a doctor, and she had made many friends. The certification exam was now behind her, and she was ready to start the practice she had wished for. She had put so much work into achieving her own personal goals, and yet she suddenly felt it was not enough. She had helped many people, especially women. But had she been able to change their lives for the better? The incident with Isabel was affecting her in ways she hadn't anticipated. The sadness of it. The cruelty of it. Ben was probably right; she shouldn't interfere when she couldn't know the consequences of her actions. But how could she live with herself, knowing what was going on and doing nothing about it? She didn't know the answer to this question. She turned her horse and continued down the road to Lost Horse Gulch.

When she entered the cabin, she saw immediately that Isabel was gone. The breakfast dishes had been washed up and set to drain. There was a note on the table:

> *Dr. Moore,*
>
> *Thank you for helping me. You are so kind. I have to go back now. I promise to pay you as soon as I have saved enough money. Please, don't come to the house and please, please don't tell the constable.*
>
> *Isabel.*

Mollie sighed. She should have expected this. Isabel must have hitched a ride and gone back to the house while Mollie was talking to Ben. That woman would probably give her hell. Isabel's running away had tied Mollie's hands by her promise—as the girl had well known it would. She couldn't go to the law now.

Thinking about Isabel's promise to pay her, Mollie felt sad. She didn't want to be paid from those earnings.

CHAPTER TWELVE

A Startling Proposal

MOLLIE KNEW SHE SHOULD MOVE to Marysville immediately. With the Empire shut down, she felt too isolated in her cabin, and there might be consequences from the incident with Isabel. There was a temporary space for a few days next door to the new Golden Leaf store, and the rooms above the *Mountaineer* would be ready for her in a week or so.

Ben brought a wagon and helped her move into town.

"I'm so glad you're coming to Marysville," he said. "I've always worried about you alone out here. Now maybe your patients will come to you instead of you riding all over these hills."

"The riding all over won't stop," she said, "it's the nature of this business. But don't worry, I always carry a riding stick with me in case one of the miners thinks to get fresh. I've never had to use it, but I make sure they see it."

In the days that followed, Mollie was so busy setting up her new office, she didn't have time to think about the man who had beaten Isabel, let alone what, if anything, she could do about it. Bill Mahurin wrote in his column, "News and Gossip," that "Dr. Moore has had excellent success in her practice since coming to Montana, and will doubtless receive a generous patronage." She was grateful for the support. She had indeed been successful, at least in her contract position. Now she would have to prove she could manage an independent practice. She knew that the attitude of the public was such that if the patient of a male doctor died, it was an unfortunate circumstance; if the patient of a woman doctor died, immediately her competency was questioned.

Moving to Marysville allowed Mollie to spend more time with the Longmaid family. Frank and Mary Longmaid's first child, daughter Irene, was born in January, and Janette Longmaid was pregnant again. Mollie kept an eye on her progress. Little Harold was thriving, and Mollie would often bring Willy up to the house at the top of Grand Street to play with the boy. The dog and the toddler became great friends, and one of the first words that Harold learned was "Willy, " which sounded more like "Wooie," but Willy certainly understood and would come running. When the baby was due, Mollie, of course, was called.

This time there were no problems with the delivery.

"I want to ask a big favor of you," Janette said to the doctor as she lay back against the pillows, holding newborn Baby Mary in her arms. "I wish you would leave Willy here with us for a few days. I think it would help Harold adjust to the fact that he is going to have to share us now with his little sister."

"That's a wonderful idea," Mollie said. "Willy is just the one to smooth things over for Harold."

The economic depression, as well as her struggle as a woman to attract a private clientele, meant business was slow. The Golden Leaf Company contract had ended, but she was fortunate to have the Longmaid family agreement. As with the company contract, the workers paid into the Longmaids' private coffers about $1.00 a month, and the family paid Mollie a monthly salary. The Longmaid wages would carry her while she built up her practice.

In April, Mollie's application for membership in the Montana Medical Association was accepted. At her first meeting, George King was elected MMA president, and to her surprise Mollie was nominated for second vice president. Even more to her surprise, she found herself elected to that position. On the agenda were reports on the smallpox epidemics ravaging Silver Bow and Deer Lodge Counties. Mollie and Dr. King brought up the need for a state board of health. The doctors agreed that the legislature should be approached.

Mollie's acceptance into the medical association allowed her to make the professional contacts she'd been hungry for ever since she had left Iowa. There were two women already in the MMA: Dr. Maria Dean, a member since 1883, and the first licensed woman doctor in Montana, and Dr. Katherine Holden, who had joined two years before Mollie. Mollie became fast friends with both these women, but in Maria Dean she found a fellow fighter, a woman who shared her convictions about public health issues and equal rights for women. Dean had been the chairwoman of the Helena Board of Health in 1885, when Montana was still a territory. She had presided over one of the worst diphtheria storms to hit the city. People died by the dozens, and many of the dead were children. As physicians, Maria Dean and Mollie felt strongly they must impress on the state legislature the urgency of the state's public health problems, particularly in the mining communities; as women, they were committed to bettering the lives of all American women.

A growing number of Montana Democrats felt that the politics-as-usual stance of their party was not addressing the economic problems of the state and the nation. In the summer of 1892, the Progressives had begun a vigorous campaign to pull many of these disgruntled

Democrats into the "Peoples' Party." At that time, Mollie was still in Bannack, far from the capital at Helena and far too busy to give much thought to the politics of her new home state. After she moved to Marysville, however, what caught her attention was that the Progressive Party not only railed against commercial monopolies and the use of strike-breakers in the mines, but was also the only party to endorse the cause of women's suffrage. To demonstrate that commitment, at their Butte convention in 1892 the Progressives had nominated a woman, Ella Knowles, for Montana attorney general. Known across the state as "the Portia of the Peoples' Party," Knowles was the first woman to pass the bar in Montana—and then only because two years earlier she had been successful in convincing the legislature to overturn a statute prohibiting women from practicing in the courts. Although Knowles, along with Will Kennedy, the Progressive candidate for governor, lost the election (only men could vote in the election, of course), the party did manage to get three of its members elected to the state legislature. Now, two years later, the Progressives were expected to take three seats in the senate and to send a number of new members to the legislature.

Mollie had met Ella Knowles in Helena at the home of Maria Dean. She found in the lawyer and the doctor two women who had fought, as she had, the prejudice against women joining traditionally male professions. Now that she had moved from the isolation of Empire, she determined that she would join with her new friends and actively take up the cause of woman suffrage. The three women were convinced that once women had the franchise, male prejudices would be forced to change.

"I haven't forgotten the incident with Isabel," she said to Ben one evening at the Peterson House where he had invited her for dinner. "You're absolutely right that I can't directly intervene in Isabel's life. What I can do, however, is fight for a woman's right to vote as a starting point for changing the social conditions that drag young women like Isabel into a life of prostitution and abuse, a life that ultimately kills them. I've been called on to establish the cause of death of many of these women and to file death certificates. It's a disheartening, gruesome experience. Their deaths usually result from a drug overdose, advanced venereal disease, or suicide."

"What do you plan to do?" Ben asked.

"First, I'm going to start a Marysville suffrage group. I'll advertise in the *Mountaineer*. I know there are lots of women here who can be drawn into the cause."

"That's a great idea, Mollie. With your energy in the game, those codgers in the legislature will never know what hit them. And second?"

"This may surprise you, Ben, but I've decided to run for county coroner on the Democratic ticket."

"Good God, Mollie!" Ben almost dropped his wineglass. "Why do you want to do that? You just said legalizing corpses was a gruesome business."

"Now, Ben," Mollie said. "Not everyone who dies in Marysville is a prostitute. But since I'm often asked to do that anyway—and let me tell you, I have yet to find a corpse willing to pay for the service—I want the job for the simple reason that a salary comes with it. Frank and J. Henry have closed the Penobscot, and the Empire's been sold to a couple of Helena men. My contract with the Longmaids has shrunk considerably. They're holding on to the Bald Butte and the Bell Boy, and they're considering buying the Belmont, but that deal's still up in the air. Frankly, Ben, it's tough times. Aside from my salary from the Longmaids, most of my private patients have paid me with eggs and potatoes, chickens and whiskey, and, last week, an offer to do my laundry. Very little cash and lots and lots of promises."

Although Mollie had intended to start her suffrage group

immediately, she decided to put it off until after the September election. The Lewis and Clark County Democratic Party did indeed endorse her as its candidate for coroner. At the last minute, however, it was discovered that women were not eligible to run for that office, so no one could vote for her.

Mollie and Ben, along with Willy, had driven out for the day to Granite Butte with their friends the Foremans, who ran the Marysville grocery. The two had climbed the butte while Myron Foreman stayed below and took care of the horses, and his wife prepared a picnic lunch for the four of them. It was a beautiful day for an outing. The late September Sunday was still warm, and the aspen leaves were thinking of turning. Willy had bounded to the top, and Ben gave Mollie a hand up the last steep stretch so that they could sit together at the summit and look out over the Divide and down into Marsh Creek canyon.

Mollie was glad that she had agreed to come on the picnic with Ben and his friends. Still, she couldn't drop her annoyance at the recent election. She had been hopeful that she would win, and could have had the salary she so badly needed.

"You see what I mean?" she said, bringing up the subject that had been on her mind since the election. "A bunch of male bureaucrats decide what women can and cannot do. Ella had to fight the legislature to change the statute banning women from practicing in court, but she couldn't even vote for herself when she ran for attorney general. And now they've reserved the job of coroner for their own kind as well. I suppose they think it's unladylike to deal in corpses. Of course that doesn't stop Pat Dillon from asking me to come down and write out a death certificate every so often.

"Sometimes I think I'd be better off in Helena. Not that women have any more rights there than here, and Helena has its economic problems, too. It's just that it's a much larger town and there would be more opportunity there for me."

Ben looked at Mollie with alarm. "You're not thinking of leaving Marysville? I didn't realize you were in such financial straits, Mollie."

"Oh, I'll be all right. What's important is that I'm doing what I really want. The practice is beginning to pick up. I'm just angry at the attitude some men have toward women, and the fact that they have the power to curtail our lives, our ambitions, and, in the case of married women, power over our bodies if they choose to use it."

The day was so beautiful, she suddenly felt ashamed to be harping on the injustices of the world. "It's beautiful up here, Ben," she said, leaning back on her hands and breathing in the sleepless wind of the mountain. She was sitting on a large flat rock, her long tattersal skirt spread out around her. Willy was at her feet. "I apologize for being so angry. I shouldn't carry on so on such a lovely day in such a wonderful place. Don't let me start on all my grievances again. Forgive me."

"There's nothing to forgive, Mollie. I support you, and I'll help you in any way I can. You know men are part of the movement, too."

"Yes, I know. And I do appreciate your support. Huseby in the House and Brosnan in the Senate are pushing for a suffrage amendment, but there's a lot of opposition, especially in the Senate. Oh, but here I go again," she said, laughing. "Make me change the subject."

"Yes, I do want to talk about something else," Ben said. "There's something I want to say to you."

"Good." She smiled at him. "What is it?"

"I want you to marry me."

The smile dropped from her face. She stared at Ben, astounded. She had been so preoccupied with her own problems and ambitions, she had not realized how serious Ben had become about their relationship. She had long ago dismissed the idea of marrying again. It wasn't the unhappy experience with Frank—she knew enough never to make that mistake again. It was her work as a doctor. It wouldn't be right to marry. She didn't want to have children; they would interfere with her career.

She didn't answer him. A confusion of thoughts whirled through her mind, as she stared out at the distant mountains. What could he possibly be thinking? He must know that for her, children were out of the question. Did he think she would change her mind? And did she even love him? This thought caught her up.

There are times when a word from another will unleash an awareness that has been straining under the surface, trapped by the mind's refusal to acknowledge it. Mollie had come to take Ben's friendship for granted. Yet what suddenly flooded Mollie's consciousness was the realization that she had always looked forward to their meetings with excitement, that she had come to value his counsel, his thoughtfulness, that when she was with him . . . she was happy.

Yet she knew the kind of happiness that marriage would offer her would disappear in a flash if she turned away from everything she had strived for. She couldn't do that, just as she couldn't do it with Frank. No, it was impossible. She couldn't marry Ben—she couldn't marry anyone. She had chosen her path. And yet his words had awakened something in her she had for years not allowed herself to feel—not since those early days with Frank so long ago.

Finally, Ben interrupted her thoughts. "Mollie, I know what you're thinking. That marrying me would cause you to give up your practice. But I would never ask that of you. I admire what you're doing, I love you for doing it. I would never stand in your way. I know how much your work means to you, and I honor that and I always will."

Mollie finally found her voice: "Ben, you are a young man, younger than I am. You will want children, a family. I can't give you that. I don't want to have children, and I have no right to deprive you. You may think now that that's all right, but in a few years, you may resent that you've sacrificed your fatherhood to my career."

Ben looked out at the sunny ridge of the Continental Divide across the valley. He didn't answer for a while, seeming to carefully consider his response. Then he turned to her.

"Mollie, don't presume to speak for me. I have thought about this for a long time. I don't want to have children. I like children, but I don't think it's right for me to bring them into this world of wars and injustice. I know what I want. I want you. I love you and I want to live with you. Of course you'll continue your practice and your suffrage work. And if someday you want to be county coroner, I promise to vote for you," he said, smiling.

The hot sting of tears rose at the edges of her eyes. "There's something about me you don't know," she said looking away from him. "I've never told this to anyone in Marysville, but I have to tell you now. I am divorced." She waited a moment to let her words sink in. "For almost ten years I was married to a doctor in Iowa. I left him and ran away to Montana. That's when I took the job in Bannack. Before coming here, I went home to Iowa and signed the divorce papers."

Ben was silent. Mollie glanced at him quickly. It was clear from his surprised expression that this was something he hadn't expected. She started nervously twisting some strands of grass that were growing at the edge of her rock seat.

Finally Ben reached over and took Mollie's chin in his hand and turned her face to him.

"Poor fellow," he said, grinning at her. "I could almost feel sorry for him, losing you. But I'm glad he did, because now I've found you."

Mollie pulled away, touched by his kindness, not wanting him to see her tears.

Ben stood up and took a few steps to the edge of the rock cliff and looked out at the Divide. Willy rose, too, and walked over to stand beside him. The noon sun was warm, but Willy's fur ruffled in the mountain breeze. The man and the dog stood at the edge looking out for some time. Then Ben turned back to Mollie.

"Don't answer me right now. I know that I've sprung a surprise on you. You need time to think. And besides"—he smiled at her—"the Foremans must be wondering by now what we're up to. They're probably already chattering about us." He reached down to help her up and pulled her into his arms. When he kissed her, Mollie began to tremble. Frank had once kissed her like that, but it was so long ago . . . she had almost forgotten.

"Come, we must go back," she said, pulling away from his embrace. Her head was whirling. His kiss had touched a passion in her she had thought was buried forever. She needed to break the spell, to race down the mountain to join their friends—to paste a proper innocence on her face, to eat fried chicken and potato salad and gossip about Marysville.

Riding back to town later, Mollie found it difficult to keep up a conversation with the Foremans. Her mind was in turmoil, thoughts racing back and forth between the absurdity of even considering Ben's proposal and the pulsing of her blood. Perhaps it wouldn't be so impossible, if Ben was sure that he didn't want to have children. But what if he changed his mind? He would feel trapped. He would want to leave, and it would be like breaking up with Frank all over again. No it wouldn't. Ben was not Frank. But he would be unhappy, and she'd have to let him go. How could she even consider such a thing? There would be nothing but unhappiness ahead.

And yet, what did she really feel for Ben? This last question was perhaps the most confusing. The friendship that she had taken for granted had abruptly changed with his kiss. He was no longer her friend. Now she would either accept his love, or he would leave her. A sudden fear of loss rushed through her.

"Mollie, I asked you a question." Myron said, laughing. "Are you here in this wagon with us? We were just talking about the time last winter when Patsy Sullivan drove you in our wagon up to Bald Butte, and the horses left you both in the snow and came back to the grocery without you."

Mollie grinned with embarrassment. "I'm sorry, Myron, I was thinking what a beautiful day it's been. I guess I was just dreaming."

Ben looked at Mollie and smiled. "Yes, I agree, it has been a beautiful day."

Ben and Mollie climbed out of the Foreman's wagon on Main Street in front of the *Mountaineer* office. Willy was already bounding up to Mollie's rooms. They thanked their friends for the lunch and the outing, and Ben accompanied Mollie up the steps. At her door, he spoke.

"Mollie, you've been lost in thought all afternoon. Is there something you would like to say to me now?"

"No, Ben. I need to be alone for a while. Thank you for a wonderful day. Let's talk tomorrow."

Ben took her hand and brought it to his lips. He released it with a smile and started back down to the street, passing Bill Mahurin, who was coming up the steps.

"Is Dr. Mollie back?" Mahurin asked him. "I've got a message for her."

Ben nodded, and went on down to the street. Mahurin knocked on Mollie's door.

"Pat Dillon asked me to tell you he wants you to come down to the station," Mahurin said when she opened the door. "He's got a body for you."

Mollie hadn't even had time to take the pins out of her hat. "Thanks, Bill. I'll be right there." She picked up her shawl and medical bag and went back down the steps and across Main to the constable station.

"Another one of the ladies, Doctor," Dillon said, opening the door to Mollie's knock. "Thanks for coming. I couldn't get hold of the new coroner. Guess he doesn't want to work on a Sunday. This one's a young one—a girl, really. A shame, it is. Carbolic acid as usual, I suppose, but that's your business."

The constable ushered Mollie into a back room of the station. A body lay on a table, covered with a sheet. Mollie pulled it back and gasped. The girl on the table was Isabel.

CHAPTER THIRTEEN

Just Another Little Whore

"WHAT IS IT, DOCTOR?" the constable asked when he saw Mollie's reaction to the corpse. "She's just another little whore who decided to end it all."

Mollie turned on him angrily: "She's not 'just another little whore.' She had a name."

"You mean you knew her?"

"Yes, I knew her. I took care of her for a couple of days. She came to my office several weeks ago, beaten almost senseless. You can still see some of the marks on her body. You wouldn't perhaps know of someone who gets his thrills beating prostitutes, would you?" Mollie glared at Dillon.

Pat Dillon was taken aback. "I'm sorry, Doctor. I didn't know you knew her. Of course I don't know anything about that. If I did, I assure you I would arrest him. He would have to answer to Judge Padbury."

Mollie had dealt with Pat Dillon on many occasions, and while she was offended by his crude remark, she trusted his honesty.

"Well, there's someone who comes to the house where this girl worked. The madam won't talk, but she allows him to beat up her girls.

I guess poor Isabel here couldn't take that kind of life any longer. She may have been a prostitute, but no one has the right to treat her like that."

"You're right, Doctor. I'll investigate this."

Mollie sighed. She doubted if the constable would be particularly zealous in his investigation of the men who frequented the brothels. And if he did try, he certainly would get nothing out of the madam. She wondered if Jim Hendricks, Pat's assistant constable, might know something.

"The madam suggested I wouldn't get anywhere if I talked to the police. Do you know what she might have meant by that?"

"I certainly do not!" Pat said angrily. "I told you I would investigate, and I will."

Mollie let it go. If the madam warned the man that the constable was asking questions, it might at least scare him off.

She signed the death certificate: death by ingestion of carbolic acid. "What a waste," she said, looking down at the dead girl. The county could take care of disposing of the body.

When Mollie left the constable's office, her first instinct was to go to Ben. But she caught herself. Not now. Not after today. She would have to decide what she was going to do about him. She walked back to her rooms. It had been more of a day than she could bear.

She felt too tired to go over to the Drumlummon Hotel, where she usually took dinner if she was eating alone. There was some bread and cheese in the cupboard in her room, and she could make tea on the gas ring. That was enough to hold her for the evening. She fed Willy and took him out for a quick walk down to Silver Creek, and then climbed the stairs back up to her room, exhausted. She lit a lamp and for a while tried to read, but she couldn't release her mind from the day's events: Ben's proposal, Isabel's death. Finally she gave up and went to bed.

The image of Isabel dead on the police station table floated in the darkness of her room. The sadness of it, the waste. Examining the body, Mollie had seen that the girl hadn't been assaulted again. But what did she have to look forward to? Her attacker would probably have come again. And even if he didn't—perhaps scared off by official inquiries— what kind of life could she have had? Ultimately, as she grew older, she would have been forced to leave the small protection that the brothel offered, and maybe join those ragged forms of female depravity in the cribs. Depressing as the thought was, in a sense Isabel had saved her life by destroying it. The girl was too vulnerable to be the whore that she was trying to be, to please the men, to please the madam. And if time and experience turned her into that whore, then her life would be meaningless anyway.

Mollie couldn't shake the sadness. She could scarcely imagine the despair Isabel must have felt when she determined to drink the acid. Something had to be done, but what? Of course Ben was right in saying she couldn't shoulder the ills of the world. But was that enough? Merely to accept such a situation as a given? She wasn't naively thinking to change the institution of prostitution, like the "purity" bunch in the WCTU. That concerned her not at all; in fact, disturbing as the idea was, she tended to agree that at some level prostitution probably was a community service. But it was a service paid for by the destruction of the women involved. If they didn't kill themselves first, as Isabel had, they would be used up and thrown onto the trash heap of human depravity to die later from drugs and disease. To be sure, a few women were able to get out of the business, or at least to turn it to their advantage. Some were smart enough to save their money and invest it. Mollie was aware that Helena was famous for the amount of real estate owned by prostitutes. Others got out by marrying one of their clients, but it was seldom; from what she had heard, such marriages were usually disasters.

197

These thoughts circled in Mollie's brain in a vortex, at the center of which was the memory of Ben's kiss. The arousal she had felt as they embraced on the mountain washed over her again and again in the remembering. And with it a panic. She would have to make a decision soon. Could she really count on his resolve not to want children? Would he someday resent her? Did she even want to marry at all? She certainly had not planned ever to marry again. Yet she hadn't planned *not* to marry again; she had simply dismissed the idea. And here it was in front of her. She knew that her surprise at his proposal was a sham, a self-deception. His intentions had been obvious for some time. Of course she had known. She had invited his interest from the beginning, accepting his invitations to dances, to dinners, to outings, all the while telling herself he was "just a friend." His kiss had jerked her into the truth. She wanted his kiss, she wanted him. But just because she wanted him didn't mean she should have him, and risk everything she had worked for.

As she finally succumbed to exhaustion, one conviction overrode all her arguments for and against. With or without Ben in her life, she knew she would never give up her profession.

The next day Mollie was so busy she had to put aside such questions as whether or not to get married and what, if anything, could be done about a dead prostitute. Frank Longmaid's baby girl was sick with croup. The Longmaids had shut down the Penobscot mine, at least temporarily, but Frank and his wife, Mary, hadn't yet moved into town. Mollie took Willy and rode out to Penobscot. Little Irene would live. Hers was more a case of parental worry than a major medical problem.

On her return, she rode over to Empire to look in on Mick O'Malley, who had been the manager of the bucket chain for the stamp mill before it closed. Mick was an old Irishman who had been in Montana since the big rush in the '60s. He had had a bad bout with pneumonia a couple of weeks earlier. She had stopped in twice last week to make sure he was on the mend. Today she merely wanted to check to see if he needed anything.

"Damn it, Mollie," Mick said as he opened the cabin door. "I'm all right, but where 'n hell d'you put the plate to the stove?"

"Well, Mickey, if you'd ever bother to make your bed, you'd find it," Mollie said, laughing. "I wrapped that stove plate in a blanket and put it in your bed to keep you warm. But that was two weeks ago."

"Aw, Mollie, me lass. Why didna you tell me? I 'bout smoked myself out a me house with no plate on the stove."

Mollie flipped back the dirty blankets on Mick's bed. The iron plate was still there in its bundle. She took the plate and set it into the iron ring on the woodstove. Then she pulled the covers completely off the bed and took them outside to air in the fresh sun.

"I'm glad to see you're okay," she said as she carried the last dirty sheet out to drape over some rocks. "I'll be back in a few days to check on you. Meanwhile"—she eyed him with mock sternness—"I suggest you get this place cleaned up and get these sheets washed. Take them in to Wing Lee's laundry. He'll get them clean for you."

Mollie was back in Marysville in time to fix herself a quick lunch and then await the drop-ins during her office hours. At four o'clock Mahurin's office boy came up the stairs with a note from Ben:

Please join me for dinner at the Bon Ton at seven.

Mollie scribbled her acceptance at the bottom of the note, saying that she would meet him at the hotel. She gave it to the boy to take to Ben's office.

How long could she put this off? Why couldn't she make up her mind? She had shared many a dinner with Ben, but this time everything would be different. Again she felt his kiss, and knew she wanted more. And why shouldn't she be happy with a man if he meant what he said? She could still carry on her career, but she had to be sure. Yet even as she thought this, she realized the folly of it. Nothing was sure in this life, only her trust in his good faith. But then her mind seesawed again: No, it was too risky. She would have to tell him no.

Mollie laid out her gray crepe dress on the bed, then sat down at her dressing table and stared at her face. For the first time she noticed that a few strands of gray had crept into the dark mass of hair she always wore pinned up in back. She was thirty-five. No longer young, not yet old. Ben was thirty-two, and handsome. Very handsome, she sighed, as she pictured her tall, lanky friend. She did want him. She wanted him with a passion she had not thought she would ever feel again, a passion that was equally balanced with fear. She wanted everything: Ben, her career. And Ben was offering her everything. Was she too afraid to reach for it?

When she arrived at the Bon Ton, Ben was waiting for her in the lobby. She felt awkward slipping her arm through his as he escorted her into the dining room. Everything was so different now. The tension of her indecision was knotting her stomach. As she faced him across the table, the litany of the past twenty-four hours ran through her head: Of course she wanted him, but it would never work. She would never give up her profession, and he would leave her when he realized the mistake he had made.

They gave the waiter their dinner order, and Ben asked for a bottle of California wine. The tension at the table was almost palpable— something important was left unsaid, but couldn't be said while trying to politely maneuver half a baked chicken away from its ribs. Scrambling for things to say, Mollie told Ben about finding Isabel's body at the constable station.

He was appalled at her story. "That poor girl. How horrible! I'm so sorry you had to see her like that."

Then she discussed her determination to start a suffrage group in Marysville.

"It's the only way I know that might help the Isabels of this world. It's just a first step, but it's a step toward someday providing women with opportunities in life that were not there for her."

Ben was sympathetic, but all during dinner they both were scratching for topics to talk about, avoiding the unstated question that Mollie must answer. Finally she could stand the tension no longer.

"Ben, I need to go home to Osage for a couple of weeks." Ben looked at her with a shock of disappointment. She looked down at her plate. "I want to tell my family—my mother and sister, and my brother if he's around—that I'm . . . that I'm going to get married."

"Mollie!" Ben's voice exploded with joy, causing the hotel guests at the other tables to turn and stare at them. He grabbed her hand. "Let's get out of here."

Ben called the waiter over, paid the check, and to the man's astonishment left a whole dollar on the table for him. He took Mollie's arm and rushed her outside, away from the light of the hotel windows. He took her in his arms and kissed her eyes and her ears and her nose and her chin. He moved his lips to her mouth, and she felt herself swirling into a vortex of desire.

Ben proposed that he and Mollie take the Overland Stage together to Garrison Junction. He had told his friends that he was going hunting, but what he wanted was to accompany her to the Northern Pacific station at Garrison Junction. She could have left on the NP directly out of Helena, but Ben had insisted on taking the stage route.

"You're being silly," Mollie said with a laugh as the coach bumped over the dusty road. "We're going to spend our lives together. You don't need to drag me on the stage all the way to Garrison."

"Yes I do," he said. "It means I can spend another day with you before you run off to Iowa."

Mollie twisted her new engagement ring around on her finger. Ben had gone to George Sugden, the Marysville jeweler, the day after their dinner at the Bon Ton. He had seen the diamond he wanted, a large stone with two small stones on either side to set it off. He had struck an agreement with George that he would pay for it over the next three months, and had presented it to Mollie that evening.

"It's beautiful, Ben," she said, holding her hand out in front of her. She had already said it countless times. The truth was that she was deeply touched. She knew it must have cost much more than Ben could possibly afford. But that was his secret.

Mollie waved Ben good-bye from the open window in the door of the train car. The train began to move out of the Garrison station, and she went to find her compartment.

The words that had come out of Mollie's mouth that evening at the Bon Ton had come without her knowing she would say them. She knew now that her heart had spoken those words for her. And yet, removed now from Ben's physical presence, the commitment she had made to him still frightened her. She would have to trust herself, trust her heart. If she would go through with this marriage, and she knew now that she wanted to, she would have to make it work as she had made everything in her life work in her favor. She would take Ben at his word. If there were trouble in the future—well, it was not like her to make a decision based on what *might* happen. This last thought gave her some peace, and she settled back in her seat and let herself drift off to the pleasant rhythmic *click-clack* of metal against the track.

Mollie was looking forward to seeing her mother and Sadie. Her brother wouldn't be there. Adelia Sophia had written that Jason had gone back to Coeur d'Alene to establish a homestead. Jason was a loner. He was thirteen when their father had died, and ever since, he had been aloof from his mother and sisters. Mollie supposed Jason had thought he would have to become the man of the family, and he didn't want the responsibility. Actually it was she, Mollie, who had taken charge of the family when her father died. At sixteen, she was the oldest, and already teaching school. When she was accepted for a high school teaching job at the Cedar River Academy in Osage, Adelia Sophia left Wisconsin with the two children, Jason thirteen and Sadie six, and settled with her daughter in Iowa.

This year Mollie's visit to Osage was very different from her visit two years before. Her family and friends immediately flocked around to admire her engagement ring. Apparently, the ring legitimized every-thing for Adelia Sophia, and she no longer seemed embarrassed about Mollie's divorce. Of course, relations were still strained between the Babcocks and the Moores, especially with Sarah. But Cora and Alice, Frank's two sisters, were always polite when they met Sadie or Adelia on the street or at someone's home. Unlike during Mollie's previous visit, Adelia invited her friends to the house to see her daughter. She even took advantage of Mollie's visit to have a small dinner party to celebrate Sadie's engagement to Mr. Allen of Waterloo.

Soon after Mollie's arrival, Clara and Charles invited her, along with Sadie and Adelia, for dinner. The first thing Clara asked her guests, after they had settled in the Bennets' comfortable drawing room for a glass of sherry, was about Willy.

"How's my favorite dog?" she asked. "Is he happy in Montana? Is he healthy, eating all right? Do you think he misses us?"

"Willy is always with me," she said, smiling at Clara. "He runs in the woods every day. Yes, he's healthy, and I'm *sure* he misses you. And I'm so lucky that Ben loves him, too."

Sadie seemed amused that most of the dinner conversation concerned a dog.

"I know you're fond of dogs," she said to her hosts, "but you people talk about Willy as if he were a friend of the family."

"Well, he is," Charles said, laughing. "After all, he lived with us for almost two years. That certainly makes him part of our family."

Mollie had a wonderful time that evening. She was so glad to be back in the good graces of her mother and sister, and to feel that Osage was no longer a place of unhappiness and shame for her. She wished Ben could have come with her to meet her family and friends.

She tried to find Rita, but discovered she had moved away. They had lost touch since Mollie had gone to Marysville. She heard that Rita had sold the apartments, but no one seemed to know where she had gone.

Two weeks in Osage, however, was long enough for Mollie. She had been worried about her mother being left alone when Sadie married, and she was relieved to know that Sadie and Jim Allen had invited Adelia Sophia to move with them to Waterloo.

Although Mollie was too proud to deliberately avoid her former mother-in-law, she was relieved that again this visit, she had managed not to run into her.

"I'm not going to slink around as if I have something to apologize for," she said to Sadie as they were walking along Main one afternoon. "But in a town of only 2,000, it's amazing we haven't crossed paths."

"Maybe Mrs. Moore's avoiding you—did you ever think of that?" laughed Sadie.

"I must confess, it would do my heart good if that was true." Mollie grinned at her sister. "Maybe she's had some time to think about the way she acted. But then again . . . probably not. Sarah's not the type for introspection."

"Well, Osage gossip will tell her that you're engaged. And now that Cora and Alice are married and busy with their own lives, maybe she'll follow her precious son to Louisiana," Sadie suggested.

"Oh, poor Frank. Don't even think such a fate!" Mollie said, laughing.

Mollie was grateful for these exchanges. Ten years older than Sadie, she had had little time to get to know her sister. Sadie was still a little girl when Mollie had married Frank, and not much older when she and Frank had gone away to Chicago. She was delighted to see that Sadie had grown into a lovely young woman. And she felt that her sister had made an excellent choice in her engagement to Jim Allen. Mollie liked the young man, and was pleased that he welcomed Adelia Sophia to join them in Waterloo.

Leaving Montana for a while had been a good idea. She found herself longing to be back, to be with Ben again. And in this longing she found relief from her worries about her marriage. She was excited about her decision; she was happy.

The Illinois Central had a branch line off its route from Minneapolis to Chicago that stopped in Osage. Mollie wired Ben when to expect her. He wired her back that he would meet her at the Helena station, and that she should be ready for a surprise.

Riding westward through prairie miles of corn and wheat stubble left from the harvest earlier in the month, Mollie wondered what Ben could have meant by a "surprise." To her, her new state of engagement was a surprise in itself. When she had made this trip in 1892 to make final her separation from Frank, she could not imagine she would be returning two years later, promised to another man. She smiled, touching the ring on her finger to make sure it was really there. She could be a wife and a doctor, too—something that had been impossible with Frank. She wondered if Frank would marry again, maybe have children. She was sure he wouldn't marry a lady doctor.

Mollie settled back into the coach chair and closed her eyes. The trip to Osage had been good for her. She no longer felt the guilt and the wrenching pain of her separation from Frank. She could think about him calmly, objectively, if still with a twinge of sadness. She had loved Frank, at least in the beginning. And that was a gift from the past she could hold in her heart. Certainly part of the blame for the breakup of their marriage belonged to Frank's parents. His doctor father had vehemently disapproved of his daughter-in-law studying medicine. Alex was of the school that taught that women belonged at home. In fact, Mollie suspected that Frank's father doubted that women had the capacity to do much other than make pudding and children. Mollie wasn't much good at the first and had refused to do the second. After Alex died, Sarah Moore had turned to her son for emotional comfort. She had been jealous of Mollie, there was no question. The whole thing was bound to blow up. Mollie could see that clearly now. She had nothing to apologize for.

Ben was waiting for her when the NP pulled into the Helena station. He wasn't alone. Standing with him on the platform were the Foremans and the Maygers and their Helena friends, the Stedmans.

"What's this?" Mollie asked as she stepped down from the train.

Ben rushed to embrace her. "We're getting married today. That's what this is. Everyone is here to celebrate."

"Ben!" Mollie exclaimed. "What are you talking about? I can't get married looking like this in my train-rumpled clothes. And besides, we don't even have a license."

"But we will. We're going right now to the county clerk to get it. Reverend Love is meeting us all at four o'clock in the rectory at Saint Peter's. I told you to be ready for a surprise. Can I help it if you didn't dress for the occasion? Besides, my darling Mollie, you're as beautiful as ever."

Myron Foreman took care of checking Mollie's luggage with the station master while Ben hailed a cabbie.

"We'll meet you at the rectory," he called to the group of friends.

"Did you think I was going to change my mind?" Mollie asked, smiling at Ben. "I must say, this is more of a surprise than I could have imagined."

"No, I didn't think you'd change your mind, but I missed you so much while you were gone that I just couldn't wait another minute. Actually this was Charlie Mayger's idea. I was mooning around town like an abandoned puppy for so long that he finally said, 'Why don't you just grab her off that train and marry her then and there?' I thought that was a grand idea and so did your friends. So here we are."

The cab stopped outside the Lewis and Clark County building, and Ben told the driver to wait. Ben ushered Mollie into the clerk's office, and they signed the license. Two women working in the office signed as witnesses, and they were off to meet their friends at Saint Peter's.

When the Reverend Love came to the part in the ceremony where he asked for the ring, Ben was suddenly flustered. He slapped at his pockets. In a moment Myron Foreman stepped forward with the ring in his hand. "Calm down," he whispered in Ben's ear. "You gave it to me to hold." Crisis averted, the Reverend Love pronounced them man and wife.

Yet another surprise awaited Mollie. She and Ben drove over to the Stedmans with their friends. "Just for us to have a celebration drink together before you two disappear," Blanche Stedman had said. When Mollie entered the Stedmans' drawing room, she was greeted by shouts of "Surprise!" The room was full of her Marysville friends. MOLLIE AND BEN was printed on a huge banner that hung across the room. Crepe streamers fluttered from the ceiling. In an alcove, a table was set with glasses and ice buckets of champagne, a tall white wedding cake in the center. The Longmaids were there with little Harold and Frank and Mary. Dr. King had come with Arthur Jordan, the new doctor in town. A number of the young Marysville ladies Mollie had chaperoned were helping set the serving table. Maria Dean was standing with Ella Knowles and Ella's fiancé, Henri Haskell. And in the midst of the party was Willy. When he saw Mollie, he came at a run, gallumpfing through the ladies' long skirts, and flung himself at her.

Mollie knelt down and caught Willy in her arms. Then she smiled up at her husband. "Oh, Ben, this is wonderful what you've done. And that you thought to bring Willy, too!"

"Mollie Atwater's wedding party wouldn't be complete without Willy," Ben said, as he bent down and kissed her cheek.

CHAPTER FOURTEEN

❧

The Marysville Suffrage Society

THE NEXT THURSDAY, Bill Mahurin noted in the *Mountaineer:*

A. Benjamin Atwater and Mary Babcock Moore, MD mar-ried Wednesday, Oct. 24, 1894 in Helena. At home in Marysville. Dr. Atwater will resume practice of her profession and will respond to all calls as before her marriage.

"At home" meant Ben's rooms, which were a squeeze for two peo-ple and a dog. Mollie still needed to keep her office over the *Moun-taineer,* and until her practice picked up more, making two rent payments meant the couple needed to be careful with their expenses. The day after the wedding party in Helena, they had taken the train to White Sulfur Springs for three days, but that was the extent of their honeymoon. Mollie had been away from her practice for almost three weeks. It was time to get back to work.

As the year turned to 1895, Mollie found that adjusting to mar-ried life was much easier than she had thought it would be. Ben, unlike Frank, was not competitive with her. After so many years of hardened defensiveness, it was a relief to just let Ben's kindness wash over her.

She found herself responding to his loving with a passion suppressed for years. That Ben adored his wife was clear to everyone. He was wonderfully funny, and like few others, he could make Mollie laugh. His accounting practice was stable, and if the pair were frugal, his work alone brought in enough for them to live on.

Mollie continued to work to increase her practice. This, however, was proving difficult. The Longmaids' Bell Boy mine was producing well, as was the Bald Butte, and Mollie still held those contracts. But many of the mines were closing or had closed, and the town was beginning to lose population. The *Mountaineer,* in 1892, had proudly boasted that "within a dozen years Helena will only be a suburb of Marysville." In 1893 the newspaper assured investors that "every dollar invested in buildings will net you at least 33 percent interest." Now in 1895 the town leaders were placing ads in eastern newspapers in a campaign to attract investors to come to Marysville to develop the mines, many of which had shut down for lack of the capital needed for deep development. But the campaign had little success. For all the boosterism of the local press, Marysville had never recovered from the 1893 depression; like so many Montana mining towns, it was in decline. That Helena survived the depression and continued to grow was no doubt because the city had withstood the challenge from Anaconda in the 1895 election to remain the capital of the state.

There was a great deal of sickness in Marysville and the surrounding area in 1895, and Mollie was concerned that contaminated well water might be contributing to the cause. The town still had not installed a water system. The Montana Company's manager, R. T. Bayliss, had sent water samples back east for analysis. Certain wells were reported unsafe. Despite the newspaper's advocacy for a water company, nothing had been done.

Clean water was not the only problem. Typhoid was always a threat, arising in areas of filth. The townspeople needed to be pushed to go outside of town to bury their dead animals and garbage, much of which was still collecting in alleys and doorways. And they were urged to wash their hands before milking their cows. Mollie was especially concerned about the milk; she suspected that bovine TB might be present in some of the dairy cattle.

To add to her problems expanding her practice, two young doctors had settled in Marysville: Dr. Arthur Jordan, in whom Mollie immediately found a friend, and Dr. Oscar Lanstrum, with whom she felt politically at odds. Dr. Lanstrum was a Republican, and Mollie strongly disagreed with much of the Republican agenda; her sympathies were with the Populists and the Democrats. Earlier, she had wished for more help in Marysville when she and George King were the only doctors. Now, however, with the population declining, the medical field was becoming increasingly competitive. And as a woman, she found herself on the losing side. What was particularly disturbing to her was that Dr. Lanstrum was luring away some of her contract patients, even though they were still paying their medical fees into the Longmaid coffers. The men simply felt more comfortable with a male doctor, and about that, there was nothing she could do.

"You know, Ben," Mollie said to her husband after a few months, "we should think seriously about moving to Helena. I'm sure you'd find work there, and Helena would be a better opportunity for me."

"You're probably right Mollie, but let's give it a little time yet. Maybe Marysville will turn around. We have so many friends here, and I have enough clients to keep us eating for now."

Mollie agreed to wait and see what would happen to Marysville. She, too, would prefer to stay if that proved possible. She decided to stop worrying about expanding her practice for the time being, and to concentrate on something she had wanted to do for some time: research the etiology of certain diseases. The Montana Medical Association was a good forum for her ideas, and she began to devote much of her time to studying. She was very interested in the reports coming out of Germany on the diphtheria antitoxin that was being perfected. If only she could have had that two years earlier. She would never forget the diphtheria epidemic she had gone through in Empire, and the terrible conditions under which she had had to operate. She thought sadly of the children, some of whom had not survived.

The conditions under which the miners worked often led to serious lung diseases. Pneumonia and silicosis could easily develop into TB. Additionally, a life spent underground contributed to problems of depression and other mental aberrations. Mollie had become increasingly aware of this in her practice. She was concerned that mental illness was often ignored by physicians, when early detection could have resulted in a cure. This last she meant to address in a paper at the MMA meeting the next year.

The incident with Isabel still saddened her, but there didn't seem to be anything she could do about it. Isabel had chosen death—perhaps wisely—as preferable to a life of prostitution. As for the man who had beaten her, there weren't any more incidents that Mollie was aware of. Not surprisingly, Pat Dillon had not turned up any information.

"I trust Pat," Mollie said to Ben as they were walking Willy one evening down by the creek, "but obviously the brothels are paying off the constabulary. Pat's people probably just go around him and take their money on the side. It happens here, it happens everywhere."

"Well, at least the beating doesn't seem to have been repeated," Ben said, "so perhaps just the fact that Pat was asking questions may have scared off whoever it was."

"I hope you're right, but I still can't get it out of my mind that that horrible man is still around here somewhere. Maybe he's just waiting for the questioning to quiet down so he can go back to making his deals with the madam."

"If it makes you feel any better, I was talking to Pat the other day, and he told me that most of the houses are closing. These days, I guess it's tough times for everyone in Marysville."

In February 1895 the lower house of the Montana legislature voted 42–12 for John Huseby's bill that would submit a constitutional amendment to the electorate giving women the vote. The Senate, however, postponed the action indefinitely, thereby killing it. Still, given that the lower house had moved so favorably, and that several labor unions had passed woman suffrage resolutions, Mollie and her Progressive friends were elated.

She had put off starting her suffrage club in Marysville because of her practice and her new interest in writing and publishing. But with such hopeful action in the House, she suddenly felt energized. She joined with her Helena friends, Ella Knowles Haskell, Maria Dean, Harriet Sanders, and several others, to put together a strategy for keeping the issue before the eyes of the legislators and the populace, and for approaching the legislature in the 1897 session with a new resolution.

The 1895 House vote had also caught the attention of the National American Woman Suffrage Association, which all at once saw Montana as another staging ground to advance the fight for equal rights. The national association sent one of its most formidable activists, Emma DeVoe, to organize the state. DeVoe helped women in several communities across Montana set up suffrage clubs. Mollie asked her to come to Marysville, and the Marysville Suffrage Society was born in Mollie's office above the *Mountaineer.*

Mollie and her friends began a weekly study group to work on a political science course developed as an educational tool by the national association. They also considered the arguments presented by lawmakers and special-interest groups for and against woman suffrage, and found themselves both amused and incensed. The argument in favor of the franchise was simple and straightforward: Denying half the population of the United States a voice in their government was a denial of those basic human rights that were the foundation of constitutional law. The arguments against equal rights for women, however, were far more convoluted. One argument was clearly motivated by power politics: If women could vote, some men feared they would be ousted from political control. Another argument was the fear that the delicate sensibilities of "pure" womanhood would be corrupted by ruthless female advocates imbued with a Machiavellian will to power. Still another concerned the belief that women, being more emotional than men, would be susceptible to control by the clergy, leading to a government by theocracy. And some of the most bizarre arguments concerned the inadequacy of the female physiology to support right thinking. Among the beliefs that proponents of this position endorsed was that women's brains, being smaller in size than the brains of men, precluded their ability to think rationally; another was that women's bodies, controlled by a disruptive menstrual cycle, made women unfit for the psychic rigors of political life. And a theory prevalent in France held that a woman's strength was in her pelvis, whereas a man's strength was in his upper body. Somehow this difference in the locus of strength meant that women were less capable of abstract thinking.

Mollie had come across an article in the September 1895 issue of *The American Naturalist* by James Weir Jr. She couldn't wait to bring it to the next meeting of the Suffrage Club.

"Ladies," she said as the meeting assembled, "I think I've now found the most absurd argument against the franchise for women that our brothers have yet devised: 'psychic hermaphroditism.'"

Laughter sounded throughout the room.

"What on earth is a psychic hermaphrodite?" asked Tressie Dunn after the laughter had quieted. Tressie was the youngest member of the group, and often had trouble absorbing the radical ideas of the suffragists. She had confessed once to Mollie that she was timid about asking a question, thinking that perhaps everyone but she knew the answer.

"Well," Mollie said, "according to Mr. Weir, you, as well as the rest of us, are a psychic hermaphrodite. Let me read you what he says:

> *I think I am perfectly safe in asserting that every woman who has been at all prominent in advancing the cause of equal rights in its entirety, has either shown evidences of masculo-femininity (viraginity), or has shown, conclusively, that she was the victim of psycho-sexual aberrancy.*

Mollie continued: "So the whole lot of us are hermaphrodites, in that our espousal of equal rights has turned us into sexual aberrants—in our heads anyway, since we're told we're 'psychic' hermaphrodites."

"Wait till Charlie hears he married a psycho-sexual aberrant!" Helen Mayger said in an aside meant to be heard. Laughter broke out again.

"Now, ladies," Mollie said, trying to keep a straight face. "Let's have a little respect here for Mr. Weir's intellectual efforts. Obviously he's given the subject his serious consideration.

"Mr. Weir fears that if women are allowed to vote, the next step—God forbid—will be they'll want to govern. This will turn American society into what he calls a retrograde, psychically atavistic matriarchy."

"And where does he get this idea?" asked one of the women.

"His evidence for this is that women who have held political power in the past were either psychically or physically degenerate—hermaphrodites or at best neurasthenic androids, as he calls them. For example, he claims that Jeanne d'Arc was a hystero-epileptic; that Catherine the Great was a dipsomaniac of unbounded and inordinate sensuality; and that Messalina, the powerful and depraved wife of Claudius, was of such lecherous and gross carnality that even the salacious Roman senators were shocked. Of course he throws Cleopatra in with this bunch; nor does he forget Elizabeth of England, that so-called virgin and megalomaniacal 'viragint' who was said by those who knew her to be more man than woman."

Again there was laughter.

"Well," Mollie continued, "we've considered small brains, the menses, control by the clergy, the corruption of our delicate sensibilities, pelvic interference with rational theorizing, not to mention humdrum political competition—which is undoubtedly the real objection. Now the problem is defined for us as 'psychic hermaphroditism.' Can anyone here top that?"

Mollie's Marysville suffragettes found these arguments pitiful at best. However, there was one male fear of the female franchise that the women did take seriously. This was the fear that if women were allowed to vote, they might vote to prohibit the sale of alcohol. And in this, the concern of the liquor industry was well founded.

The Women's Christian Temperance Union was a staunch supporter of woman suffrage. But it was widely understood that the WCTU ladies were not interested in "temperance" at all. Their aim was the outright prohibition of the sale and consumption of liquor. Union members were not particularly concerned whether or not the denial of suffrage was a transgression of women's natural political rights. Suffrage was a tool to effect a transformation of the moral order of society. And about this, Mollie and her friends were extremely concerned. As a physician, Mollie had seen the effects of the "cult of pure womanhood" on women's health, both physical and mental. The "purity" movement that many of the WCTU members endorsed was the political consequence of the cult. Although not all members agreed with this movement, Mollie worried about the campaign the union was waging to impose its ideas of morality on American society as a whole.

In drafting a Montana constitution for proposed statehood that would be acceptable to Congress, the 1889 territorial legislature had not wanted to include in that document anything the least controversial, anything that might delay or hinder the approval of statehood for Montana. Hence, rather than permitting a future legislature to determine whether women should have the vote, the state constitution stipulated that suffrage could only be allowed as a constitutional amendment, requiring a two-thirds vote of each house in order to present the proposal to the electorate for ratification. This made the work of the suffragists doubly difficult. Not only did they need more votes in the legislature than a simple majority, but they would also have to convince an electorate composed only of men to approve the amendment. In order to achieve this, many of the suffragists saw the involvement of the WCTU in the movement as a distinct liability. They feared the men would not endorse an amendment supported by a group identified with prohibition. On the other hand, the union was extremely well organized and had a large membership in Montana and across the country. The suffrage clubs could well use the organizational networks of the union, as well as its money and the influence of the numbers of prominent women the union could bring into the fold. Indeed, there was often a crossover of membership in the suffrage clubs.

In September, Mollie's Marysville group, along with clubs from Bozeman, Great Falls, and Butte, met with the Helena club to hold a convention, and the statewide Montana Woman Suffrage Association was formed. Susan B. Anthony, president of the national organization, sent to Montana, along with her congratulations, one of her top guns: Carrie Chapman Catt. Mrs. Catt was to assist in organizing the new association.

Mollie addressed the convention, outlining the association's objectives.

"I don't expect woman suffrage to revolutionize the world," she said. "Rather we must abolish sex prejudice in order to share opportunities and recognition. Our state has adequate property statutes for women, but as professional women we find many positions closed to us, and we are not regarded as eligible for paying positions in state or company institutions." She had not forgotten being denied the opportunity to run for county coroner. The convention stimulated much excitement among the women's groups and elicited statements of support from a number of influential men, including Governor Rickards.

As winter turned to spring, Mollie found herself spending more and more time in Helena. She had been elected treasurer of the new state association. Since it had become increasingly difficult to maintain her medical practice given the economic problems in Marysville, she decided that at least for the present, her suffrage work would take precedence over her practice.

The second convention of the Montana Woman Suffrage Association was held late in 1896. Mollie's friend Ella Knowles Haskell was elected president of the association. Ella was now the assistant attorney general, and had married the attorney general, Henri Haskell. Mollie was reelected treasurer. The purpose of the convention was to devise a strategy for support of the new suffrage amendment bill to be introduced in the legislature by the Democratic representative from Missoula.

It was a cold, snowy January morning when the House Committee on Privileges and Elections met to hear the suffragists' testimony. Despite the weather, the women were present in full force. The previous day they had deluged the legislators with 2,500 petitions from all parts of the state, asking them to submit the suffrage issue to the voters. Although many of the committee members were ambivalent about woman suffrage, they were nevertheless impressed with the number of petitions and recommended the bill be printed. The women rewarded them with boxes of apples.

When the House Committee of the Whole met to consider the amendment, tension was high in the hearing room. So many women flooded the room that there was standing room only, and even that was full. Ben had come to the hearing to see for himself what Mollie was up against.

Representative Hill of Missoula, the women's proponent, rose to speak.

"What I ask of you, my fellow representatives, is that we allow the question of equal suffrage to be submitted to the voters. To date I have not heard a valid reason for denying women the right of participation in their government." Hill's final line brought down the house with applause: "Have women ever been consulted as to who will speak for them?"

When the clapping had quieted, Hill made an extraordinary move. He requested that Ella Haskell, as president of the Montana Woman Suffrage Association, be allowed to speak. Some of the solons were incensed at the request. Such an action was unprecedented. House rules did not permit nonlegislators to speak. And now a woman . . . ! However, Ella wasn't just any woman, she was the state's assistant attorney general. A majority voted to suspend the rules.

Ella was careful to make her points quickly.

"Representative Hill has stated he has heard no valid argument to deprive women of the vote. Do the men of this legislature consider the women of Montana of lesser intelligence than the women of Idaho, of Colorado, of Wyoming? Has the franchise in these states overturned the government? Are we any less trustworthy? We ask only one thing of this legislature: that the sixty-eight members of this body permit the equal suffrage amendment to be submitted to the 50,000 men of Montana. We have presented you with 2,500 petitions. How many more do you need? Tell us, and we will have them for you." Ella stepped down to a thunder of applause.

Then it was the opposition's turn to speak. One representative claimed to have heard of a woman bragging she had voted eighteen times in a school district election. Another brought up the theocracy fear. A third facetiously suggested the bill be amended to allow woman suffrage only in cases where husband and wife bear children alternately. Others implied that suffragists simply were frustrated in their inability to find husbands and become mothers.

By far the most eloquent of the opponents, however, was Representative George Ramsey of Bozeman, who expounded for an hour and a half on the folly of the misguided suffragists.

"Woman is the queen and the absolute ruler of her God-given sphere," Ramsey assured the assembled, "but the Bible decrees that men should rule the state. Therefore woman suffrage is un-Christian. A female lobbyist is a most pitiful and revolting sight. But," he wound up his diatribe, "I revere woman for her purity. May she never grow less divine."

The House measure lost by three votes of the required two-thirds. The Senate killed it.

Mollie and her friends had worked so hard, they could scarcely believe the legislators would simply ignore all the women's petitions, ignore even the support within their own ranks.

"You know, Ben," Mollie said to her husband after the vote, "I'm afraid a few of the women didn't help things by snickering at some of the speeches. When Representative Ramsey suggested that suffrage was un-Christian, and that a female lobbyist was a pitiful and revolting sight, there was tittering all over the room. But when he had the gall to say he hoped women might never grow less divine, a couple of the women guffawed out loud. I could hardly keep my face still, either, but that sort of thing didn't help our cause."

"You're right, Mollie," Ben answered. "I was embarrassed by that, too, especially after Ella had spoken so eloquently. But the women's tittering was nothing compared with those foolish men carrying on about how 'divine' woman's place is in the home, or that the whole movement is about the frustration of women who can't find a husband. It was shameless. I was embarrassed for all of you."

Defeat sparked the energy of anger. The suffragists licked their wounds and prepared for an 1899 attack on the legislature. Mollie kept her Marysville group busy with projects every week. Her group was now meeting in various members' homes, and was praised as the most active of any in the state. Another convention was planned for November.

At the April 1896 meeting of the Montana Medical Association, the applications of her Marysville colleagues Dr. Lanstrum and Dr. Jordan had been accepted. A demonstration of Roentgen rays was given, and Mollie was fascinated. She had read about Roentgen's invention, but words couldn't compare with seeing the X-ray machine actually working. She knew immediately that the X-ray was going to revolutionize medical diagnostics.

In between her political activities, Mollie had still found time to carry on her medical research. She had been working on the mental problems of the miners in the Marysville vicinity, and had prepared a report on the results of her research for the association meeting. After the Roentgen demonstration, she was asked to present her paper, "The Borderland of Insanity." The paper was a warning that physicians should pay attention to symptoms that point to coming nervous degeneration. It was the responsibility of the physician, she argued, to educate the public that nervous diseases, if caught soon enough, could most often be cured. She pointed out that there was no line between normal and not normal. However, when a given individual began to act differently from what had been previously considered "normal" for him, the physician must pay attention, especially to the patient's hereditary history.

Her paper was well received, but some of the more conservative doctors were offended by her final statement and did not hesitate to tell her so. Mollie had written:

> . . . why anyone should be considered sane who believes in an
> orthodox God and an orthodox hell, the writer cannot tell. It
> is no wonder that too much religion unseats the intellect of its
> devotees when one remembers the improbable fables and the
> unscientific statements they are called on to believe.

Although Mollie had many colleagues who agreed with her post-Darwinian beliefs, her comment was not the most politic to make to the somewhat stodgy MMA. But then, what should they have expected from a woman who had just married the secretary of the Marysville Agnostics' Club?

In April 1897 Mollie and Ben moved out of their cramped rooms and rented Mrs. Bojay's house on Grand.

"This is wonderful, Ben," Mollie exclaimed after their friends had finished moving in the last of their furniture. "I've been living so long in miners' cabins and cramped rooms, I hardly know what to do with all this space."

"Let's celebrate by inviting our friends to a housewarming whist party," Ben suggested. "Lord knows we owe everybody invitations."

"You're right, Ben. We are in debt to so many friends. But I don't know when I'm going to find the time." When she saw his look of disappointment, she smiled at him. "Well, don't worry, I'll think of something."

Willy was delighted by the move as well. Now he had a fenced yard where he could move freely, and where he could watch the children going by on their way to school.

Mollie was so busy juggling her practice, her research and writing, and her suffrage work that she had little time to enjoy her new house, let alone entertain her friends. She was spending much of her time in Helena, organizing the suffragists for the next confrontation with the legislature. If Ben was free of clients for a couple of days, he would sometimes accompany Mollie to Helena, where they would stay over with friends. On these occasions Willy would camp at the Longmaids' with little Harold. Otherwise Mollie would take the train in to the capital alone, returning in a day or two. Ben would meet her at the depot, and they would go to one of the hotels for dinner on their way home.

One evening when Mollie returned from a Helena suffrage meeting, Ben was waiting for her train. She could see immediately he was extremely upset.

"Something has happened," she said when she saw the look on Ben's face. "What is it?"

"Come, let's go home first," Ben said.

"No," Mollie insisted. "Tell me right now what's going on."

Ben took Mollie's arm and led her over to a bench along the wall of the depot. "I'm so sorry, Mollie." Ben seemed to be struggling for words. "Willy got out of the yard last night. I think someone let him out. It wasn't until this morning that I realized he was gone and I went to look for him. I found him dead."

Mollie gasped. "Oh no! How could that be?"

Ben put his arm around her. "Mollie, someone took him in the night and shot him, then dumped his body on our doorstep. There was a note on his collar."

Mollie was silent for a moment. Then she groaned out in a whisper. "Tell me what it said."

"I hate to tell you this, but I know I must. It said, *'This is what you get, bitch doctor, for sticking your nose in a man's business.'*"

Mollie pulled away from Ben. She stood up and walked slowly past the depot office to the end of the station platform; Ben waited without following her. She knew instantly that the man who had abused Isabel had taken out his revenge on Willy; this was his way of paying her back for sending Pat Dillon to ask questions at the brothel. She stood there for several minutes, staring blankly out at the town. Then, her face grim, she walked back to Ben.

"Where is Willy's body? I want to see him."

"You can't, Mollie. I took him out to the woods this morning and buried him. Charlie Mayger helped me. We didn't want you to see him."

She sat down again on the bench, leaned back against the station wall, and closed her eyes. "I suppose you're right. I don't know if I could bear to see him like that. Thank you, Ben."

Mollie and Ben walked silently up the street to their house. She had controlled her emotions until they reached the door. But then, looking down at the step, she saw the smear of Willy's blood. It was too much.

Ben held her on the sofa while she cried out her grief and rage. "The cruelty of it, the meanness. That sweet, innocent animal! I know it's that beast who beat Isabel. It has to be. How am I going to tell poor little Harold?"

When she finally calmed down, she got up and lit the gas burner to make some tea. Then, holding the cup in both hands, she paced back and forth across the living room without saying anything. Her life with Willy ran through her mind: finding the hungry little puppy in the alley behind the apartment she and Frank had shared in Chicago; Willy, joyously assaulting her when she went to get him in Osage; Willy, lying on the floor beside her bed on lonely winter nights in Empire; his concern for her when she was angry or upset. There had been times in the last ten years when he had been her only companion. Her face hardened. Ben waited her out in silence. Finally, she sat down again on the sofa and faced him.

"Ben, it's time for us to leave Marysville. It's not just this business with Willy, although this makes everything ugly. But the town hasn't turned around as we'd hoped. There are rumors that even the Drumlummon is closing. Our friends are talking about leaving, too. My practice is going nowhere here, and it seems like we're as often in Helena as we are here. I am, anyway. There's no future for us here. Even the Longmaids are talking about moving to Helena."

"I know, Mollie," Ben said. "Charlie was telling me today that he's going to Helena, and the Kesslers are leaving, too. I've got some contracts I need to finish up, but I think by the end of the year I'll be ready to go."

225

"It won't be too soon for me." She stood up and pulled on his hand. "Come. Come to bed with me. I don't want anything to eat."

CHAPTER FIFTEEN

A Surprising Diagnosis

J. HENRY WAS IN BANNACK checking on the Golden Leaf operation there when the incident with Willy occurred. Mollie discussed with Janette how to tell young Harold the dog was dead. It would be the first time the five-year-old would experience the death of someone he loved. Willy was already ten years old, but his life might have gone on for a few more years. She left it to his mother to talk to him. Sooner or later Janette would have to have such a talk with her son.

When J. Henry returned and heard the story, he arrived at the Atwaters' in a rage. Ben was there alone, working on a client's accounts. J. Henry was even angrier when Ben told him the whole story of Mollie's experience with Isabel and the probable connection between Willy's death and the man at the brothel.

"I'm going to talk to George Padbury about this. Anyone mean enough to beat a girl like that, let alone kill an innocent animal, should be run out of town."

"I suppose the irony," Ben said, "is that the houses are closing anyway. Pat supposedly investigated the incident with the prostitute, but didn't turn up anything. Now he tells me he, too, is joining the

Marysville exodus. If his associates were on the take, they're gone now. There's nothing Judge Padbury can do if there's no one left to investigate. I'm terribly sorry for Mollie and for your boy, but all we want to do now is to pack up and move away from here. We'll be going to Helena at the end of the year."

"I don't blame you for that." J. Henry had calmed down somewhat. He had been pacing the room, chewing on the end of a cigar, but now he settled on the sofa. "The town is certainly going down. I suppose it's futile to try to find the miscreant now. He's probably left town anyway, and the law's almost nonexistent. There are a few solid citizens who act as sheriff's deputies in an emergency, but that's all."

"A lot of the saloons are closing, too," Ben said, "which is just as well. They're where all the trouble in town starts. Back in '92, when Marysville was really booming, I counted sixty saloons."

"My God," J. Henry said, laughing. "I didn't realize there were *that* many." He got up and picked up his coat and hat from the chair. "Please tell Mollie how sorry I am about Willy. I know how much she loved that dog." He went to the door and opened it. "I've got to get back to the Bald Butte now. The water shortage is really hurting us up there. I'm going to miss you and Mollie. You've both been good friends. And she's been a great help to my family and the company. Janette and I will probably join you before long. She's been talking about it. Right now, though, I've got a couple of mines that are still producing."

Now that she and Ben had decided to leave Marysville at the end of 1897, Mollie gave up her Marysville practice completely. She had presented her paper on the etiology of pneumonia to her colleagues at the medical association in April and was pleased with the acknowledgment she received. She was appointed, along with Drs. Riddell and Grigg, to coordinate MMA members' publications in the *Medical Sentinel*, a journal published in Portland, Oregon.

Much of Mollie's time, however, was devoted to preparing for yet another political assault. The same old stuffed shirts were in power in the legislature, and the women's strategy that year at the suffrage association convention was to canvass every county in the state, soliciting even more petitions to present at the upcoming hearing. A new slate of officers was elected, with the actress-singer Roena Medini as president. Soon after the election, however, Medini had had to leave Helena, and Mollie was elected president.

As soon as the suffragists' convention was over, Mollie and Ben prepared to make their move to Helena. A popular couple, they were feted at several going-away parties given by their Marysville friends.

"These parties make me sad," Mollie told Janette one afternoon, as the two women were having tea in the sunroom of the Longmaid house. "Not sad that we're leaving; we do want to go to Helena. But sad because life here just isn't what it once was. I have the feeling that these farewell parties are in a sense good-bye parties to the town itself. Soon, I doubt any of the people at these affairs will be living here."

"I know what you mean," Janette said, as she offered Mollie a plate of scones. "Life was such fun and excitement here just a few years ago. And now I have the feeling Marysville is on its way to becoming a ghost town."

Mollie had come to see Janette specifically to spend some time with the children before she moved. Baby Mary was almost two and a half, a bright little girl with curly dark hair and a sunny smile. At the moment she was busy climbing on Mollie and pulling on her earrings. Mollie would try to settle her long enough to take a gulp of tea. Harold was playing with his puppy, Duke, throwing a stick under the furniture for the pup to chase.

"Look, Dr. Mollie!" Harold shouted, grabbing her arm in his excitement. "Duke's learning to bring the stick back."

"That's wonderful, Harold. But I'm not surprised he's so smart. I've met his mother, and she's a smart one, too."

"It was so good of you to bring him this puppy," Janette said quietly to Mollie out of Harold's hearing. "Harold is so happy now. He's forgotten how sad he was just a few days ago."

Duke's heritage, like Willy's had been, was a little bit of everything. He was smaller than Willy, with sharp pointed ears, and his fur was black with a white patch on his chest. Mollie had gotten him from her diphtheria patient, Jerry McCullaugh; Minnie had recently had puppies. Harold had cried over Willy for several days, but now he was caught up in the joy of having his own dog.

Ben and Mollie found a place on Grand Street, opposite the Hotel Helena, that was big enough for a residence with an extra room for Mollie's office. It was a rather ugly, squat little house in Mollie's opinion, but right downtown and convenient for her patients.

"At least there's a big spruce tree in the front yard," Mollie said to Ben. "Maybe someday we'll have enough money to buy a pretty house, and I'll be able to afford a separate office."

"Of course we will, my darling," Ben said, as they were packing their things for the move. "I know we'll both be better off in Helena once we get settled." Since Ben had not yet found work in Helena, Mollie was concerned, but she was grateful for his enthusiasm. Ben closed out his few remaining Marysville clients, and early in December 1897 they moved into their new home.

For the past three years, both Cuba and the Philippines had revolted against Spain, and the United States had been drawn inexorably into war. The U.S. battleship *Maine* had been blown up in Havana harbor, killing 266 American sailors. President McKinley demanded independence for Cuba, but Spain refused. U.S. troops were sent to the island, and while ultimately successful in helping Cuba win its independence, the troops fell victim to malaria, dysentery, and other tropical diseases. They were quickly shipped back to the United States for treatment. The war then moved to the Philippines, and McKinley sent out a call for nurses and doctors to accompany the troops.

"I really should go," Mollie said to Ben as they were reading the paper one morning in their new house. "It's my duty. Those boys caught all sorts of diseases fighting in Cuba, and the same thing is going to happen to them in the Philippines."

"My God, Mollie," Ben suddenly flared, "what will you come up with next? We've just moved here. I thought you were eager to establish a new practice. Now you're talking about running off to the Philippines. I know I told you I would support you in whatever you want to do. But the Philippines? That's too much! I mean . . . you could get killed!"

Something in Mollie stiffened. She did not intend for Ben or anyone to interfere with what she determined to do. He had married her with the knowledge that she was a doctor and, as such, would respond to a situation whenever she was called.

"Are you suggesting that you will oppose my going there?" Her voice was a razor. She and Ben had never had a serious fight before, although they had skirted around the edges at times when her interests had become more and more demanding of her time.

"Mollie, there are plenty of nurses and doctors who can go there. You're not the only one. I thought we were going to set up a new life for ourselves here. And what about your new practice? I don't know how to take your sudden desire to abandon Helena and me for something that isn't really necessary."

"I'm not abandoning anyone or any place. And *I* will decide what is necessary for me." She smashed the paper down on the breakfast table and went into her office. She sat there for several minutes, examining her feelings. Was Ben really crossing her, or did he have a point in saying that for her, such an expedition wasn't necessary? Why did she feel she should do this? Was it a true conviction, or was she maybe bored; was she using the excuse of "duty" to justify an adventure?

Usually when there was strain between them, Ben would come to her to work it out. This time he did not come. After a few minutes, she heard him leave the house.

Mollie knew that Ben would not try to stop her. If she decided to go to the Philippines, she would. But did she really want to risk her marriage? Was she just being stubborn? Much as she loved Ben's kindness and support, she did indeed expect to have everything her way. All her life she had expected that, and she had manipulated people and circumstances to make that happen. But this time Ben had stood up to her.

There was a lesson in this for her, and she knew it. She had always gotten what she wanted, and she had gotten Ben—when she finally decided she did indeed want him. But as his wife, she had also made a commitment to him, to her marriage. Doctor or no, there were times when she would have to live up to that commitment, even if it curtailed her freedom to do as she wished. But only if his concerns were reasonable, and she had to admit that in this case they were: It was not necessary for her to answer this call.

Fortunately for Ben and Mollie both, no one was called from Montana. There had not been a verbal resolution between them, and neither mentioned the subject again. It was their first major fight, and they both felt subdued, treading carefully around each other. Ben had not pressed her, but it was clear that she considered he was right. Over the next days life returned to normal. Or at least as normal as living with Mollie was likely to be.

Mollie embraced her new life in Helena with her seemingly inexhaustible energy and enthusiasm. She advertised in the *Helena Independent* and the *Record,* and gradually over the weeks the patients started to come. Knowing her concern about public health issues, Maria Dean put in a word for her, and Mollie was appointed chairman of the Helena Board of Health. In addition to her private practice, this was precisely the kind of work she wanted to do. Her position in the city, plus her work with the MMA, would allow her to move the legislature toward the establishment of a state public health office. She joined the Helena Women's Club, and also became president of the Dorcas Society, a charity arm of Saint Peter's Episcopal Church. Although she was not a believer—she had made that very clear in her paper to the MMA meeting—she felt an attachment to the church of her childhood, and the Dorcas Society was active in bringing aid of all kinds, including medical, to the poor. And always there was the ongoing work of the suffrage association.

However, Mollie was concerned about Ben. He had not had time to establish a clientele, and to make ends meet he had taken a job as manager of the Parlor Cigar Store on North Main. She felt a twinge of guilt. She was actively building her practice and spending hours at her volunteer work. Yet until she could bring in enough money on her own, she was dependent on Ben to support her. For all the talk a couple of years earlier about the importance of maintaining *her* career after they married, it was suddenly Ben's career that was suffering.

"Don't worry about me," Ben said to her more than once in those early weeks in Helena. "Something will turn up, I'm sure of it. I have several applications in with Helena businesses, and I'm confident I'll have a job soon."

"I just want to know that you're happy. I would hate to think that my career is somehow dragging you down."

"Stop talking like that, Mollie. We're in this life together now. I'll find something, I know I will. Meanwhile, I'm having a great time at the cigar store. It's the gossip station of Helena. The men stand around and smoke and talk, and I'm all ears. Every day I learn more and more about this town and the power structure that runs it. Who knows, it may be just the education I need to get an accounting contract."

If she had time between patients, Mollie sometimes would drop into the cigar store to meet Ben for lunch. Actually, she had an ulterior motive. If there was an interesting conversation in progress, Ben would appear to be busy and would tell her she would have to wait for a few minutes. This little conspiracy allowed her to surreptitiously overhear what was being said.

Mollie was concerned that the governor, Robert Burns Smith, although a Democrat and a Populist as well, was not supportive of the suffrage amendment. This was surprising, given the man's political credentials. One day when she came into the cigar store, Ben silently directed her attention to a discussion going on in a corner. She recognized the governor and a couple of the Democratic legislators. Fortunately, there was a newsstand near the men, and she picked up a copy of the *Helena Record* and pretended to be engrossed.

"I can't understand your position on the women's amendment, Bob," one of the legislators was saying. "What is it you're concerned about?"

"I know the party endorses it," the governor replied, "but I just don't believe the time is right. You know I hail from the South. I watched the government make a total mess there with their so-called Reconstruction. The Fifteenth Amendment gave all those former slaves the vote, but they were so uneducated they didn't know how to vote or why or what to vote for. It was a disaster. The government admitted it, but not until after seven years of chaos. They finally agreed not to enforce the amendment. I don't want that kind of mess here in Montana with uneducated women voting."

"I don't think you can compare our women with a group of men who only a few years ago were slaves," argued the other legislator.

"I'm not so sure," replied the governor. "A lot of the women are wives of illiterate foreigners who've come here to homestead or work in the mines. I'm not crazy about those men voting, either, since they pretty much do what the mine owners tell them to. But we certainly don't need their women voting as well."

"But you're a Populist. What about their rights as citizens?"

"I'll be happy to vote for women's rights when they can show us they are educated and informed as to the issues on which they are expressing their opinions."

Mollie had heard enough.

"Let's go, Ben," she said, whispering to him. "Obviously, Governor Smith doesn't have the wits to look around him and see who it is he's talking about."

Ben nodded to his assistant that he was leaving. "I'm glad you stopped in just when you did," he said as soon as they were out on the street. "I was hoping Smith would be here. He comes in often to buy a cigar, and usually a discussion starts up. I've heard him express this view comparing the suffrage movement with Reconstruction before."

Before the next year was out, Ben was offered a job as accountant for the Union Mercantile Company. The president, Lou Hillebrecht, was a steady customer at the cigar shop. The pay was good, and Ben had accepted immediately.

"I'm delighted you've landed a good job, but I'll miss those wonderful eavesdropping opportunities," Mollie said when Ben told her about the job offer. "I can't very well hang around the cigar shop if you're not there. That would look very odd indeed. They might even think I was a spy—which of course I am." She laughed.

Mollie was relieved. The job for Ben came at a time when she and her suffragist friends were struggling with their latest proposal to the state legislature. At least she didn't have to worry about her husband. But as it turned out, she had plenty to worry about at the legislative session. The Democratic representative from Missoula had offered a suffrage bill in the House, and Mollie, as president of the state organization, had coordinated a presentation by supporters. However, other problems besides sending a suffrage amendment to the electorate were pressing in the legislative session. Montana had sent Butte's William Clark, one of the so-called Copper Kings, to the U.S. Senate. When Clark arrived in Washington, the Senate refused to seat him. He had bribed his way into winning the election, and had brought Washington's ridicule down on Montana. The embarrassed lawmakers didn't bother with the women. This year when the vote came in on the proposed amendment, it was a defeat worse than the previous one.

As president, Mollie tried to rally enthusiasm at the next suffrage convention in October 1899. Her main concern was to keep the organization from dying. But even with Carrie Chapman Catt present, the troops were discouraged, and little was accomplished. By 1900, besides the floundering statewide organization, the Helena Equal Suffrage Club was the only local club still active.

Maria Dean took over the presidency of the state suffrage association from Mollie. Together, the two doctors promoted their cause at the Democratic and Republican conventions. They needn't have bothered. The legislators were far more interested in the economic problems of the state to concern themselves with another suffrage bill.

Adding to the setbacks that Mollie and Maria Dean and their fellow suffragists faced as the year turned to 1901 was the spectacle of Carrie Nation running berserk around the country, slashing saloons with a hatchet.

"Damn that woman!" Mollie said to Maria and Ella. The three leaders had met for a strategy meeting for approaching, once again, the upcoming legislature. "She's going to undo everything we've worked for."

"I know," said Ella, "but it's impossible to separate ourselves from the prohibitionists. I've been anxious about this from the beginning. They want suffrage so they can vote to close down the saloons, we want suffrage as our natural human right. We both want suffrage, and that's all most people can see."

"Nation claims her 'hatchetations,' as she calls them, are inspired by a divine call. Apparently God has chosen her to personally chop up every den of iniquity this side of hell," Mollie said. "Most of the prohibitionists don't even support her, but try to convince some bartender of that when he's being threatened by an army of wild-eyed females wielding hatchets in his face. Can't say I blame him, either," Mollie added with a rueful grin.

The relationship of the Women's Christian Temperance Union with the suffrage movement in Montana continued to be a subject of strain for the suffragists. Some of the most steadfast workers for the cause were members of the WCTU. Mary Alderson of Bozeman was a close friend of Mollie and her suffragist colleagues, and was a member of the executive board of the statewide suffrage association. Furthermore, Ben was a friend of Mary's husband, Matt Alderson. Although a WCTU member, and therefore concerned to prohibit the sale of liquor, Mary was an active suffragist for the same reason that her Helena friends were: to overcome the political injustice of denying women the franchise.

The presentation of the 1901 suffrage amendment at the capitol that year was halfhearted at best. The bill died an early death, and the suffragists didn't have the energy or even the interest to try to resurrect it.

Mollie had dropped out of the campaign earlier in the year. In late February she had begun to feel unwell. There was a bad flu going around, and she complained to Ben that she didn't seem to be able to shake the symptomatic upset stomach. In fact, it seemed to get worse as the days went on.

She was forty-three. Her illness might be the flu, or perhaps it was connected to the onset of menopause. As a physician, she knew that menopause could come to women as early as the late thirties, or as late as the early fifties. But also, like many physicians, she didn't feel confident diagnosing herself. As days went by and she didn't feel better, she decided to consult her friend Maria Dean.

"It may be a lingering flu," she said to the doctor, "but I don't seem to be able to shake it. Or maybe it's just the change of life. I've missed a period, so it may be that. But still, I'm concerned. I've felt nauseous for almost a month now. I'm worried I've got something serious—an ulcer, a tumor. I just don't know."

Maria Dean gave Mollie a thorough examination. When she finished, she told her to come back the next day. She wanted to be sure of what she had found. Mollie went home full of trepidation.

"I'm really worried, Ben," she said when he came home that evening. "I know that Maria's found something. She's an excellent doctor, and she's going to make me wait until she's sure what she's got before she'll give me her opinion."

Ben's face clouded with fear. He pulled Mollie down with him on the sofa. "Oh Mollie . . ."

She realized she shouldn't have said she was worried. There was no point in alarming Ben when she didn't know what she was talking about. "Don't worry," she said, pulling away from him. "Whatever it is, I'm sure Maria can take care of it. Let's not jump to conclusions here." She smiled, hoping that a smile would reassure him—and herself as well.

Mollie was in Maria Dean's office promptly the next afternoon.

"Well, Mollie," Dr. Dean said, smiling, "let me be the first to congratulate you. You do indeed have a tumor, a little tumor growing in your womb. You're going to have a baby."

Mollie gasped. "Oh my God . . . That can't be! . . . You're absolutely sure? . . . But I've been so careful . . ."

Maria reached across her desk and took Mollie's hand. "Yes, Dr. Atwater." She smiled at her friend. "I'm absolutely sure."

Mollie sat back in the doctor's chair, stunned.

No longer smiling, Maria looked at her steadily.

"Mollie, are you telling me that as a doctor, you didn't know you were pregnant? Is having a baby something that is so unacceptable to you that you would deny the symptoms in yourself that you would easily recognize in another woman?"

Mollie looked at Maria in alarm. Was what she was saying the truth? Had she really been denying to herself what she had suspected all along? And was this such an awful revelation?

She left Maria's in a daze and walked home to her Grand Street office. She had another patient yet that afternoon. This one was a pregnancy that was not going well, and the woman was terribly afraid she might lose her baby. It was her first.

Mollie reassured her patient that she shouldn't give up hope; although the baby had turned too early, everything might still be all right. She advised the woman to stay in bed and rest. She would see her every few days until her time came.

After her patient left, Mollie sat alone in her office. She wasn't yet ready to face Ben.

Her patient's distress shamed her. Here was someone desperately concerned for the welfare, for the potential for life of her unborn baby, while Mollie was aghast at the news of her own pregnancy. And what would Ben's reaction be? He had agreed with her when they married that they wouldn't have children. He had said, already eight years ago now, that he didn't want to bring children into this world. The thought crossed her mind she could have an abortion and not tell him. Or maybe do tell him? Maybe that's what he would want. She didn't know what he would want. And what did *she* want?

What she desperately wanted was that Maria had made a mistake. It seemed to her at that moment that everything she had worked so hard to achieve, her successful practice now that she was in Helena, the respect, even the admiration, of her colleagues in the MMA, her work for the city as chair of the board of health—all of that was for nothing. She would have to give up her practice, just when she had finally developed a name for herself and was bringing in a substantial contribution to the maintenance of the household. With Ben's new job as accountant for Kessler's Brewery and the income from her practice, they were finally reasonably well off. But what would happen now?

She was ashamed that the thought of abortion had crossed her mind. She was a doctor—doctors didn't kill life because it was simply inconvenient. How many women had she advised against this—and with what moral authority. But now that it was her life . . . suddenly that was different? What a hypocrite!

Mollie didn't know how long she sat in her office, desperately trying to come to terms with what Maria had told her, what at some unconscious level she had already known to be true. No, she knew there would be no abortion. She could not kill the child inside her, the child that she and Ben together, however unintentionally, had made.

It must have been after six o'clock when Ben knocked tentatively on the door that separated her office from their living quarters.

"I hope I'm not disturbing you, Mollie. I didn't think you still had a patient with you. It's getting late, and I'm concerned that you're in here alone so long. You must tell me what Maria said."

CHAPTER SIXTEEN

The Fight for a Suffrage Amendment

THE CONVENTIONS OF VICTORIAN DECORUM dictated that Mollie drop out of sight once her "interesting condition" became obvious. She had no patience with such nonsense. She continued to practice into her seventh month, when she began to tire too easily.

When she had told Ben about the baby that late afternoon in her office, she saw, once the shock had settled, that for all his talk about not bringing children into this world of woe, he was as happy as any father-to-be. Perhaps the both of them had something to learn from the experience. They had denied themselves a part of their humanity, the expression of their loving, with the thought that other things were more important. Yet abruptly their humanity had been now thrust upon them.

For the first few months, Mollie struggled with a deep resentment. It was not directed at Ben, but at the vagaries that life had played on her. It wasn't until she began to feel her baby moving beneath her heart that finally she was able to put regret behind her. The life that was taking command of her body began to command her spirit. She didn't confide to Ben what she fervently hoped: that the seed he had planted in her was a girl. She would raise her to be a strong woman, a woman who would face life as Mollie had, but in a better world. Her daughter would have the rights and opportunities that Mollie was fighting for at that moment, and would continue to fight for until she was successful. She knew she risked great disappointment by fixing on the idea that her child would be a girl. Yet if it was a boy, she would raise him to be a fighter for women's rights, too.

If initially, Mollie had felt herself unfortunate in becoming pregnant, the birth of her daughter on October 3, 1901, made her feel that once again her life was working out as she wished. She had come to terms with the fact that motherhood would cost her her practice, at least for some years; she would not give over her daughter to be raised by someone else. She was aware that if she tried to continue her practice, she would be putting her child in danger. She had read of several cases where the children of woman doctors and nurses had been exposed to the diseases the mother was treating. Mollie could see no alternative. And so the intensity that she put into all her undertakings, she put into loving the tiny female creature who had sprung from her womb.

As Mollie began to care for her baby, to nurse her, to change her, to bathe her, to knit tiny clothes as she sat evenings with Ben that first winter of her motherhood, she began to realize that her efforts to live life as she chose—to become a doctor in the face of male ridicule, to fight for equal political rights, to work for the health of the public— were now for a future that was no longer the abstraction she had only vaguely sensed. Now that future had a face, the face of her own baby. For Mollie, this was indeed a revelation. She had never before acknowledged to herself the extent of her self-centeredness. She had always managed to do what she wanted: to have a career; to divorce Frank; to force the world to acknowledge her rights—even to marry Ben, with all the insistences she had put on him. She did love Ben. She relished his kindness and warmth, and she valued his support. But she had indeed married him on *her* terms. And then life had suddenly grabbed her and shaken her so hard that she had finally come to see herself as a part of something grander than she had ever imagined. She now had a far more important reason than self-centeredness to live the life she had chosen. She was a part of the future. And for this, she was thankful. She named her baby Dorothy, the gift from God.

Still, Mollie couldn't help feeling sad when she and Ben moved from Grand Street to a temporary apartment on Benton. It meant that her office was closed, that her practice was over. Maybe in the future she would be able to start again; she determined she would keep up with the changes in medicine that were happening so rapidly. She packed her surgical tools and books to take with her, and put the office equipment in storage.

Mollie considered how she would organize her life now that she was a mother. Her days would be largely taken up with caring for Dorothy, but occasionally she could call in her cleaning lady, Mrs. Washington, if she needed help with the baby so she could attend a meeting. Although a full-time medical practice was out of the question, she could certainly continue her suffrage work, since those meetings could occur in the evening, perhaps at her house. She would not have the time to continue as chair of the Dorcas Society and the Helena Board of Health, but there was plenty of work she could do through the MMA. Her new life would be a matter of juggling time, of finding occasional child care help, and of enlisting Ben to take charge in the evenings. And when Dorothy would be old enough, Mollie fully intended to take her daughter with her to the suffrage meetings; she should be initiated into the cause as early as possible.

Despite the women's efforts, once again that year the lawmakers couldn't be bothered with the suffrage amendment.

"You know, Ben. I'm beginning to wonder if suffrage in Montana is a lost cause." Mollie was rocking Dorothy in the front room of their Benton Avenue apartment. "Maybe the only way to proceed is the national route. This is what Carrie Catt thinks, although given what's happened to the Negroes in the South with the government refusing to honor its own constitutional amendment, the prospect for national suffrage is bleak, too."

"I know, Mollie. The hypocrisy of these solons is appalling. But you keep losing every time by just a few votes. You mustn't give up. One of these years they've got to come around."

"Oh, I won't give up. But I'm not sure I share your optimism. At least we got the money to establish a state board of health last year. It certainly took long enough. Those legislators have been far more interested in corrupting each other than in looking out for our welfare. Enough of them have to get hit themselves with diphtheria or smallpox or TB. And that's what I saw at the hearing. Two of the legislators had lost children, one to diphtheria and the other to smallpox. Unfortunately, that seems to be what it takes to make them think about something besides their deal making."

Mollie was indeed encouraged that the legislature had finally established a state health board. She had lobbied hard with the MMA to bring this about, spending hours writing to legislators in an attempt to impress upon them the seriousness of public health problems in the state.

In 1902 the argument of the suffragists took a new turn, one that disturbed Mollie considerably. Rather than insisting that a woman's equal right to the franchise was a matter of fairness based on natural

human rights, the thrust of the campaign was that there was an immediate *social* need for women in politics. This was the approach pro-
pounded by the National Suffrage Association. Carrie Chapman
Catt—replacing Susan B. Anthony as the national president—brought
two assistants to campaign in Montana, particularly in Butte, where the
labor unions strongly supported the suffragists. In her campaign
speeches Mrs. Catt alluded to the ignorance and criminality attributed
to foreign immigrants in Montana, especially in the Butte area, where
more than a third of the people had been born abroad, and most of
those were men. Catt's argument was that the women's votes would
dilute the votes of this undesirable foreign element, thus preserving
American social values and the political power of the native-born
American male.

Mollie didn't like this chauvinism. It countered the very arguments
of fairness that were the spirit of the U.S. Constitution. Now, for the
sake of political expediency, the national association had made the
thrust of the movement the need for morally superior women to save
men from themselves.

Mollie hosted a meeting of the Helena Business Women's Suffrage Club
at the Atwaters' Benton Avenue apartment in November. There were
six members present, along with a guest who was visiting from Butte.

"Ladies," Mollie opened the meeting, "you certainly know from
the convention two months ago that National has switched arguments
on us. Now our pitch is to be that we women are so virtuous and
morally superior that the men need our votes in order to protect society from their own male perversions. It seems it's up to us to preserve
American values. I, for one, cannot abide this attitude."

"I'm with you, Mollie." Maria Dean spoke up. "Mrs. Catt is taking over this campaign. I appreciate help, but this is our state and we need to keep control."

"I was in Butte last May," said Ella Haskell. "Carrie had an open meeting—" The discussion was suddenly interrupted by a plaintive wail emanating from the bedroom.

Mollie got up and went to the back of the apartment, emerging in a minute with a blanketed bundle of misery. She sat down in the rocker and started to rock and coo at the crying baby until she had quieted her.

"Please go on, Ella. Dorothy and I apologize for the interruption."

"Yes, I was going to tell you about Carrie's meeting in Butte. It was an open meeting, mostly of labor union men. I was embarrassed by what I heard. She talked about the influx of 'foreign ignorance and criminality.' She argued that extension of suffrage to women would safeguard the superiority of the American male."

"Aren't we forgetting something here?" said Mary O'Neill, the new press agent for the suffragists. She was the guest who had dropped in on the meeting. "What's the point of going down with the ship of natural rights and human equality and all that, if we can get the vote by claiming to be morally superior? You ladies want to stand on your principles. I want to get the vote, and I think this 'eternal feminine' approach looks like it might work."

No one answered her argument, and she excused herself, saying she had another engagement. Mollie got up from the rocker and carried her sleeping baby back to the bedroom.

"She's probably right," sighed Ella after O'Neill left. "If anyplace brings in the votes for the amendment, it's going to be Butte—the labor unions there have endorsed us. That's where the bulk of the foreigners are, and, of course, that's where the reaction against them is going to be strongest."

"Well, I can't stand to campaign with such an attitude," Maria said, "but I'm certainly not going to argue with our own people in public. We've got enough problems with the WCTU image out there. If National can get us the vote with this virtue business, maybe that's what's important for now. Meanwhile, we need to put together some words for Governor Toole. He's promised to introduce the amendment request again, so let's get to work."

"I tried out some wording this afternoon while Dorothy was taking her nap," Mollie said, crossing the room to take a paper off her desk. "Tell me if you agree with this:

> *We, the undersigned, believers in the enfranchisement of women, hereby petition the Eighth Legislative Assembly of the State of Montana to submit to the qualified electors of the State for their approval or rejection at the next general election a constitutional amendment so framed as to secure to the women of the State equal political rights with men.*

Everyone agreed to Mollie's wording. It was simple and to the point without any mention of morally superior women or criminal elements.

But in the 1903 legislative session, once again the major political parties would not consider Mollie's amendment, even though Governor Toole—elegantly and effusively arguing the wisdom of the male electorate—supported submitting it to the voters.

So again the women were defeated. However, during this legislative session, the suffragists discovered that they were up against a new enemy, one far more powerful than the liquor lobby: the political machinery of the Amalgamated Copper Company, aka Standard Oil. Amalgamated Copper was sure that woman suffrage was not in its corporate interest. Elected women might challenge the corporation-corrupted legislators, and with their vote make life difficult. The Copper Kings, as the corporation heads were dubbed, controlled several of the newspapers, and they used those tools effectively to promote their interests. The last thing the Copper Kings wanted was any more power in the hands of the people, whatever the gender. Not to menton that most of the foreigners whom Mrs. Chapman Catt disparaged were working for the corporate mine owners, and could be relied on to vote as their superiors dictated. They certainly didn't want the voting process "diluted" as Chapman Catt had advocated. The *Helena Record,* a corporation-controlled press, advised the women to forget trying to run the government and to look to their own hearths to see if there might not be room for improvement there.

Two years later the seemingly indefatigable suffragists tried again. They attended the committee meetings and this time presented legislators with petitions of 6,000 signatures. The result was the same as before.

"Look," Mollie said to her friends after the vote, "we're wasting our time. Montana industry is so wracked by corruption and greed, and enough of the politicians have been bought off, that we'll never get anywhere until the corporation mess is cleaned up. Maybe Teddy Roosevelt can do something about this, but we certainly can't. As far as I'm concerned, woman suffrage in this state is a dead issue."

"I agree with you for now," Ella said. "We can't do anything about the jobbery in the legislature because we can't vote the bums out of office. When the men get around to facing the corruption in this state, we can try again. Until then, however, I—and I'm sure the rest of you—have better things to do."

Mollie felt the sense of defeat bitterly. She had spent ten years banging her head against the stone wall of male arrogance. And now the cause was caught up in corporate politics as well. She had promised herself that Dorothy would live in a better world. At the moment, that world seemed very far off.

After 1905 the few remaining suffrage groups in Montana ceased to exist. Mollie turned her energy to a project that had concerned her since her experiences in the mining camps: stemming the spread of tuberculosis and the need for a state-funded treatment facility. The new state board of health was challenged in every direction: Something had to be done about spotted fever; smallpox and typhoid were prevalent in several areas; whole towns relied on contaminated water; the death rate in Butte from tuberculosis was twice the rate in the nation. With a budget of only $2,000, the board hardly knew where to begin.

A few years earlier Mollie's friend Dr. Thomas Tuttle had been appointed state health officer. Dr. Tuttle's first effort as head of the state board of health was to educate people to the dangers of spitting. He published articles in the newspapers, pointing out that spitting spread the germs of tuberculosis. Tuttle insisted that hotels, theaters, and especially railway coaches put cuspidors within easy shot of "expectorators." Prior to this, people simply spat on the floor. Spitting was particularly dangerous in the railcars, Tuttle said, because the janitor would come through and sweep up the floor, swirling the dust and germs through the air in the enclosed space. If a consumptive had spit on the floor, the TB germs were spread into the lungs of the passengers. Tuttle prohibited smoking on streetcars, not because it was damaging to the lungs, but in order to prevent spitting. The state board instituted a fear campaign: Anyone caught spitting in public, unless into a cuspidor, was arrested. Schoolchildren were taught that "spitting is death."

The board members attempted to convince the public that tuberculosis, if caught early enough, could be cured. Despite their efforts, however, the perception remained that the "white plague" was hereditary and incurable. This defeatist attitude was one of the factors that made tuberculosis the leading cause of death of adults in America.

Mollie could only watch from the sidelines for the first few years of the new state board's activities. But she was an eager observer. She was especially encouraged when the board tackled the problem of bovine TB. Ever since the Montana land boom at the beginning of the century, certain unscrupulous cattle dealers from the East had been unloading their diseased animals onto Montana ranges, infecting the healthy herds. A testing system was soon established that discovered hundreds of infected cows, all of which had to be destroyed.

The ranchers were furious. Many of them were foreigners, and since cattle hadn't been tuberculin-tested in the countries they had come from, they couldn't understand why this was an issue on the wide-open plains of Montana. Some of them assumed the testing requirement was merely political graft and tried to bribe their way out of compliance. When this approach didn't work, they often pulled out ear tags and switched animals in the herds. The veterinarians finally found help through the intercession of a Catholic priest from Butte, who was able to convince his parishioners of the dangers of infected milk. Further research confirmed what Mollie had suspected for some time: The bone TB that was common in children was shown to be directly attributable to the milk of infected cows. Further, it was determined that glandular and abdominal tuberculosis—as well as hunchback, caused by spinal tuberculosis—was traceable to contaminated cattle.

In a few years Dorothy was old enough that Mollie felt she could return to her profession, although not to full-time practice. In the first decade of the century, Montana was hit with several severe smallpox and typhoid epidemics, and Mollie was frequently called on to help the overworked doctors in various parts of the state. Mrs. Washington was hired to spend the days with Dorothy, and Ben took over at night.

Since woman's suffrage in Montana seemed to be moribund, Mollie's main interest during these years remained the public health problem of tuberculosis. An unfortunate, if perhaps inevitable consequence of the educational programs initiated by Dr. Tuttle and the state board was to turn the "consumptive" into the "tubercular." Previously, the consumptive often had been treated in the home by concerned family. When Dr. Tuttle's campaign convinced the public that the disease was infectious, the tubercular was shunned as a menace, not only by the public, but often by his own relatives. The irony of this was that to be kept away from public places and from intimate contact with family members was precisely what was necessary to prevent the spread of the disease—yet often at great psychological cost to the sufferer. It was a classic case of the needs of the society versus the needs of the individual. Many doctors didn't bother to report tuberculosis deaths, or the family didn't want them to. Furthermore, TB in its incipient state often had no outward physical signs; if they were present, they could be easily confused with other diseases. This situation made it difficult for the board to convince the legislators of the magnitude of the problem, and hence to convince them to release money to fund an all-out anti-TB campaign.

Dr. Tuttle lobbied the legislature to require physicians to report all cases of tuberculosis so that patients could be monitored and could avoid giving the disease to others. He was not successful. The legislature refused to pay attention to the problem, even though everywhere was fear and ostracization of the sick. Restaurants refused to serve tuberculars, landlords refused to rent to them, hospitals turned them away. It was the situation all over the country. As in the case of the lepers of the

Middle Ages, one state even considered a bill requiring the tuberculars to wear cowbells around their necks. Fortunately, the bill was not enacted. But the problem remained: Where could the sick person go? There was no facility in Montana specifically to treat tuberculosis.

The challenge brought out the fight in Mollie. She could not maintain a full-time private practice, and she was forced by political circumstance to put off for a time the cause of women's rights; however, she could launch a crusade for the rights of the tubercular.

Since the board of health was unable to convince the legislature to act, and the members of the Montana Medical Association were dragging their feet, Mollie decided it was time to bring *real* pressure to bear: It was time to mobilize Montana's women to action. Her experience with the suffrage movement—although as yet the movement was still unsuccessful—had taught her how powerful women could be when they took up a cause.

Mollie contacted her friend Elinor Walsh, who was president of the Federated Women's Clubs of Montana. She argued to Elinor that the women should challenge the legislature to provide a state-supported facility for the treatment of tuberculosis. As wife of the U.S. senator from Montana, Mrs. Walsh was close to the political power to support the cause. The vehemence with which Mollie made her case convinced the senator's wife that, together, they would unleash the power of Montana's club women on the public, and ultimately on the legislature.

Elinor sent Mollie to a meeting of the Federated Clubs in Glendive to speak for the new campaign.

"Let me begin," Mollie told the assembly, "by telling you that tuberculosis is the greatest killer of all the horrible diseases we are subject to in this country. It is the leading cause of adult deaths, both here and abroad. It is spread by spitting in public, and by the crowded living conditions many of our poorer citizens must endure. The miners are especially vulnerable because their lungs are weakened from working in the dust. When the bacteria enter the lungs, the infection causes a defense reaction that destroys the lung tissue. We call it 'consumption,' because in addition to fever and coughing, there is a serious loss of weight—that is, the body is literally 'consumed.'

"It is also called the 'white plague,'" she continued, "because the destruction of the lung tissue leaves cavities that fill with a white material that looks like cottage cheese. Since the tiny blood vessels are destroyed in this process, the victim coughs blood until finally a massive hemorrhage occurs."

Mollie could see that some of the women were feeling repulsed by her description. She knew their discomfort was a good sign: The more upset she could make her listeners, the faster she would get their attention.

"Let me stress," she went on, "that the pulmonary tuberculosis I have just described is a common form of the disease, but by no means the only form it will take. And let me also point out that your children are particularly susceptible, often infected by contaminated milk— milk that is readily available to all of your homes."

There was a murmur throughout the audience, and a tension could be felt in the room.

"Regardless of what you may have heard," she said, "tuberculosis is *not* hereditary. It is extremely contagious and its victims must be isolated. *But*"— she stressed the word—"if cases are caught soon enough, they don't have to be fatal. We have reports from treatment centers in other states that under controlled conditions, the disease can be cured.

"Caring for our suffering citizens is the challenge I put before you. It's a big undertaking, but we can swing it, and we will!"

Mollie's enthusiasm for her cause caught the women's support. The

255

federation asked the local clubs to assess a per capita tax on their members for the prevention of TB. As well as arousing statewide awareness for a treatment center, the women raised $3,000 for public education.

Elinor Walsh formed a committee of four prominent women to carry out the public education campaign. Mollie was in charge of twisting the arms of the medical establishment.

At the next MMA meeting, held in Missoula, Mollie brought up the subject of Montana's need for a sanatorium. When she had finished her presentation, one of the doctors said, "It's a lovely dream, but impractical."

Another added, "It's a wonderful idea, and you're a great girl. We're sorry your dream is impossible of accomplishment."

"How sorry are you?" Mollie asked, smiling at him.

"What do you mean?" her colleague asked.

"I mean, how sorry are you in *cash?*"

She collected $10 from the man. Then Dr. Tuttle stepped forward to give a rousing speech in support of Mollie's proposal; she returned to Helena the next day with $100.

"It's not much," she reported to Elinor Walsh, "but it's a start. At least it will help toward our printing bill."

Mollie's commitment to the antituberculosis cause and her hard-nosed fund-raising earned her the sobriquet "our militant member" from her club associates. With the other committee members, she gave educational lectures, staged exhibits, and handed out literature at public gatherings. By 1911 the women's antituberculosis committee was ready to make a presentation to the legislature.

The representative from Silver Bow County, Jim McNally, introduced the bill for the establishment of a state TB sanatorium. The issue was a personal one for McNally: His brother had died of tuberculosis. When his brother was on his deathbed, McNally had promised him he would work for the prevention and cure of the disease. Mollie briefed Representative McNally on the statistics. The representative pointed out to the assembly that half of all TB deaths in the state occurred in the Butte area. This was due, he told the legislators, primarily to the silicon in the dust created by underground drilling, but it was also due in part to the miners' superstition that there was no cure for consumption—or the "con," as they called it. Since death was inevitable, they believed, there was no point in visiting a doctor. McNally's statistics impressed the legislators, and they agreed to study the proposal.

"The miners would rather admit to syphilis than to 'miner's con,'" Mollie said to Dr. Tuttle after the hearing as the two were riding the train to Butte to attend a meeting of the public health board. "They know that syphilis can be cured, but when it becomes known that a miner has the 'con,' his friends shake their heads and say, 'one more clean shirt'—the shirt he will wear in his coffin. I tried to reason with them when I was working in Marysville. I hate to think how far consumption has spread because they just won't listen."

"Well, McNally seemed to have finally caught the attention of some of the legislators," said Tuttle. "Now let's hope we can get through to the miners in Butte. The statistics you gave McNally may have turned things around for the state."

Another reason the death rate was so high in Montana was that the mine owners feared they might be faced with compensation costs, as was the case in Canada, where they were already paying out hundreds of thousands of dollars. The last thing the owners wanted was for the board of health to arouse public opinion by distributing information on the causes of the disease. And in this they had been helped by the legislature, which had consistently refused to require doctors to report tuberculosis cases.

Despite intensive lobbying by the mining industry, McNally's bill passed. A sanatorium was authorized, and McNally graciously acknowledged that his success was due in large part to the indefatigable efforts of Mollie and her club friends. But alas, as with so many well-meaning efforts, the original bill, which had proposed $200,000 for construction and $100,000 for maintenance, ended up authorizing $20,000 and $10,000—a reduction indicative of the solons' continuing lack of concern. Still, like Mollie's first $100 from the Missoula doctors, it was a start. The following year a pared-down Montana tuberculosis sanatorium was built at Galen, and Dr. Tuttle became the facility's first director.

The same 1911 legislature that authorized the passage of the sanatorium bill saw the reintroduction, after a hiatus of six years, of yet another woman's suffrage amendment. By this time outside as well as locally owned corporations had a death grip on Montana politics. In fact, it was commonly acknowledged that the corporate rulers were more powerful than the state government. Progressive political leaders saw the value of woman's suffrage as a way to help break this hold. Furthermore, there was momentum for the idea since the state of Washington had approved a suffrage bill the year before. Instrumental in that campaign was a young Montana woman, Jeannette Rankin. After the Washington victory, Rankin returned to her home state. She joined with the old guard of women's rights activists and threw her efforts into reviving the issue.

The Women's Christian Temperance Union had persuaded the Dawson County representative to introduce the suffrage bill in the House. In a supposedly chivalrous gesture, the House chamber was decorated with flowers for the women. Mollie, Maria Dean, and the WCTU leader, Mary Alderson, sat on the speakers' platform. They informed the assembly they would defer their time to Miss Rankin.

Jeannette Rankin began her presentation with the statement that she was born in Montana. This was politically astute, and raised a loud applause. She continued: "Men want women in the home, and they want them to make the home perfect. Yet how can women make it so if they have no control over the influences of the home?"

She went on to discuss the effects of woman suffrage in other states. Washington had just passed its referendum in 1910, and Wyoming women had enjoyed the franchise since 1869. Rankin pointed out that obviously the government had not fallen in states with women's suffrage. She ended her brief talk with a reminder from the beginning of the country's history as a nation: "Taxation without representation is tyranny."

The reward for her efforts was a bunch of violets, presented to her by her leading adversary.

Mollie was disgusted.

"What do they *think*?" she said to Rankin after the women's presentation. "That you'll be so flattered to receive a bunch of flowers from that man that you'll forget all about our equal rights? How insulting! And I wonder which of them decided to decorate the chambers for us. Do they think we're too stupid to not know when we're being patronized? That all those flowers would make us feel better about losing?"

As the representatives discussed the bill over the next two days, it was clear that the proposal would fail. Again. One opponent had repeatedly obstructed the discussion with facetious amendments, such as a requirement that only women with six or more children could qualify for the ballot.

"There's only one thing I'm grateful for," Mollie said to her friends after the final vote. "At least Ella didn't have to see this." Ella Knowles Haskell had died the week before.

What angered Mollie most about the hearing was that Jim

McNally, who had been so appreciative of the help that she and the women of the tuberculosis education committee had given him in support of his sanatorium bill, turned out to be a fierce opponent of woman suffrage.

"Talk about blind ingratitude," Mollie fumed to her friends. "He doesn't even see that the political savvy of our group of women is what turned the legislature around on his sanatorium. He couldn't have gotten his bill through without our help, and yet he has the gall to oppose our amendment."

Mollie had to take the next year off from her Montana politicking. Dorothy had had a mild case of strep throat earlier in the fall, and it had turned into rheumatic fever. Mollie was worried that the fever might affect her heart. She had insisted her daughter stay in bed until all trace of the fever passed. This meant Dorothy would miss school. Mollie got her schoolbooks from the teacher, and she and Ben helped her keep up with her class at home. But then Dorothy developed a nervous tic in her facial muscles and tongue, and her arms would give spasmodic jerks. Mollie recognized the symptoms of rheumatic chorea—Saint Vitus' dance.

Ben and Mollie discussed what should be done.

"This childhood chorea is very unpleasant for a while, but she'll recover. It's certainly not fatal," Mollie told him. "But I'm especially concerned that it doesn't affect her balance. She'll need some exercise therapy." Dorothy had been studying dance, and young as she was, she showed considerable talent. "I'd like to take her to the seashore for a few months. I think the sea air will help her recover faster."

"I don't like the idea of you and Dorothy abandoning me," Ben said, "but of course I want what's best for her."

"We'll miss you, you know that, Ben." Mollie smiled at him. "But I do think this is the right thing to do for her. I have a colleague in California, an excellent pediatrician. I would like to put Dorothy in her care for a while."

"Well, she's already eleven." Ben said. "I think she's old enough to understand the implications of her disease. We might as well talk to her now."

They went upstairs together to Dorothy's room. She was sitting up in bed, trying to do her homework, but was having trouble controlling her hands enough to write her arithmetic problems in a notebook. Her eyes were wet with tears of frustration. Mollie and Ben exchanged painful glances. They sat down on either side of the bed.

"Dorothy," Mollie said, "I'll help you with that in a little while." She took the notebook away and set it on the night table. "Right now your father and I want to talk to you about your sickness. The nervous tics you have developed in the past week are actually symptoms of a disease. It's called Saint Vitus' dance."

Dorothy was suddenly fearful. "What does that mean? Am I going to die?"

"No, no, darling, it doesn't mean that, not at all," Ben was quick to assure her. He looked into Dorothy's wet, gray-green eyes. They were unnerving, jerking in nervous spasm. "You'll get better, but it will take some time."

"Yes," Mollie said. "You and I are going away for a while to California. I know you'll get better faster by the ocean."

"I don't want to go to California."

"I know," said Ben, "but we think the sea air will help you get well, and then you can come home right away."

"Will you come, too?" Dorothy asked.

"I wish I could, Dorothy, but I have to stay here and work."

"I want you to come, too." Her eyes were brimming.

"It won't be for more than a few months," Mollie said, taking her daughter's hand. "You can catch up your lost semester at school there. And I know you'll love living at the seashore. As soon as you feel well enough, you can go swimming in the ocean. You've never done that before. It's lots of fun to jump in the waves."

Dorothy did not seem convinced. Mollie thought she was probably afraid of the separation from Ben. As an only child, Dorothy was the focus of love in their little family. Except for Mollie's occasional trips around the state for meetings or temporary medical assignments, the three of them were always together.

"Poor little girl," Ben said later when he and Mollie were back downstairs. "I guess this is one of the bumps of growing up. You can't always have your life work out the way you want it."

"Don't worry too much, Ben. She'll have a marvelous time on the beach. I'll probably have to drag her back here. You'll see."

CHAPTER SEVENTEEN

A Close Win

MOLLIE RENTED A SMALL COTTAGE just steps from La Jolla Cove. As she had hoped, Dorothy's health improved quickly in the warm Southern California air. With the help of daily physical therapy, the palsy completely disappeared. Dorothy was enrolled in her last semester of grammar school, and Mollie had to wait for her to graduate before they could return home.

That semester was a trial for Mollie. In her mind she had never left Montana. She felt sure the suffrage movement was gaining significant momentum from the spirit of reform that had finally begun to move the state political parties. The grip of the corporations and the legislators who supported them was being challenged, and she hoped the groundswell for reform would sweep the suffrage movement along with it.

She had never been idle in her life. It was not in her nature to sit watching waves surge and fling themselves against the sand, or to meander along the promenade at the edge of the cliffs, listening to the crashing against the rocks below. Perhaps others would have felt lulled by the timeless rhythm of one of the loveliest beaches in America. For

Mollie, that rhythm was anything but timeless. Every meaningless advance and retreat of the waves was like a sand clock marking minutes passing from her life. Afternoons she waited impatiently for the mail from Montana. Maria Dean kept her informed as to the campaign, and Ben wrote regularly about Helena news and gossip.

One afternoon when she went to pick up the mail at the La Jolla Post Office, there was a letter from Ben with a clipping from a Helena newspaper. She walked down to the promenade to sit in one of the gazebos above the water to read it. The clipping told of the arrest of a prominent Helena businessman, whom she remembered from their Marysville days. She had met the man and his wife occasionally at Marysville parties and recalled that the couple had left Marysville about the same time as she and Ben. The article said that a man was arrested for beating a prostitute at "The Castle," Helena's most notorious bordello. Mollie had no doubt it was the same man who had beaten Isabel and killed Willy. She had not known him well, but she had disliked him immediately on meeting him. There was a crudeness about him that had repelled her. As she thought about him, she remembered what the madam had said that day years earlier, when Mollie had confronted her in the Marysville brothel: "You *don't want* to know who he is."

She wrote to Ben immediately:

> *Isabel's suicide has been nagging at the back of my mind for almost twenty years, and now at last I can let it go. Perhaps it is small of me to rejoice in this. I'm sure his wife must be disgraced beyond belief. But I do feel relieved that finally here is the justice that Isabel disparaged as ever applying to the likes of her.*

As soon as Dorothy finished her school year, Mollie rushed her back to Montana. She was eager to get back to the suffrage activity now that the politicians were talking about reform. Jeannette Rankin had formed a new state central committee, and had visited every county to organize the campaign. The women championed their cause especially forcefully in Butte, where suffrage opponent Jim McNally—Mollie's former colleague in the fight for the sanatorium—was up for reelection. Rankin had managed to get party endorsements from the Democrats, the Progressives, and, to Mollie's admiration, the Republicans as well.

Mollie was back in time to help with the last of the campaign. Democrats swept the state in the 1912 elections, and the Democratic governor-elect, Sam Stewart, promised to support the suffrage amendment as part of the package of his party's reform agenda. Still, the women were worried. Even with this strong support, there were a number of antisuffrage conservatives in both parties in the legislature—among them Jim McNally, who had retained his seat in the House. This year, however, when the women's amendment finally came up for the vote, party discipline held the conservatives in check. The holdouts—this time even McNally—grudgingly went along with their platform promises. At long last, after almost twenty years of the women's efforts, the amendment, with only two negative votes in each house, would be sent to the electorate for ratification.

The excitement at the outcome in the legislature's action spread all the way to New York. The national association held a mass meeting in Carnegie Hall to raise money for Montana's upcoming referendum. Speakers and money flowed into the state from the East. James Laidlaw, a New York banker and president of the Men's League for Woman Suffrage, organized a Montana men's league, with Jeannette Rankin's brother, Wellington, at the head. Among the league members were several prominent men, who added an endorsement of male approval to the effort.

The opposition jumped into the fray. The liquor interests' Protective Association was determined to prevent the adoption of the amendment. Flyers sailed back and forth from both sides: one side arguing the necessary contribution women would bring to political life; the other predicting that the saloons would close.

As had happened before, the women themselves were divided over the approach they should make to the electorate. The Temperance Union wanted to tie the vote to prohibition, and courted the immigrant vote. Rankin's group, now loosely formed as the Montana Equal Suffrage Association, wanted to disassociate itself from the WCTU and brought up Chapman Catt's ethnic prejudice again. Mollie was uncomfortable with both camps.

"I can't go along with the WCTU," she told Ben and Dorothy one evening at dinner, "because I think it may be disastrous to tie suffrage to prohibition. But at the same time, I dislike Jeannette's ethnic prejudice as an argument for women's suffrage. On that score the WCTU has the right attitude, as far as I'm concerned. They recognize that the immigrants are with us to stay, and what we need to do is educate them to their civic responsibilities, not drown them out by the votes of us lily-white women of virtue."

"I think this attitude has been underlying the suffragists' approach right from the start," Ben said. "Certainly your friend Carrie Catt has been talking this way all along."

"I know," Mollie said with a sigh. "And that's why Maria has been cool about our contact with National. Here we are struggling to claim our place in democracy and at the same time contriving to deny others that place."

"Politics always forces one into a corner," Ben said. "It's forever a matter of how much compromise one can stomach."

Mollie was disturbed by the divisiveness between the WCTU and the suffragists for personal reasons as well. Several of the women had a foot in each camp, and friendships were strained. Her friend Mary Alderson was now state chairman of the WCTU. Alderson had worked with the suffragists all along and had served with Mollie on the board of the original state suffrage society they had formed in 1895.

Shortly before the amendment was to be voted on, disagreements came to a head in the planning committee for the suffrage parade at the state fair in September 1914. Jeannette Rankin had initially invited the Temperance Union ladies to participate in the parade under their own banner, but then thought better of the idea and withdrew the invitation.

"We've got to disassociate ourselves from the temperance women," Rankin argued at the meeting. "I don't want those people in the parade. We've got to keep to the single issue. If people see the WCTU marching, we will very likely lose this referendum."

"Mary Alderson is going to be furious." said one member. "You know how hard she's worked all these years."

"I know, but this is our big chance. We can't afford to let them parade. It's hard enough playing the political game in Butte, cozying up to the anti-immigrant folks, telling them how we're going to dilute the foreign vote, and at the same time telling the immigrants that suffrage would give them more power. The last thing we need is for them to think the bars are going to close."

Mary Alderson was indeed furious. She appeared at the next planning meeting. "The WCTU has been working for woman suffrage in this state longer than most of you have even been here—before some of you were hardly even born." She glared at Rankin. "And we will continue to do so. I'm not taking orders from you. The union will carry on its own suffrage campaign. It's laughable how considerate you are of the liquor industry." Alderson stood up from her chair and slammed out of the meeting.

The two groups were wise enough to keep their dissension under wraps. And although she did not admit it, perhaps Alderson may have recognized the political wisdom of toning down the temperance association long enough to get the vote. At any rate, she finally acquiesced to the suffragists' insistence that WCTU members could march as individuals, but not under the WCTU banner.

September 25 was a perfect day for a parade. The air was crisp and clear, not yet cold. Thousands of marchers, both men and women, assembled at the state fairgrounds. As the parade stretched out along the Helena streets, it grew to a mile in length. Marchers came from every county, and some from the adjacent states. Anna Shaw, national president succeeding Carrie Catt, headed the procession. She was followed by Jeannette Rankin and Maria Dean holding a huge yellow suffrage banner. Women from states where suffrage was legal carried American flags; yellow flags were for states with campaigns, as was Montana on that day; gray flags were carried by women from states with partial suffrage; and black flags were carried by those from holdout states. The WCTU women marched, dressed in white, but they did not carry a banner. The Boy Scouts carried signs that said I WANT MY MOTHER TO VOTE! There were bugles and banners and bands, cars and horses and floats. Dorothy had a new yellow dress for the event, and Mollie wore a yellow shawl around her shoulders. One woman was dressed as Sacajawea, with a sign that read THE FIRST MONTANA SUFFRAGIST. Ben marched with the men's league, and there were as many men as women in the parade.

A small group of women who opposed the vote had opened a stand at the fairgrounds. They handed out flyers arguing that a woman's proper place was in the home, not in the voting booth, but they attracted little attention. Thirteen-year-old Dorothy proclaimed the march the most thrilling event of her life. The excitement was tremendous; Mollie and her friends hoped it would hold over to the November referendum.

For the two weeks before the referendum, the women handed out little yellow flags that read VOTES FOR WOMEN. Children went to school wearing yellow headbands; volunteers handed out flyers printed on yellow paper; telephone poles were adorned with yellow posters.

On the day of the referendum, the women were on the alert all over the state—with good reason. They didn't trust the opposition. The California vote had been almost lost through fraud, and the suffragists were convinced they had been tricked out of a victory in Michigan. Jeannette Rankin assigned her troops to watch county ballot boxes throughout the state. Mollie's job was to watch the polls in Jefferson County, and she took her daughter with her.

"I can't think of a better civics lesson," she said to Dorothy. "I only hope it will be civics at its best."

"How *could* they not vote for us?" Dorothy said to Mollie and the other women who were watching the ballot box. "It would be so unfair."

Mollie had to smile. Indeed how could they not? Dorothy was getting a tiny taste of the frustration Mollie had felt for the last twenty years.

"Well, darling," she said, putting her arm around her daughter, "if it turns out that Jefferson County doesn't understand what's fair, it doesn't mean we've lost the state."

It took several days for word from the counties to trickle in. Early in the week, the results looked like the women were in trouble, but Jeannette Rankin refused to admit defeat. Missoula had stood by them, but Helena, the suffragists' headquarters, voted against them. Butte was breaking even. Jefferson County, where Mollie and Dorothy had stood guard on the ballot box, voted them down. Dorothy was both excited and discouraged; she watched the newspaper every morning as the progress of the vote was reported.

As the suffragists had expected, something smelled fishy in Anaconda, the Deer Lodge County home of Amalgamated Copper. Election officials were required by law to lock one copy of the referendum results with the actual ballots for safekeeping until the count could be verified. But inexplicably, for several days no report at all was sent in from Deer Lodge County. Even the newspapers, which sent special reporters to the polls in Anaconda, were unable to get information.

"I know their game," Jeannette Rankin said to National's Anna Shaw, who had come to Montana for the election. It was already the fifth day that no report had come in from Anaconda. "They're going to wait to stuff the ballot boxes at the last minute if they think they can swing the vote against us."

"That's what they tried to do in California. I was there," Shaw said, angrily. "And I'm convinced that's how we lost the vote in Michigan. But this time I'm calling out the Associated Press, and I'm going down there with our lawyers. Why don't you round up everyone you can find, and we'll all go down there together."

By late afternoon a crowd of suffragists armed with a cadre of lawyers and reporters descended on Deer Lodge County. If Anaconda officials had indeed been planning such shenanigans, they didn't have to bother. The county soundly defeated the amendment anyway. It wasn't until six days had passed that enough votes came in from the outlying counties. The women had won the state by a slim margin. It was not the sweeping victory they had hoped for, but the important thing was—they had won.

"Whatever are you going to do now the fight's over?" Ben asked Mollie the day after the results were final. "Don't tell me you're going to run for Congress. I just can't see myself at those infamous Washington booze parties—or you, either, for that matter."

Mollie laughed. "Come now, my dear. Were you worried that was my intent with this effort all along? No thanks. I think I'll leave Congress to Jeannette. I'll bet you anything she runs two years from now. And what's more, I'll bet you she wins."

"Well, she'll have my vote," Ben said. "After watching her revive the moribund suffrage movement in Montana, I'd say she'll have Congress wrapped around her little finger."

"This last push for the vote was tremendously exciting—and exhausting," Mollie said, "but now I've got to do something about the TB sanatorium at Galen. The place is not only too small, it's bleak and depressing. That stingy legislature didn't give us enough money to build an adequate facility in the first place, and now we're turning people away, letting them just die because there's not enough space."

"Mollie, you are amazing. Where do you get the energy for all these challenges?"

"I really don't know, Ben." Her face was suddenly serious. "Something inside me won't let me sit back and watch things happen—bad things I know I could do something about. Or at least try."

What concerned Mollie about the situation at Galen was that not only were there far too few beds, but there were no separate facilities for women or children, either. Once the legislature had authorized construction in 1911, the members apparently thought they had fulfilled whatever obligation they had to Montana's tuberculars. Because of the taboo, especially among the miners, about even admitting to TB, the patients referred to Galen were often so far along in the disease that their cases were terminal. Dr. Tuttle requested that only hopeful cases be sent. But again and again he had to inform families that they had waited too long. And yet, as he tried to explain to the public, if he could have reached these people early enough, very likely they could have recovered. The death rate at Galen did not bode well for the reputation of the sanatorium, particularly in the minds of the legislators.

The state board of health was extremely concerned that men, women, and children were all together in the same facility. To remedy this was the challenge that Mollie took up. Again working with Senator Walsh's wife and other women from the Montana women's clubs, Mollie and her fellow club members started a fund-raising campaign for a separate woman's facility at Galen.

At the same time, she and Dr. William Cogswell, who had replaced Dr. Tuttle as secretary of the board, worked diligently to convince the medical association that a state tuberculosis association must be formed. The board of health had too many problems to have the time to focus on a single issue. The tuberculosis epidemic required a special organization to oversee the advance of the disease and to keep accurate statistics on its spread and intensity, the rate of recovery, the rate of mortality. And such an oversight organization was needed to lobby for funding and improvements at Galen.

Finally in 1916, through the campaigning of Mollie and her club women, as well as the MMA, the state board, and especially Butte pathologist Dr. Caroline McGill, the Montana Tuberculosis Association was founded. Mollie was pleased that her old colleague from Marysville, Dr. Oscar Lanstrum, took an active, constructive role in the association. Lanstrum and Mollie had had their political differences, but these didn't extend to their mutual concern for the welfare of the tuberculars. They both served amicably on the board of directors.

From 1915 to 1917 Elinor Walsh, Mollie, and several women from the Montana Federation of Women's Clubs raised funds for the national Christmas Seal campaign to build a separate woman's tuberculosis facility. They were hugely successful. However, Elinor was in Washington in 1917 with her senator husband when the Helena women got the news that she was dying of cancer. Mollie was shocked with grief. After so many years of working together, she and Elinor had become intimate friends. Mollie was determined the women's facility would go forward as a memorial to her friend. But this project, like so many socially important endeavors across the country, was put on hold by America's entry into the Great War.

Mollie's prediction that Jeannette Rankin would run for U.S. Congress was correct. In 1916, with the help of the newly enfranchised woman electorate, Rankin was sent to the House of Representatives as the first congresswoman in U.S. history. Additionally, Montana voters elected two women to their own state legislature.

Unfortunately for the liquor industry, however, that same election precipitated what it had feared most about the passage of the suffrage amendment: The Prohibitionists voted the state "dry." It was not just the women's vote, although that certainly helped. The Anti-Saloon League was primarily a men's organization, largely controlled by the clergy. And the new homesteaders out on the eastern plains were a tough lot, many of whom didn't believe in liquid indulgence. The new law gave the saloons until January 1, 1919, to pack up and get out.

"Better stock up, Ben," Mollie said to her husband with a grin. "We needed the Prohibitionists to get us the vote, but we knew the price we'd pay: no hooch at all, or undercover stuff at exorbitant prices. I can't really blame those women, though," she added. "The numbers of dead and diseased from alcoholism in this state are appalling. Maybe they're right that the only thing to do is to just cut off the supply—even if it does mean our Sunday sherry."

"I'm glad I'm not working for the brewery any longer or I'd be out on the street," Ben said. "But I'm sorry for Charlie Kessler. It's a shame, seeing that family business go down. Old Nick Kessler started that brewery in Bannack back in 1865, and now it's a thriving business. Helena's going to lose a lot of jobs when Kessler's has to close."

Woodrow Wilson won his second presidential term in 1916 on the promise that he would keep the United States out of war. The desire to stay out of the madness across the Atlantic was strong in the nation. After all, Europeans had been killing each other for centuries, and on a grand scale since Napoleon had walked all over the continent. Why should Americans get involved? However, as German aggression in Europe increased, and as American lives were lost by German submarine attacks on Allied ships, including the 124 Americans of the 1,200 victims lost when the *Lusitania* was torpedoed, Wilson felt compelled in April 1917 to ask Congress for a declaration of war.

The congressional vote was not unanimous. Fifty-five congressmen voted against entering the war. But as the only woman in Congress, Jeannette Rankin's vote against American involvement unleashed a torrent of disapprobation across the country. Because she was a woman, she was accused of being soft, incompetent to stand up to political realities. Some newspapers called her a traitor and a coward, at best a sentimental fool. The *New York Times* proclaimed her vote proof of the "feminine incapacity for straight reasoning." It didn't seem to occur to the national press that it took great strength of conviction to vote one's pacifist principles against the rising clamor for war.

CHAPTER EIGHTEEN

A Monster Is Killing the People

WHEN MOLLIE PICKED UP the *Helena Independent* from her porch steps late in September 1918, the front page carried, as it had for months now, the latest overnight progress of the war in Europe: The Kaiser's troops were mobilized on the Western Front; the American Expeditionary Force had launched its first major offensive near Verdun; General Pershing was calling for more troops. It was the daily harrowing account of a war that was slaughtering millions. And Montana had sent 40,000 of its young men and women to the front, nearly a tenth of the state's population.

As they did every morning, Mollie and Ben read the paper over their breakfast coffee. They, like all war-weary Americans, followed the daily reports of the grueling advances and retreats across the fields of France, the appalling numbers of Allied dead and wounded. There seemed no end to the horror.

On this morning Mollie was the first to read the daily casualty list, "Dead in the Battle for Democracy."

"Oh no!" Mollie cried. "The Stevens boy from over on Gallatin Street is listed here. Oh poor Dorothy. They were such good friends.

He took her to the high school prom last year, remember? I hate to tell her this."

"She's probably already heard it today at school," Ben said, shaking his head. "I'm so sorry for her. It's the first time this horrible war has touched her directly."

Besides the name on the casualty list, there was another report on the front page of the *Independent* this day that caught Mollie's attention. A short news release from Washington: 3,000 new cases of influenza in the U.S. Army camps, bringing the total number of cases to 23,000. This was the first mention in the paper of the flu since the report of a mild attack of the so-called Spanish flu the previous spring. The Spanish flu had sickened some eight million in Spain, including King Alfonso XIII, but had been relatively light in the United States.

The next morning the *Independent* announced that the draft call of 142,000 troops was canceled. The military camps were under flu quarantine at a time when America's massive offensive into the German lines at the Argonne-Meuse sector had just been launched. The need to relieve the exhausted troops, let alone fill in for the dead and wounded, was urgent.

"My God, Ben," Mollie said, handing the paper over to her husband. "They've canceled the draft, and now the troops are quarantined. Washington says the flu is now an epidemic. The government thinks it's maybe another invidious German assault, brought here in their U-boats. It's already killed 12,000 Americans! The Kaiser may win this war yet."

The flu added another dimension to the agony of the war for Americans. This was a war that had already astounded the world with forms of violence and weaponry not seen before: the German submarine; the machine gun; the glass ball shrapnel; the artillery barrages; the cruelty of mustard gas; the carnage in the trenches at the Somme and

Verdun. And now this strange and seemingly incurable disease that was killing Americans by the thousands, both at home and abroad.

A few days after Mollie and Ben read the first report in the *Independent*, the flu arrived in Montana. It struck in the small, northeastern town of Scobey and quickly spread into the rural areas. Three hundred fifty cases, four deaths so far. The Scobey schools were closed. By the second week of October, the disease was surging across the state like a giant tidal wave. Public gatherings were prohibited; schools, churches, theaters, dance halls, libraries, restaurants, and saloons were shut down.

Bartenders in Butte and Helena, as well as a good lot of the public, put up such a vehement protest over the order to close the saloons that a compromise was reached: Bars could sell package liquor to be consumed off premises. No single drinks could be served. People could not congregate, and chairs must be removed. The bartenders argued they only had a couple of months left before the state went dry anyway. It was unfair to force them to shut down early.

"This flu can be cured by alcohol," one bartender argued to the state health board. "You people don't understand that liquor is good for you."

As the days moved farther into October, the flu reports from the military camps and the eastern cities became more and more gruesome. A hundred recruits a day were dying at Fort Devens near Boston. In Philadelphia there were 2,600 dead at the end of the first week; by the end of the second, 4,500. Reports telling a similar story started coming in from San Francisco, from Louisville, from Seattle, from Chicago. Although wartime censorship blacked out much of the news from other countries, reports still seeped in from around the globe: The pandemic was worldwide.

The flu hit Montana especially hard in Butte. Mollie read the autopsy reports sent over from Butte by her friend Dr. Caroline McGill, the Silver Bow County pathologist. As a physician, Mollie was no stranger to the malignancies and physical corruption to which the human body can fall victim, but Dr. McGill's description of the condition of the influenza victims had Mollie confounded. She had never witnessed death occur in such a horrifying manner and in such frequency as these reports revealed. Butte was burying bodies at twenty a day.

On October 15 Dr. William Cogswell, the state director of public health and a longtime friend, called Mollie. "We need your help, Dr. Mollie," Cogswell said. "We're desperately shorthanded. Everyone who could get free has gone to France. I'm asking Surgeon General Blue to send Montana twenty-five nurses, but I doubt we'll get that many. This flu is a monster. I want you to come down to the morgue right away; you have to see for yourself. I'll have one of my assistants show you what it's doing to us."

When Mollie arrived at the Lewis and Clark County morgue late that afternoon, there were two bodies waiting for autopsy. The public health pathologist was just finishing work on a third. Mollie gasped at the sight of the corpse he was working on. The body was grotesquely discolored, a purplish black, especially dark at the feet. Mollie went quickly over to the washbasin. She removed her hat and stretched a net over her hair. She took a surgical mask from her purse and a clean lab coat down from a hook by the basin. She washed her hands and joined the doctor at the autopsy table.

"These three were sent over from Saint Peter's a couple of hours ago," said the doctor. "This young man was admitted just day before yesterday. Only thirty years old. The hospital report says that on arrival he was coughing and had a fever of 104. Yet he had claimed he'd felt fine until the night before he was admitted.

"Look at these lungs, Dr. Atwater," the pathologist continued, scooping up a bluish mass from the dissecting tray. "I've never seen such a case of pulmonary edema before. Two sacs of bloody froth. The poor man drowned in his own blood!"

Mollie inspected the lungs closely. The sight took her aback. "No I've never seen this before, either," she said, grimacing. She looked down at the purple corpse: "Look, Doctor, the froth is oozing out of his nose even now. And look at his neck . . . my God, what a venous engorgement."

"The other two are flu cases also," the pathologist said, "but they'd been sick for a week or so, and the cause of death is pneumonia. Let's go have a look."

Mollie followed the doctor over to a white enameled table where a corpse lay covered by a sheet. The doctor pulled the sheet back, revealing the body of a young woman. She looked to be barely twenty. "How horrible," Mollie said. "This monster is killing the young ones."

"Yes," the pathologist said, nodding. "I had a baby in here yesterday, and a couple of days ago we had two elderly men. But most of the dead are between, say, twenty and forty. It's very strange. Ordinary flu picks off the old ones and the infants, but not the young healthy ones like this does."

Mollie stood at the table across from the pathologist. The girl's face in the repose of death was still lovely. She hadn't been dead for more than three or four hours. Her long brunette hair still had some pins caught in it. Mollie watched the doctor cut into the girl's chest, peel back the skin and fatty tissue from the young breasts, and sponge away the blood that slowly dripped down into the well at the edge of the autopsy table. A fear gripped Mollie; she could barely stand to watch. The girl was only a year or two older than Dorothy. What if Dorothy caught the infection . . . it could be she that was being cut like that.

"Look here, Dr. Atwater," the pathologist was saying. "The pathological process in these lungs is completely different from what we just saw."

With a shudder, Mollie took hold of herself. She leaned over the cadaver and looked into the exposed chest cavity.

"Yes, that's pneumonia," she said. "I can see the tissue is toughened, and the body isn't as cyanotic as the young man's. Maybe the flu attack was milder in this girl than in the man we just looked at, and that gave the pneumonia time to get into her lungs."

"Could be, Doctor," said the pathologist, closing the girl's chest and covering the body again with the sheet. He walked over to the sink and washed his hands. "The truth is, we don't know anything about this disease. We don't know how to treat it or even if it can be treated. It's killing thousands across the country either directly or by the pneumonic process, and there's nothing we can do to stop it. What's more, the doctors are so busy they don't even have time to report the number of cases. The surgeon general thinks there are at least twice as many as are being reported everywhere in the country. The best we can hope for is to try to make infected victims as comfortable as possible, and try to keep it from spreading. But we haven't been very successful at that, either."

Mollie took off her mask and net, and tossed the lab coat into the laundry hamper by the washbasin. "Thank you for taking the time to show me this," she said. "When I read Dr. McGill's reports, I couldn't imagine from her descriptions the severity of the pathology."

The doctor put his hand on Mollie's arm and gripped her with his eyes. "We need your help, Dr. Atwater. We need all the help we can get. Dr. Lanstrum and Dr. Copenhaver have volunteered, but you know as well as I there are whole areas in this state that have no medical presence at all. One of our workers stopped by a farm outside Miles City a couple of days ago. He found the mother and father and three children dead. One of the children had tried to get out, but he found her on the ground outside the house. Their starved animals were dying. And outside Havre, we found a family of eleven, all of them sick and lying three to four to a bed with all their clothes still on. We've asked the Red Cross for nurses, and I understand we will receive seven, but most of the nurses who could have helped us are overseas in the war. The few who are still in the country are urgently needed in the big cities. We need every doctor and nurse who can possibly help to volunteer. This is a pandemic, and I'm afraid this may be only the beginning."

Mollie couldn't hold his gaze. He was challenging her; they both knew it. She held out her hand to say good-bye. "I know," she said. "I'll let you know right away."

Mollie escaped out into the brisk afternoon air of the city. She walked up toward the city park on the side of Mount Helena. In the distance she could see the clear outline of the soft-molded hills of Marysville. A breeze coming up from the Helena Valley moved a wisp of hair loose from under her hat. The mountain air seemed so clean and fresh, yet it was secretly carrying the indiscriminate spores of death. She was still in shock from what she had seen. The cyanotic skin of the young man's feet and legs was like the skin of an eggplant, the lungs a froth of disease. Even in rigor mortis, his features were still twisted into the terror he had faced at the end. She had to admit that for once in her life she was frightened. What if this happened to Ben, what if . . . to Dorothy?

Mollie belonged to the Volunteer Medical Service Corps, a pool of civilian physicians deferred from national service because of health, age, or local need. She knew no one was forcing her, but as a member of the corps she had an obligation to serve in place of the doctors called to the war.

She knew the doctor was right. She should go; she should help those people. It was her responsibility. If she were to become infected and die, Dorothy would be all right—she had just turned seventeen. Mollie remembered how Dorothy had gone up to her room and sobbed that day after school a couple of weeks back. She had not heard about

Bradley Stevens at school, and Mollie had had to tell her. But she was still so young . . . Mollie balked at the thought of leaving her daughter. Again she saw the lovely dead girl in the autopsy room. If Dorothy came down with the flu, and she was not there to take care of her. . . .

Perhaps only once before had Mollie felt out of control of her life—the day Maria had told her she was pregnant. Now suddenly she was confronted again with a situation she couldn't control, a situation that threatened what she loved most in the world. As a doctor she had been exposed to epidemics of typhoid, smallpox, diphtheria, and more. But she had had the tools, the knowledge, and the medicine to protect herself and her patients. There was no medicine that would stop this killer. It seemed no more than a game of roulette as to who would survive and who would succumb. And she was being called to leave her family to this callous game of chance so that she could help others survive.

On October 17 the *Independent* announced there were 5,000 cases of flu so far in Montana. "All schools and churches in Helena are closed. All public gatherings of any sort are prohibited. By police order, all chairs and tables are out of the saloons."

On October 18 the *Independent* reported that the flu had spread to Marysville and Gloster. "East Helena is closed," said the announcement. "Absolutely no public gatherings are permitted, no exceptions. Lock-up is complete."

On October 19 the paper announced thirty-one new cases in Helena. Later that day Mrs. Holloway from the Helena Women's Club called Mollie on the telephone.

"I can't go, but you can," she said. "And I can take care of your daughter while you're away."

Mollie thanked her. "I haven't decided yet," she said to her friend. "I'll let you know."

The next day the newspaper announced that Lewiston was closed. "Everyone is urged to wear a mask." Citizens were asked to volunteer to manage the households of the sick—cooking and cleaning and caring for the stricken.

"I have to go, Ben," Mollie said that morning to her husband. "I just can't stay here knowing what is happening to those people out there in the towns. Bill Cogswell called again yesterday. The public health officer in Whitefish is desperate. Bill wants me to go up there. There's only one doctor for the whole area, and now he's sick."

"I know, Mollie," Ben said, looking intently at his wife. "I was wondering how long you were going to let this go on. I know you're worried about Dorothy and me. But don't. We'll be very careful. I'm not going to let her out of this house if I can help it—at least not without her mask. Since school's closed, she doesn't have to leave here, except to go down to the store for food—that's all."

"Mrs. Holloway said she'd help out," Mollie said. "I could ask her to come over and cook for you a couple of times a week."

"Stop worrying, will you? Dorothy and I will be fine. We don't need any help. Dorothy's a good little cook already. You know that. You have to go. There's no need to discuss it any longer." Ben got up and set his coffee cup in the sink. "I've got to get down to the station. I'm taking the train up to Great Falls to work on that lumber company's books. I'll be back on the seven o'clock. You get your things ready."

"Please, Ben. You must wear your mask on the train."

"Of course, Mollie. Stop worrying. I'll be careful."

It took Mollie a few days to organize her life. She didn't know how long she would be gone, and she had to consider that she, too, might become infected and possibly die. Nor could she shake the sense of anxiety about leaving Ben and Dorothy.

The face of the dead girl in the autopsy room haunted her. And yet, in the end, it was the memory of the dead girl that made her realize that she had to go. She must do what she could to stop this horror.

Early on the morning of the thirty-first, a white van with a big red cross painted on the doors stopped in front of the Atwaters' house at 516 Hayes. Ben carried Mollie's bag down the front steps and handed it into the van. Dorothy and Mollie came out onto the porch. Mollie hugged her daughter, then turned abruptly and hurried down the steps. She briefly embraced her husband, turning her face so he wouldn't see what she couldn't hide. She put on a smile and waved up to Dorothy, then climbed into the van that would take her to the Northern Pacific for Whitefish.

CHAPTER NINETEEN

The Flu and the Doctor in Whitefish

AT THE STATION, THE MAN AT THE NEWSSTAND had some back copies of the *Whitefish Pilot*. Mollie bought them all. The porter carried on her suitcase, and she stashed her medical bag on the net shelf above her head. As she settled in her seat and opened the newspaper, she didn't know which crisis was more horrible—the war or the flu. On the war front, the paper reported the final death toll of the British at the Somme and Passchendaele was a million and a half; another million French were dead at Verdun. She couldn't conceive of such carnage. Disbelief gave way to nausea. It seemed to her she could smell the stench of the rotting bodies halfway across the world. In Russia, she read, Lenin was solidly in control. Trotsky was organizing the Red Terror, and the Bolsheviks were murdering the Mensheviks. In this country the government was launching its Fourth Liberty Loan, asking people to buy more war bonds. The reactionary Montana Loyalty League was threatening to ". . . combat and destroy every influence, individual, clique, set, class or organization . . . that in any way interferes with or fails to assist in our program." The Red Cross was asking people to save nut shells and fruit pits to make charcoal for gas masks.

Montana was reported to be behind in its nurse quota; there was a plea to the women of the state to give their services. Margaret Hughes, head of Red Cross training in Montana, was giving a six-week crash course in elementary nursing for war volunteers: first aid, hygiene, and dietetics. Mary Roberts Rinehart, the popular mystery writer, had become a Red Cross nurse and was urging all nurses to go to France. In one hospital in France, there was one nurse for fifty wounded. There weren't enough nurses for the war, and now they didn't have enough to combat the killer destroying Americans here at home.

The flu reports were equally appalling. By this time 11,000 people had died of the flu in Philadelphia. "In the city morgue, the corpses are piled three and four deep like cordwood, unembalmed and mortifying," Mollie read. "The stench is ghastly. There are not enough undertakers, not enough coffins, not enough grave diggers. Special trains are needed to haul away the bodies. In some cases the dead are left in their homes for days."

In Montana, Bill Cogswell was asking people not to call a doctor unless it was a matter of life or death. The doctors were exhausted, some of them working as long as forty hours without rest. There were now 1,500 cases in Butte. The little town of Whitefish, where Mollie was headed, had a population of 3,800, with 300 cases reported and fifteen deaths so far. And Cogswell thought there might be twice as many as reported. She hoped they had help for her. She knew she couldn't handle this alone.

Dr. Lees, the local health officer for Whitefish, met Mollie at the station.

"Thank God you're here, Dr. Atwater." the doctor said, taking Mollie's suitcase. "We don't have enough nurses. The ones who were here have gone to Europe. The flu's as bad there as here, let alone the war casualties. Our hospital is overflowing, and we've been using the domestic science building at the school. We're still looking for additional space. The city teachers have volunteered as nurses, but two of them have already come down with the flu."

"How many cases do you have?" Mollie asked.

"As of now, only 300 reported, but I suspect two to three times that many. The people are angry, especially the businesses, about the quarantine. And the saloons are giving us a bad time. We have the police checking up on them, making sure they're really closed, which just adds to the anger."

"I know, I hear it's that way all over Montana. People actually think that alcohol will protect them. And the businesses are mad because of all the money they're losing. But we've got to keep enforcing this."

Dr. Lees held the station door open for Mollie, and they went out onto the street. It was almost deserted. A couple of masked women hurried by with bags of groceries, but the bar across the street was closed. The empty town emanated an eerie quiet.

"The first thing we have to do is train the volunteers and the public how to treat the victims, " Mollie said as she climbed into the doctor's Model T. "You work on finding us space, and I'll set up the training and public information."

Mollie checked into the Northern Hotel on Central Avenue. She stayed in her room long enough to wash up from her trip before going over to the domestic science building. There the cots were squeezed in side by side.

"We've got to move these people as soon as possible," Mollie said to the volunteer teachers. "The patients are much too close together. The germs must be jumping from one patient to the next. These people have to have air."

Dr. Lees found room for Mollie's temporary hospital in the two-story Masonic temple. The upper floor would serve as the makeshift hospital; the lower floor would be for convalescents. An appeal went out to the community for the temporary donation of beds—cots and singles—and bedding. By the end of the week, all the patients from the school building had been moved into the temple. Many were single men who lived alone and had no one at home to care for them. Mollie had five volunteer teachers and a railroad brakeman to help her in shifts.

She organized a class for the volunteer nurses; some were family members of sick patients, and many were schoolteachers.

"You must keep the patient isolated," she stressed. "Sanitation is essential. We've got to keep this disease from spreading. You must wear a mask, and be careful not to touch it. Change the mask every two hours. The masks must be boiled for a half hour after washing. All dishes and utensils must be boiled after use. The patient must be kept warm, and any cloths that have been spit or coughed or sneezed into must be burned immediately. Please, don't try to wash them. They must be burned. For those of you who are caring for a victim at home, it is important that no one sleep in the same room as the patient. Make sure he is warm and leave the windows open. Children should play outside as much as possible, but alone in their own yards.

"I must emphasize," she concluded, "there is no cure for the flu. Do not let yourself believe that any of the nostrums that are advertised as cures are anything other than a waste of money. All we can do in the face of this epidemic is keep the victims isolated and as comfortable and clean as possible, and take every precaution that the germs are not spread."

She repeated this information for publication in the *Pilot*. She couldn't hold a public meeting, since all meetings were banned.

Mollie was in touch with Ben almost every evening by telephone.

"We're fine, Mollie." Ben would say more or less the same thing every time she called. "You're the one who's constantly exposed. You be careful, don't worry about us. Dorothy's incredibly bored, but she's staying inside as you wanted her to. If this keeps up, she'll have read every book in the house."

On November 11, three days after Mollie had set up her hospital, the war ended. The last fighting had been the day before, when General Pershing's troops attacked over a front of 71 miles from the Meuse southeast to Lorraine. Kaiser Wilhelm had abdicated and fled to Holland. Cities across the United States erupted with crowds screaming and waving flags in a patriotic pandemonium of joy and relief.

It was the worst thing they could have done. The epidemic was at its height. Masses of people were packed together, shouting in each other's faces. The flu spread through the crowds like wildfire, but there was no stopping the celebrations. Especially in the rural districts, the number of cases rose dramatically because the country people rushed into the towns to celebrate.

Mollie checked the flu reports every day. By the middle of November, Cogswell had reported 1,252 cases; there were seventy-two deaths in Helena. Deaths in Whitefish had reached twenty-five. Philadelphia was so far the worst hit in the country, with well over 32,000 reported deaths. One Philadelphia nurse reported finding a man dead twenty-four hours in the same bed as his wife, who had just given birth to twins.

In early November the army released a vaccine that officials were quick to say was "experimental." Dr. Cogswell was worried and decided not to use it. Another vaccine was developed in Minnesota, and although this one was also experimental, Cogswell determined it might help; at least he felt it was not harmful. The Rosenow vaccine, as it was called, was tried in a few towns, including Helena, but it wasn't very effective.

Mollie telephoned Ben as soon as she heard the vaccine was available: "I'm not sure about that stuff," she told him. "I don't want you or Dorothy to get vaccinated. I think you are safest if you just stay home and avoid everyone."

In addition to the reports of legitimate researchers attempting to find a preventive, there were rumors and reports of quack nostrums, as well as celestial explanations for the epidemic. One story reported a hopeless flu case being cured by eating boiled onions soaked in turpentine. Death would be one sure way to cure the flu. Another assured the public that the epidemic was the result of a certain conjunction of Jupiter with other planets. A report from California advised using coaguline to thicken the blood to avoid hemorrhaging of the lungs. That a side effect might be heart attack wasn't mentioned. The makers of the Hyomel Inhaler reported their product would "absolutely destroy germs of influenza." An article quoted from the *Christian Science Monitor* claimed that the whole epidemic was the result of fear, and that it was the duty of editors to protect the public by only printing constructive news.

The religionists decried the end of the world: The flu was the manifestation of the plague prophesied in Revelation. The Lamb had broken the Fourth Seal, and Death stalked the land, killing with sword, with famine and pestilence, and by wild beasts of the earth. Mollie supposed one could consider the prophecy another possibility; after all, the machine gun had replaced the sword, and the pestilence was thought to have started with birds and pigs.

Mollie insisted in the *Pilot* that drugs were impotent against the flu. "Aspirin, quinine, or Dover's Powder might help relieve the fever," she wrote, "and Vicks VapoRub might make one's chest feel a little better, but cures they are not."

Mollie was exhausted. The makeshift hospital was cold and drafty. It was November, and winter had already blown in to the little town at the top of Montana. Her brakeman-nurse, when he wasn't helping her with the patients, was constantly chopping wood, tending the woodstoves, and burning contaminated cloths in a large incinerator outside the temple. Human waste had to be carefully disposed of directly into the city sewer system. If there was a moment when a patient didn't need her or one of her volunteers, then there was the washing and preparation of new masks. The masks were needed in a constant supply; each nurse would use at least six or seven a day. Clean cloths had to be continually provided for coughing and sneezing and spitting, and then burned. Sheets had to be changed and laundered. And throughout the days and nights, tired as they were, she and the volunteers had to remain positive and supportive of the patients. She seldom had time to go back to the hotel. She just rested or, if possible, slept an hour or two on a cot in the convalescent ward on the lower level.

One case had Mollie especially worried. A young woman of twenty-five was brought to the temple by the Reverend Sanford in the middle of the night. The reverend went into homes all over Whitefish to check on people. He had found the woman delirious, her two little children untended and crying.

Mollie was sleeping when they arrived. The brakeman woke her, and then he and the reverend supported the woman up to the second floor of the temple. Ida Murphy, the volunteer teacher on night duty, quickly made up a cot for the new patient.

"It's tragic, Dr. Atwater," the Reverend Sanford said, pulling Mollie aside as she came upstairs to the hospital room. "I stopped by to see Mrs. Hardmeier a couple of days ago, and she told me she had received word from the War Department that her husband was killed in the last assault on the Meuse. I was worried she was probably coming down with the flu when she got the notice, that's why I went back to check on her this evening. The neighbor has the children now; they're all right, but scared. They don't know about their father, they're really too young to understand, but they're terrified about what's happened to their mother."

"My God, how horrible," Mollie said. "The poor woman. Her grief may be too much for her to fight this disease. I'll try to have one of the volunteers with her as much as possible."

The reverend left to go back to his rounds, and Mollie examined her new patient. She was feverish with pneumonia. Mollie was afraid to use the thermometer while the woman was delirious, but a hand on the forehead was all she needed to register the temperature. The woman's wailing was broken by coughs, and she was having trouble breathing. Mollie checked her pulse; it was rapid—140 beats. She could hear the congestion in the lungs.

"I'm going to give you some quinine to lower your fever." Mollie spoke gently to the woman. There was a flicker of acknowledgment.

"I want you to drink this. It will help you sleep." Holding a cup to the woman's lips, Mollie was able to get her to swallow most of the solution. The delirious wailing quieted as the quinine began to take effect. In a few minutes the woman was asleep.

"I'm going back downstairs to try to get some sleep," Mollie said to Ida Murphy. "Keep an eye on her. This one's going to need a lot of help. If she wakes up and asks, be sure to tell her the children are safe, that a neighbor is taking care of them."

As Mollie crawled back under the covers, she was overcome with the misery of what she had just witnessed. That, and her own exhaustion, brought tears to her eyes. But nothing—not even the fever of despair on the floor above—could keep her awake.

The next morning Ida shook her gently.

"Jessica will be here soon, Dr. Atwater. I'll be leaving now. Our new patient woke about five o'clock. I was able to take her temperature. Her fever is down to 102, but she's crying. She doesn't seem delirious like last night, she's just crying."

Mollie roused herself and washed. In a few minutes, Jessica Reed, another of the teacher volunteers, would be bringing food for breakfast for the patients and Mollie. She went upstairs to check on her charges.

Of the fifty or so patients who had passed through the temple hospital in the last three weeks, she hadn't lost anyone. And she shouldn't lose Cynthia Hardmeier if she could keep the pneumonia under control. The question was if Cynthia would have the will to live.

The woman's crying continued on and off all day. Mollie stopped by Cynthia's bedside several times. She tried to get her to talk, but Cynthia would turn away. From time to time she would cry out for her children. In the afternoon Mollie called the Reverend Sanford.

"Of course I can't let those children come in here for her to see them," she said to the pastor, "but is there someone we can contact? Someone from her family who can give her support? This poor woman is going to cry herself to death."

"I'll see what I can find out, Dr. Atwater. Maybe the neighbors will know."

Mollie watched Cynthia Hardmeier over the next day. Her fever still hovered around 102. She didn't seem to be getting any better or any worse. She was in a kind of limbo.

Toward evening the Reverend Sanford telephoned Mollie: "I've found her mother, Dr. Atwater. She's coming from Missoula. She should be here tomorrow afternoon."

Mollie was relieved. The woman could be sent home if there was someone to care for her. Her flu crisis had passed. She had avoided the hypoxia that would have killed her, but the pneumonia was still dangerous. She would need several days of bed rest. What Cynthia Hardmeier desperately needed in order to survive for her children was love, and while Mollie knew that love was an integral ingredient of the alchemy of Cynthia's healing, she was helpless. This was an epidemic: There was no time to give the woman the care she needed beyond medical treatment. Only someone close could help Cynthia, could give her that love. Women who died of grief were the further casualties of the brutality in Europe, and those who did survive were not counted among the statistics of mutilated faces, missing limbs, shattered minds, and shaking bodies.

Patients were still being brought into the temple hospital, but gradually over the last week of November, there were fewer and fewer cases. Mollie began to feel there might be light at the end of the darkness. Cynthia's mother had come to take her stricken daughter back to her home. Mollie told her the children could come home, too, so long as they stayed out of their mother's room. It was with great relief that Mollie saw her go. The woman's grief had elicited such pity from the other patients that recovery was that much harder for everyone.

At the end of November, there were 350 cases reported in Whitefish and twenty-seven deaths. The health department, however, estimated some 1,000 cases, more than a quarter of the town's population. The flu was subsiding. Most of the patients in the temple were in good enough condition that they could be released to home care. Mollie still had eight serious cases, but there was room now to transfer these to the hospital. The public was told they could come to reclaim the cots and bedding they had donated.

Mollie gathered her volunteers and thanked them. The *Pilot* publicly acknowledged that she had constantly risked exposure, and thanked her for her help. Dr. Lees, the Reverend Sanford, and Dr. Taylor from the hospital accompanied Mollie to the train station.

"We can't thank you enough, Dr. Atwater. Without you we would have lost many more victims," said Dr. Lees, shaking her hand.

"I'm so glad I could help you," she said with a tired smile. "It looks like the flu is almost finished here, or at least it's subsided." Turning to the reverend, she said, "Be sure to look in on Mrs. Hardmeier every so often. She'll survive the flu, but she's going to need your help facing her new life."

"I know, Doctor. When she's well enough, her mother's going to take her and the children back to Missoula for a while."

The porter handed her bag up into the train. The whistle sounded. Mollie climbed up the steps and waved good-bye to the three men.

CHAPTER TWENTY

The Nineteenth Amendment

MOLLIE RETURNED TO HELENA EXHAUSTED. At the station she hailed a taxi, then sat back with her eyes closed as the cab clattered up the shoulder of Mount Helena to Hayes Street. When she had called from Whitefish, Ben had wanted to meet her train, but Mollie insisted he stay home: The flu was subsiding, but it had not yet passed. Ben and Dorothy were watching for her from the front window of the house. Ben hurried down the front steps when he saw the taxi coming up the street.

"I feel I could sleep for a month," Mollie said to him as she stepped out of the cab. Ben paid the cabbie and picked up her bag. Together they climbed the steps. "It isn't just the lack of sleep every night, it's the worry. I was very fortunate to have wonderful volunteers. We didn't lose a single case, but it was not for lack of worrying."

Dorothy was waiting for her mother on the porch. She had tears in her eyes as she threw her arms around Mollie's neck.

"I was so worried you'd catch the flu. You were exposed to it all the time!"

"And I was worried about you," Mollie said, smiling at her. "But I see you are healthy and beautiful as ever."

Dorothy blushed. Mollie realized that her daughter never seemed to know how to react to compliments. She knew that she was tough on her daughter, but she didn't like to see insecurity. She was going to have to straighten Dorothy out about that very soon.

"Dorothy, I need to count on you to fix dinner tonight. I want to hear what you've been doing all month, and I'll tell you all about Whitefish. Right now, though, I'm going up to rest." Mollie started up the stairs to the bedroom she and Ben shared. Halfway up, she looked back over her shoulder. "Ben, would you come in a few minutes? I'd like to talk to you."

Mollie closed the bedroom door and took off her traveling clothes. She put on a robe and sat down to look at her face in the mirror above her dressing table. She was sixty years old, and she looked seventy. She grimaced, observing the dark circles under her eyes. Her hair seemed grayer than it had a month ago.

She lay down to wait for Ben. Her mind was swirling with the experiences she had just left behind. The pity, the grief, the fear, the stress on herself and the nurses. The uncanny quiet of a town stalked by an invisible killer. She needed to talk, she needed to be loved, she needed Ben.

Ben came in with her suitcase and shut the door behind him. He lay down on the bed and put his arms around her.

"I'm so tired, Ben. I don't think I could have held out much longer. The stress was incredible. And the flu isn't over yet. It's subsided for now, but another wave can come."

"I know. I read in the paper that the schools will remain closed. Poor Dorothy, she's so bored."

"Speaking of the paper," Mollie said. "I didn't have time in White-fish to read anything other than the flu reports. Of course I know the war is over, but what else is happening in the world?"

"Well, nothing at all has happened in Helena, because we've been shut down. I read the 'Dead for Democracy' column every day, but other than the Stevens boy we saw earlier, there was no one we know. Some of the war numbers are beginning to come in. It looks like Montana lost 1,700 boys."

"I suppose we should be grateful there weren't more," Mollie sighed, "when I think of the millions lost in Europe. A whole generation gone. The armistice is a Pyrrhic victory at best. I don't see how the survivors over there, whatever side they were on, can bear the horror."

"The survivors here are having a bad time of it, too. There was an article in yesterday's paper about all the spiritualism and séances that are going on across the country. Half the men killed have no known graves. People are desperately trying to contact the dead through séances, since they can't know where—or even if—their loved ones are buried."

"My God, how awful. As if things aren't insane enough in this world. Séances." She rolled over to face away from Ben. "I have to rest now, but please stay with me until I fall asleep. Everything is so sad. I need to know you are here."

"Of course, my dear Mollie." Ben held his arms around her, and after a moment she turned back to him in a desperate intensity of desire.

Mollie was right that the flu had not finished with Montana; nor had it finished with the world. By Christmas and into the spring, a third wave attacked. This one was milder than the second wave, the killer wave, that had washed across the country from September through November. And it was noted that those affected by the milder first wave the previous spring were found to be immune to the second and third attacks.

Nevertheless, by the time the final third wave subsided in late spring of 1919, it had claimed another 1,266 lives in Montana, bringing the total known flu deaths in the state to almost 4,500, and, in the country, when the count was finally tabulated, to some 675,000. Relative to population, Montana was one of the hardest-hit states, on the same level as Maryland and just below the worst state, Pennsylvania. Fortunately for Mollie, the Volunteer Medical Service Corps wasn't called on again to administer to the third-wave victims. After the armistice, most of the doctors and nurses returned from Europe, and this time there were enough to handle the situation.

Mollie being Mollie, she wasn't down for long. The U.S. constitutional amendment that would guarantee woman suffrage, assuming ratification by the states, was working its way through Washington. The House of Representatives had voted to support it in January 1918. Later that year President Wilson had addressed the Senate, urging the senators to support the amendment as a war measure, arguing that women had earned it. He eloquently acknowledged that the war could not have been fought without the service of women "upon the very skirts and edges of the battle itself." Fine words indeed, but they made no impression on the senatorial opponents, who carried the day. Except for a couple of northern antisuffrage senators, the problem was the South. The southern argument for states' rights was primarily a cover for the fear of giving the vote to Negro women. Carrie Chapman Catt decided that the national suffrage group should work to "retire" certain senators who were up for reelection, and campaign for favorable replacements. In this the women were partly successful. They had lined up all but one state's needed vote at the Sixty-sixth Congress. That vote was solicited by transatlantic cable to the senator from Georgia by President Wilson, who himself was suffering from the third wave of the flu at the armistice conference in Paris.

For Mollie, the victory in the Senate on May 19, 1919, that would send the amendment to the states was clouded with sadness. On that same day her closest friend and confidante, Dr. Maria Dean, died. For thirty-five years Mollie and Maria had worked together as professional colleagues in the fight for women's standing in the medical profession, for public action in the prevention of infectious diseases, and for equal political rights for women. And now Maria would miss the reward of final ratification she had worked so hard and so long to achieve. Her death gave Mollie a renewed sense of determination.

Having finally received Senate approval, the proposed amendment would have to be ratified by three-fourths of the states. Mollie and the old guard of suffragists were back in action, sending letters, making phone calls and appointments, urging the Montana legislature to ratify the amendment. In this they were successful, and on August 2, 1919, Montana became the twelfth state to ratify. Across the country the supportive states gradually fell in line. But women were still worried. Thirty-six states were needed to pass the amendment, and the South seemed solidly against. Tennessee was the thirty-sixth state to consider the amendment, and the opposition was out in force. Suffrage opponents poured into Nashville. The liquor, the railroad, and the manufacturing lobbies were fighting. Legislators who favored suffrage were blatantly threatened with the ruin of their businesses, or their professional or political careers. The liquor interests plied the legislators with booze the night before the hearing, apparently hoping that a hangover would keep them away or at least confound their ability to think. Carrie Catt commented that there were even some antisuffrage women appealing to "Negrophobia and every other cave man's prejudice."

Despite these terror tactics, the last and deciding vote was squeezed out of the Tennessee legislature in August 1920. The country had taken a giant step toward that better world for women that Mollie had promised her unborn daughter nineteen years before.

Dorothy had graduated from high school in the past year. She was dancing now in a professional group, touring Montana, but Mollie planned that Dorothy would go to the university in the fall.

"We need to talk about Dorothy," she said to Ben one evening after dinner. It was early spring, and the smell of lilacs hovered in the city. They had gone to sit out on the porch and enjoy the fragrance of the night air. "I think she should go to Missoula. There are good professional schools at the university, and she can decide in a year or two what direction she would like to take."

"Mollie." Ben reached over and took his wife's hand. "Mollie, listen to me. You aren't seeing Dorothy for who she is. All along, you've expected her to be like you, but she's not. It's clear to me that the girl is in awe of you, but she doesn't have your drive. She's not a fighter, she would never be the doctor or the lawyer or whatever kind of professional business woman that you seem to contemplate. But she's a very good dancer. Her future should be dancing."

"I guess I can't see dancing as a career," Mollie said, "other than being a Broadway showgirl, and for that, she's hardly the type."

"No, she needs a career that will allow her to keep dancing for her own joy. You know how she loves it. Perhaps as a teacher of physical education. Those two things would blend beautifully for her."

"I suppose you're right," she said. "It isn't what I imagined for her, but she doesn't seem to have the drive, as you say. I was hoping that it might develop in her, but it doesn't look like that's going to happen. If she's going have a career as a dancer, though, then she should be the best. I like the teacher she's had for the last two years, but I think we can find someone better, someone more professional."

"Oh, Mollie. Here you go again. You push Dorothy too hard. Let her find her own way."

"She's not strong enough to find her own way," Mollie bristled. "Professional dancing, like anything else, is hard work. She should have the best teachers, and I'll find them for her."

"You had better face the idea that one of these days she may bring some young man home for dinner, and that will be the end of it."

"What do you mean, 'the end of it'?" Mollie said, an edge of anger in her voice. "I hope she won't, but if she does decide to marry, that's no reason she shouldn't continue her career."

Ben let the subject drop. He and Mollie had had this discussion before; she had made her views on a woman's right to have a career very clear.

"When will she be back?" he asked, changing the subject.

"They have a performance in Butte tonight and one in Billings tomorrow. They should be back on Saturday. And then next week the troupe is going to Salt Lake."

"Good. Let's talk to her about her plans on Saturday. But please, Mollie, be careful. You mustn't be disappointed in her. Society needs dancers as well as doctors, and Dorothy is a beautiful dancer. She has much to give."

Dorothy had indeed thought a great deal about what she wanted to do for a career. She had decided on her own that she should go to normal school and study physical education, just as Ben had suggested. She assured her parents that she was very serious about continuing her dancing career.

A few months later, as Ben had predicted, Dorothy did bring a young man home for dinner. Hugh was a southerner from Georgia, an engineer for American Telephone who had been sent by the company to work in Helena.

When Mollie heard Hugh's strong southern accent, it took her immediately back to the year she had spent in Louisiana with Frank. It elicited unpleasant memories for her, not just of her unhappy marriage, but also of the negative attitude southerners held about her because she was from the North. And perhaps worse, the negative attitude of southerners toward a woman professional. As a doctor, she had been made to feel she was a social oddity, a woman who didn't know her proper place. Hugh seemed very nice, but Mollie was concerned he might hold these same attitudes.

"Tell us about your family," Ben asked the young man as they sat down to dinner. Mollie and Dorothy had set the table in the dining room and brought out the good china and sterling for the event. Occasionally, there had been young men invited for dinner before, but Dorothy had made it clear to Mollie that this one was special.

"My father was a farmer," Hugh told them. "But he is no longer alive. My mother and three of my sisters live in Atlanta."

Mollie wanted to find out his family's attitude toward northerners, but she couldn't just ask him outright. "I lived for a year in Louisiana," she ventured. "Of course that was a long time ago, but I felt that the people there were still fighting the Civil War."

"Yes, I'm afraid that's true for some of us southerners," Hugh said. "But I assure you I don't have such feelings. I must confess my father felt that way because he fought in the war as a teenager."

Mollie found this news disturbing. If Dorothy was serious about this man, would she be welcome in Hugh's family, even with the father gone? Mollie had been a child during the Civil War, and she still carried a child's horror of things she had seen. She had her own prejudices.

Over the next few months, as Dorothy's relationship with Hugh grew closer, Mollie came to realize that whatever his family might think, Hugh was free of any regional antagonisms. This was a relief to her, but she still was concerned that her daughter might not be accepted by this southern family.

"Well, Mollie," Ben said to her, "there's nothing we can do about history. One can only imagine the hatred in Atlanta after Sherman burned down the city. But if Dorothy wants to marry Hugh, they can just stay here in Montana. She doesn't have to deal with any of that."

"Yes, I suppose you're right." She sighed. "I just don't want her to get hurt; I hope his family will accept her."

Hugh and Dorothy were soon engaged, but Dorothy insisted on finishing her physical education studies and working for a year before she married. And she wanted to continue to build her career; she was becoming well known as an interpreter of East Indian dancing. Mollie had come to like Hugh very much, but she was relieved that Dorothy was not in a great hurry to get married.

Mollie had returned to her work for the Montana Tuberculosis Association. It was a period when the state's death rate from tuberculosis was alarmingly high. There were several reasons for this. The 1918 killer flu had damaged the lungs of the survivors, leaving them highly susceptible to tubercle attack. The years after the Great War brought drought to the prairies, and unemployment and poverty to the mining regions—malnourished bodies were easy prey for the bacillus. And some physicians had been careless about noting and reporting early signs of illness, waiting until the disease had a death grip on its victim.

Mollie was especially concerned for the women and children who were stricken; there were no separate facilities for them at Galen. Through their fund-raising efforts before the war and their continuing work now, she and her women's club friends, with the help of the Montana Tuberculosis Association, the state, and a private donation from Senator Walsh, collected enough money to fund a special women's facility at the sanatorium. Her colleagues in the association thought that the facility should bear her name, but Mollie insisted it should be named for her friend who had worked so hard on the project, but had died before it could be completed. She did, however, agree to be the administrator of the facility. At the 1920 groundbreaking ceremony, Mollie laid the cornerstone to the Elinor Walsh Memorial Cottage. In her dedication speech, she noted:

> *We might have built a great monument to Mrs. Walsh, erected an ornamental fountain or a tall marble pillar; but we prefer to perpetuate her memory and her worth with something enduring that will typify the life of service she devoted to others.*

The brick-and-frame cottage would accommodate ten recuperating patients in a homelike atmosphere, with a fireplace and a small kitchen. The idea was to give women who were recovering the chance to get away from the austerity of the hospital setting.

The problem of children at the sanatorium was perhaps even greater. Galen accepted children for treatment, but since there was no special facility for them, they were housed with the adult patients. This created tremendous difficulties for patients and staff, since a major requirement of the recovery process was quiet and bed rest. Keeping children, ranging in age from two to sixteen, disciplined and quiet— even when they were sick—was close to impossible. There was far too much shouting and fighting and crying brought on by the sheer boredom of being cooped up in a hospital for many months—even a year or more. One story was reported of an adult patient being hit by rocks thrown by a very sick and very disturbed little boy.

Children had to wait their turn along with the adults for a bed in Galen, sometimes dying before space became available. Studies showed that often tuberculosis developed in childhood, and a 1921 survey of Montana schools turned up at least 500 tubercular children. Mollie told the members of the Federated Women's Clubs that it was their obligation to keep an eye out for symptoms in the children of their communities, and to urge the parents of children suspected of infection to take them to a doctor. She followed this advice with the admonition that their own children were at risk if they played with a diseased child.

Poorer children suffered the most. With Mollie's urging, the women's clubs and the Tuberculosis Association together raised the funds to build "sunshine camps" for those children, where they were exposed to a sun cure for up to an hour a day and received nourishing meals to build up their strength.

But clearly a children's facility was needed at Galen. Mollie was on the political and fund-raising campaign trail again. This time pressure on the legislators resulted in a $16,000 appropriation to construct a Sunshine Pavilion. The sun cure was very effective, but it took from six months to a year. At the end of that time, however, if the initial community watch had been successful and the disease caught in the early stages, the child was most often completely cured.

Hugh was becoming increasingly insistent that there be a wedding soon. He had waited while Dorothy finished her normal school training and then waited again while she worked for a almost a year as a physical education teacher in Saskatchewan. He implored her not to make him wait any longer.

"I heard today I have a chance to be transferred to the San Francisco office," he said one afternoon as he was walking Dorothy home after they had seen a moving picture show. She was home for the summer break from teaching. "It's a much better job than the one I have here in Helena. If I want to take it, I'll have to decide very soon—in a few weeks. But I don't want to go there without you."

Dorothy was taken aback. She hadn't considered that Hugh would want to leave Helena. When she got home, she told her parents that he was considering going to San Francisco.

"I mustn't hold him back from advancing in his career," she said. "I just hadn't realized that marrying him might mean leaving you and all my friends. I guess I just assumed he would be content to stay here. He never talked about leaving before. But I do love him, and we are engaged. Of course I will go with him wherever he wants"—this last said with resolute determination. "We will need to marry very soon."

Mollie was shocked at Dorothy's announcement. She, too, hadn't considered that Dorothy would leave. But the girl was already twenty-two; under the circumstances of Hugh's wanting to move to San Francisco, there was no way to convince her not to marry immediately. Not only did Mollie struggle with the thought of losing her daughter, but she was still concerned that Dorothy should continue her dancing career. Ben agreed with her that they would miss their daughter terribly, but he saw the practical side of the situation. He was sympathetic to Hugh's need to pursue his career wherever it might lead him.

"Mollie, you can't control Dorothy's life, and you mustn't try," Ben said to his wife later that evening. He and Mollie were having dinner; Dorothy had gone out to a party with Hugh. "We have to let her go.

I'm sure it's harder for us than for some parents, because she's our only child. But it's her life now."

"Look, Ben," Mollie said, angrily. "I would never interfere with Dorothy's happiness. How could you think I would try to do such a thing?"

"No, of course I know you wouldn't consciously do that. But I worry about your influence over her. I don't want her to feel you wish she wouldn't marry, and I don't want to turn Hugh against us. Besides, Dorothy herself says that the San Francisco area would be a better place for her to continue her dancing. There are more professional opportunities there, and better teachers."

"Yes, I'm sure that's true," Mollie conceded. "Montana isn't exactly the culture center of the country. Thank God, at least he doesn't want to take her to Georgia. I just worry that she'll get pregnant and that will interfere with all her ambitions."

"Are you sure they aren't your ambitions, Mollie?"

Mollie glared at him, shoved back her chair, got up from the table, and left the room.

That Mollie's own pregnancy had to a large extent halted her career as a practicing physician was a subject that still hovered between them. Mollie had made her choice those many years ago, and she never made reference to it. Nor did Ben. She admitted to herself that she held regret in her heart; but it was a regret that was more than balanced by the almost desperate love she felt for her daughter. Her medical training had stood her in good stead to pursue the many public health interests she had embraced over the years, and later on she had been able to practice again on a part-time basis. But her life after Dorothy's birth had not been the one she had envisioned for herself. She was determined that her daughter not give up her chance at a career as she had had to do.

Mollie understood that Dorothy was caught between the desire to live up to her mother's expectations and her desire to marry Hugh. The girl had assured her mother that she didn't intend to have children for many years, and that she would continue to dance after she was married. Mollie was placated, but she knew she wouldn't prevail against Hugh, if it came to that. She also knew that Ben was not on her side; that he was concerned about the power she had over her daughter. That Dorothy idolized her mother was clear to everyone who knew them. Ben's only interest was that Dorothy be happy, no matter what she chose to do with her life; Mollie was convinced that real happiness could only come through the hard work of personal achievement.

A wedding was planned for the garden of the house on Hayes Street, and Dorothy Atwater and Hugh Barron were married in July 1923. Within a few weeks of the wedding, Hugh's job was transferred from Helena to San Francisco. After twenty-two years of unexpected parenthood, Mollie and Ben were left alone to face each other over the breakfast table.

CHAPTER TWENTY-ONE

A Last Move

BEN HAD LEFT HIS JOB at Kessler's Brewery in 1915, just in time to miss the Montana vote for Prohibition. He had anticipated the vote, and had completed the federal civil service examination. Senator Walsh put in a word for him, and he landed an accounting position with the federal Bureau of Internal Revenue. After spending years preparing tax returns, he found himself in the position of auditing—this time from the government's point of view—the returns of some of his former clients. One of the clients from his accountant days was a lumber company in Great Falls.

"Mollie," Ben said to his wife one morning in mid-January 1931, "I have to go to Great Falls to audit that lumber company's books today. I'll need to stay over. I'll be back on the late train tomorrow."

"That's fine, Ben. I have a women's club meeting tomorrow night, so I won't be home, myself, until late. We'll probably be back about the same time."

This conversation was the last Mollie had with her husband. She received a phone call that afternoon from Great Falls. Ben had had a heart attack and died while working on the books in the lumber company office.

The body, accompanied by a Great Falls revenue agent, was sent down by train to the Opp and Conrad funeral home in Helena. Mollie put off the funeral until Dorothy could get there from California. She asked the funeral home to bring Ben's body to the house on Hayes Street for a short while. She wanted to sit with Ben one last time while she waited for her daughter.

An usher from the funeral home, sporting a white carnation in his lapel and a carefully modulated demeanor, escorted wife and daughter to the family pew of the Opp and Conrad chapel. Mollie listened to the Reverend Daniels of Saint Peter's Episcopal Church intone the funeral rites. She thought back to Ben rushing her from the Helena station to the rectory at Saint Peter's for her surprise wedding thirty-seven years before. What a happy time that had been. Their life in Marysville had seemed perfect. And then suddenly without warning, Marysville had died, just as Ben, too, lying there in front of her, had died without warning.

Ben's friends, one after another, rose to commemorate him. Harry Picket, Ben's oldest friend, gave the formal eulogy:

> *Perhaps, Ben, you can see us here, among the flowers you loved, gathered to pay tribute to the man you were, and to tell you across the silence, something of our love for you. . . .*

Throughout the service, Mollie held herself like a statue, staring at the coffin. She had asked in the newspaper that no flowers be sent, but the chapel was full of wreaths. She couldn't stand their sickly sweet smell. To her they had the smell of death—a death that was somehow diminished in its reality by all this show. Still, the funeral was for Dorothy and for their friends, so if they wanted to send flowers, she was willing to grant them the gesture. She had taken her leave from him alone, the night before in the house in which the three of them had been happy together.

She was pleased that so many of Ben's friends and colleagues and lodge brothers had come, but she had no use for their pious mouthings. Why couldn't they just accept the reality of death? Ben was gone. He wasn't going to "see us here, among the flowers, gathered to pay tribute." Her beliefs concerning the meaning of death had not changed over the years. She became aware of Dorothy's attempt to stifle her sobs. Without shifting her eyes from the coffin, Mollie reached for her daughter's hand.

After the funeral Mollie and Dorothy stood outside the chapel for the ritual acceptance of condolences from their friends. Then they walked back up the hill in the cold January snow to Hayes Street. The funeral home director had offered to drive them, but they had declined. After the enclosure of the funeral, they both wanted the freedom of the cold, fresh winter air.

While Dorothy fixed coffee in the kitchen, Mollie stood looking out the front window to the street. It had started to snow again, spreading a white film over the leftover tracks of the morning traffic. The young elms along the street stretched their bare arms into the drifting air. She watched a man and a little girl, bundled against the cold, hurrying hand in hand along the sidewalk.

Dorothy laid out cups and saucers and some cookies she had found in the pantry. She poured the coffee and called Mollie to come. Mother and daughter settled at the breakfast table to talk about the people who had come to the funeral, about how their lives would be without Ben. They both felt the loneliness of the empty house that had once been full of life and love. Dorothy couldn't control her tears.

"Please come to California with us." she managed to say through her sobs. "You shouldn't stay here alone. Hugh and I have talked about this. We're going to start our family soon and we want you to be part of it. We're looking for a house in Berkeley big enough for all of us. Please. We want you to come."

"Thank you, Dorothy," Mollie said. "You and Hugh are wonderful to ask me, but I don't know how to answer you right now. Ben's death was so sudden . . . I just don't know . . ."

Dorothy couldn't stay long; she had a dance recital scheduled in San Francisco. She returned to her life in California, and Mollie was left alone to consider what she would do with hers now that Ben was gone. His death had been so sudden, she had not had time to think of her future. What future she might have left. She was already seventy-three. Somewhat older than Ben, she had always assumed she would be the first to die.

Suddenly she felt tired. She had never once stopped working since those long-ago days in Bannack. No, she realized, even earlier—not since she was sixteen and teaching school in Wisconsin and then Iowa. She supposed Dorothy was right. Why should she stay here alone? Her work in Montana was done. She and her friends had fought for the vote and finally won, but equality—social and professional—was another matter. That fight she would have to leave for a younger generation to take on.

Dorothy called full of excitement: "We've found a big house in Berkeley that has a little apartment on the side for you. You will come, won't you? I know you'd like it. It's on a quiet street with lots of trees."

"Yes, Dorothy," Mollie said to her daughter, her voice carrying a certain tone of resignation. "Thank you. I will come."

As word spread that after forty years in Montana, Dr. Mary Atwater was planning to leave, she was besieged with invitations to dinner, invitations to speak at public gatherings, invitations to going-away parties. As a sudden widow, she had to admit that this flurry of attention was in some ways a welcome distraction from her grief—in other ways, a trial.

The Montana Tuberculosis Association, which Mollie had been instrumental in organizing back in 1916, gave a farewell banquet in her honor. Mollie was overcome with emotion as she heard the outpouring of acclaim from the colleagues and friends who came to wish her farewell. Bill Cogswell gave the keynote address, citing his long association with Dr. Mollie and her work to make people aware of public health issues, especially her efforts to educate them about the myths of tuberculosis—the "white plague" or "miner's con," as it was called in the days of the gold mines. He told the story of her service in Whitefish during the flu epidemic, and how she had not lost a single patient in her makeshift Masonic temple hospital.

Dr. Cogswell was followed by Dr. Charles Vidal, the director of Galen, who told the audience that it was Mollie and her arm-twisting influence at the Montana Medical Association, and with the women's clubs of the state, that was the impetus behind the establishment of Galen, even before Jim McNally had been elected to the legislature.

"Tuberculosis deaths in the state are down to half what they were in 1912 when the facility was built," Dr. Vidal noted. "And for that we can thank Dr. Atwater and her dedicated colleagues in the Montana Tuberculosis Association."

Senator Walsh spoke of how his wife and Mollie had determined to build the women's facility at Galen, and how grateful he was that Mollie had seen the project through to completion after his wife's death. He thanked her for remaining as administrator of the cottage for several years afterward.

Jeannette Rankin gave a brief history of the suffrage movement in Montana and Mollie's role in it since her presidency of the Montana Woman Suffrage Association in 1895. Mollie was grateful that Jeannette mentioned the women who had passed on and who had been so important in the early years of the movement, especially her dear friends Ella Haskel and Maria Dean.

"Because of the efforts of women like Dr. Atwater," Rankin concluded, "she and I and the women of America have voted in the last four presidential elections. We thank you for that, Dr. Mollie." She gave a bow to where Mollie was sitting; there was a groundswell of applause.

The final speaker was a surprise. Although he and his family lived in Helena, Mollie had lost contact with them over the years. The man who walked up to the podium was Harold Esterbrook Longmaid, the baby Mollie had delivered at the beginning of her career so long ago in Bannack. She had not seen him since J. Henry's funeral, some years earlier. In addition to becoming a prominent businessman, Harold was an accomplished landscape artist. He presented Mollie with a watercolor he had painted of the Empire mill in Lost Horse Gulch outside Marysville. In thanking him for the painting, she laughed and told the guests that if it weren't for Harold, she might never have come to Montana.

Harold picked up on Mollie's comment. "Indeed, if it weren't for me," he told the crowd, "her name might not be Dr. Atwater. Our family has stories about her. When my father told my mother that a woman had applied for the position of mining camp doctor, my mother insisted he hire her so she could be present at my birth. And as you can see"—he gave a grandiose bow—"it went well." A laugh rippled through the hall.

"I'm told that there was some grumbling among the miners when they learned the Golden Leaf boss had hired a woman to doctor them," Harold continued, "but I understand the grumbling faded quickly when Dr. Mollie showed the complainers her horse whip, and then got on with curing whatever ailed them."

The crowd applauded with a roar when Harold finished his talk. Mollie had a lump in her throat, but she managed to smile graciously. Remembering those days in Bannack and Marysville, she knew in her heart they were the happiest of her life. But the life of the mining camps was over, not only for her, but also for Montana and the West. The mines had yielded their treasure; the abandoned tunnels and dilapidated buildings were dead now, empty of all but the ghosts who still haunted them in the minds of the living. There was nothing to regret.

Mollie sold the house on Hayes Street. As she was sorting out the things she would take with her, they brought back to her the people and events that had formed her life. There were still a few pieces of china and crockery the family had brought with them to Wisconsin when they moved from Vermont. They were precious, speaking to her of a time of childhood happiness when her father was still alive. Sadie had sent them to her after Adelia Sophia died. She still had the cut-glass perfume bottle Frank had given her on her birthday so long ago, and the gold watch, his gift for her graduation from medical school. Once, these things had made her happy. She had learned from friends in Osage that Frank had died in Missouri several years ago. There were pictures of Willy at her cabin in Empire, and a picture of Willy at her wedding party in Helena. There had been other dogs in her life before and after Willy, but none was as special in her heart. He was the one who had shared the loneliness of her divorce, the happiness of her love for Ben. She picked up the picture of Ben that always stood on her dressing table: a young Ben, dapper with his mustache and sideburns. It had been taken in a studio in Helena shortly after they were married. There were countless pictures of Dorothy as a baby, Dorothy on the beach in La Jolla, Dorothy dancing, Dorothy as a bride in the garden outside. The pictures and the objects were signs along the journey of her life—ever westward, like the nation. She had come this far, from Vermont to Iowa to Montana; it must be her manifest destiny to die in California.

Mollie shipped her trunk of clothes and books and a few pieces of furniture to Berkeley. Then she packed her old black medical bag, Harold's painting, and Ben's ashes, and took the train west to await the birth of her grandchildren at the edge of the Pacific.

Epilogue

IN THE SPRING OF 1980, I left my husband in charge of our two sons and drove north from my home in La Jolla toward a past that was mine in blood, but about which I knew very little. Indeed, I did know the stories, but I needed to find who it was who had lived those stories. I was headed for Montana, in search of my grandmother. If I could find her, maybe she would tell me something about myself.

The last time I saw her, I was four. She was eighty-two then, and lived in a little mother-in-law apartment with a separate entrance at the side of our house in Berkeley. In my mind she was always dressed in old-lady black that smelled of the little packets of dried lavender she kept in the drawers of the Victorian highboy in her bedroom. My strongest memory of her was when my mother banished me to the bathtub in my grandmother's apartment after my seven-year-old brother and I had decided to run away from home. A policeman found us in a park several blocks away. Riding home in the shiny black-and-white patrol car was even more exciting than running away. As soon as we were delivered to our frantic mother, she put us into bathtubs—my brother into the tub upstairs, and me into my grandmother's tub.

I was the lucky one. While my mother scrubbed my brother, my grandmother, who wanted to hear all about our adventure, washed me. Later that year I was told she had left us; my mother thought I was too young to go to the funeral.

It wasn't because I didn't go to the funeral that I knew my grandmother never died. My grandmother never died because I am my grandmother. As far back as I can remember, whenever I brought home a good report card, or showed skill in sports or music, my mother would smile and say: "I'm so proud of you—you're just like your grandmother." But then when I talked back to her or sneaked off to do something I knew I wasn't supposed to, her face would flush with rage, and she would shout, "I might have known you'd be just like your grandmother!" Whatever I did, good or bad, I was my grandmother all over again. Of course my mother would get angry at my brother, too, but being a boy, he was never compared to her. My father, a quiet man, paid no attention to these rows.

Still, my mother could be gentle and loving. Sometimes I would sit in her lap, and she would show me her photo album, pictures of her when she was growing up in Montana. One of them was taken in a photographer's studio, my pretty, sixteen-year-old mother in a white lace dress, empire style, with her long dark hair falling down her back. One was of her with my grandfather and grandmother sitting around a campfire—she looked about ten. Another was of a fire hydrant gushing a column of water high into the air. We always laughed about that one; it was so funny to see a fountain shooting out of the sidewalk.

"I don't know where this picture came from," my mother had said. "It was one my mother had, and I just stuck it in the album because it was so funny."

At bedtime my mother would tell me exciting stories about my grandmother's life as a doctor on the frontier and as a fighter for women's rights. These stories made me proud to be like her. And they made me just as proud—something my mother never seemed to realize—to be compared to her when I was bad. In the stories my grandmother was always wonderful, yet she was thrown in my face if I misbehaved. There was something mysterious here, something I didn't understand.

My only lead to finding my grandmother was the address for a nursing home in the Helena Valley. The woman who lived there had been the wife of the local pharmacist. She and her family had lived next door to my grandmother, and although she was much younger, the two had been close friends. She was now eighty-eight years old. I had never met her; my mother had dug her address out of a box of old Christmas cards.

"Fanny didn't answer my card last Christmas," my mother said, "so I don't know if she's still alive."

I hoped not only that she was alive, but that her memory was still with her. My grandmother had been gone for such a long time; this address was all I had.

Two days out from California, I pulled into Helena late in the evening. I registered at the Last Chance Motel, named for the main street of the city, which, in turn, was named for the gulch where four prospectors—or so my guidebook said—discouraged and ready to leave the territory, decided to take one last chance. They struck a bonanza. I was exhausted from driving and slept fitfully, dreaming of a ghostly old lady in black, scrubbing me in a bathtub.

The next morning I went to the motel office, checked the directory for the number of the nursing home, and dialed. I asked if I could please speak with Mrs. Fanny Reynolds. To my delight, the woman who answered told me to hold on and she would find her. So she really did exist! Now if only she still had a mind.

A thin, frail, but determined voice came on the line. I told her my grandmother's name and asked if she remembered her.

"Of course!" the voice answered. "Everyone remembers Dr. Mollie." I wondered who, after forty years, was "everyone"? I told her I'd like to talk with her, and she gave me directions to the nursing home.

I drove out to the valley and found the place—a large, settled, homey structure that looked like it had been built in the 1920s. A wide veranda crossed the front of the building, shaded by huge cottonwoods. Groups of white wicker chairs furnished the veranda. As I walked up the front steps, a tall, white-haired, still-elegant woman rose from one of the chairs to greet me.

"You must be Mollie's granddaughter," she said, smiling and extending her hand to me. Her next words stopped me cold: "I've been waiting years for you. Sooner or later I knew you would come."

For a moment I thought maybe she had indeed lost her mind. I had never heard of this woman until a couple of weeks before. What could she possibly mean?

"Sit down with me here on the veranda," she said. "I have lots of stories to tell you about Dr. Mollie and Dorothy. I know that's why you've come. You need to hear them." I sat down on a wicker swing seat facing Fanny.

"Dr. Mollie was an amazing woman," Fanny began.

"Yes," I said, "I have heard so many wonderful stories about her. But what I want to know is, what went wrong? Why, when I was a child, did my mother compare me to her with such awe and devotion, and then tell me I was just like her when I did something that made her angry?"

"I knew this would happen," Fanny said, almost as an aside.

"What do you mean?" I asked.

Fanny sat quietly for a few moments, as if she were considering carefully how to tell me her story. Then she looked up and said, "You modern girls have no idea how hard it was for a woman to become a doctor in those days. Just to get anyone to take you seriously, to acknowledge that you could be competent. Dr. Mollie was the strongest person I ever knew, stronger than any man I ever knew. Yet she was a 'lady' in the extreme—a proper Victorian, divorce and all. Although she married again, she was determined not to have children. Children would interfere with her career."

"So what happened when my mother was born? Did she change her mind?"

"No, not at all," Fanny said. "She got caught. Her pregnancy with your mother was an accident."

"Oh, Fanny," I said. "My mother never told me that!"

"I don't know if Dorothy knew. Possibly not—at least not consciously." Fanny was quiet for a moment. She seemed to be thinking how to continue.

"Mollie and I were next-door neighbors. She and I often had coffee together early in the mornings after the children left for school. One day she told me what had happened when she found out she was pregnant. At that time Mollie must have been in her forties. For the first two months, she told me, she was in denial. Can you imagine a doctor not knowing she's pregnant?"

"Why do you think she didn't terminate the pregnancy?"

Fanny was thoughtful. "I don't know," she said finally. "I just don't know what she struggled with. She was torn between her own biological reality and her career. And remember, she was a doctor; she had sworn an oath to do everything possible to preserve life. What I do know is that when she finally came to terms with the fact she was going to have a child, she determined that she would devote her life to that child. After all the struggle she had gone through to achieve her own practice, she had to give it up."

"Oh my God," I said. "I think I'm beginning to see what happened."

"Yes," Fanny continued, "Mollie put all the force and energy she had previously poured into her work into raising her daughter. I could see the consequences of that when Dorothy was growing up. Mollie controlled everything your mother did—what she thought, what she studied in school, even what she wore to school. Mollie managed her down to the last minute of the day she died. It wasn't that she meant any harm. It's just the way she was."

The grandmother in me came out. "Why didn't my mother rebel?"

"She couldn't rebel," Fanny said. "She was in awe of Mollie. And clearly her mother loved her, loved her almost desperately. But Dorothy had to compensate for the sacrifice her mother had made for her very existence.

"Not that Mollie gave up being an activist. She was an avid suffragist and an ardent advocate for public health programs, but these things, important as they were, were not the profession she had worked so hard to achieve and which had she wanted to pursue. Later, of course, she was able to work in medical emergencies, but it was never the private practice she had wanted. Dorothy must have been resentful, but she couldn't admit that to herself. So she buried it deep inside and never let herself go near the thought. All she could think was that her mother was the most wonderful woman in the world. And the problem was—it was true."

As we sat together in the warm, leaf-stippled sunshine of the veranda, incidents from long ago that had left me confused and angry suddenly began to make sense. Fanny was answering a lifetime of questions, giving me the reasons I had wondered about for so long: Why my mother's anger had always seemed to my little-girl mind far in excess of the merits of my transgressions. The power she had never had as a child over her own life, she wanted to exert over mine. But I was a rebellious brat, and her life as a mother must have been equally as frustrating as her life as a child. These conflicts had roused an antagonism in me that was a constant source of strife between us. After I was old enough to leave home, my mother and I were never close.

Fanny and I were quiet for a while. I stared out at the breeze-ruffled cottonwoods shimmering in the morning air. So my mother's life was an accident—an accident that had cost my grandmother the chance to practice the profession she had worked so hard to achieve. Today, most likely she would not give up her career, but that was another time.

We continued to talk for another hour. I felt I was in the presence of a psychic. Fanny seemed to know everything about me, yet what she knew came from her understanding of the dynamic between my mother and my mother's mother. Just as with my own father, my grandfather was apparently not a significant player in this dynamic. It was something between women.

One of the stories Fanny told me was about teaching my grandmother to drive.

"It was the late 1920s," she said, laughing, "after your mother had married and moved to California. Mollie must have been close to seventy. Your grandfather had bought a used Model T, and Mollie asked me to teach her to drive it. She never did get the knack of it. She was the scourge of Helena, especially after the day she backed into a fire hydrant on Last Chance Gulch and a fountain of water spewed 30 feet into the air. Water was all over the place before the fire department got there to fix it."

So that was the funny picture in the album, I laughed to myself.

I knew that my mother had taken dancing lessons when she was growing up. In the photo album there were pictures of her dancing in exotic costumes. By the time she met my father, she was quite accomplished, dancing in professional groups. Fanny told me my grand-mother's reaction when my mother announced she and my father would marry.

"One day when I was working in the pharmacy," Fanny recounted, "your grandmother came in, wanting to buy a birth control device for Dorothy. 'She should not have children,' Mollie had said. 'It will ruin her dancing career.' I asked her if she didn't think that should be Dorothy's decision. She glared at me and marched out in a huff—without the device.

"After the wedding," Fanny continued, "your mother and father went to Marysville to stay in a cabin for their honeymoon. People from around here did that, there was a little resort out there in those days. After a couple of days had passed, your grandmother asked me to drive her out to Marysville to check on them. 'Oh, Mollie,' I said. 'For heaven's sake, it's their honeymoon. Leave them alone.' But she insisted, so we went. Dorothy seemed delighted to see her mother. Mollie saw that the cabin floor was dirty. She got a mop and a bucket and mopped it clean. Hugh gave me a look I will never forget."

"You've got to be kidding," I said. "She went out there and did that on their honeymoon?"

"Yes," Fanny replied. "She really did, she mopped that floor."

I couldn't imagine such a thing, but I could well imagine what my father must have thought.

For several minutes a delicious smell of roast beef had been waft-ing from the open door of the nursing home. The morning had passed so quickly; it was time for Fanny to go in for lunch. "Thank you, Fanny," I said as I stood up to leave. "I can't tell you how important this visit has been for me."

"I think I do know," Fanny said, as she rose to her feet. "I could see what was happening all those years, and I was pretty sure that the resentment would come out in some form. I thought it unlikely your mother would ever let such thoughts surface to her own understanding, and I feared they would be projected onto her children. And here you are."

I left Fanny and drove back to the Last Chance, amazed that this wise woman had been waiting in Helena, Montana, all these years, wondering when I would come. And I felt a poignant sadness. She was eighty-eight years old; I had come just in time.

Lunch was a hamburger in a cafe next to the motel. I spent the rest of the afternoon exploring Helena, imagining what it once must have been like when my grandmother lived there. Was one of the pharmacies I saw in the older part of the city the one that had belonged to Fanny's husband? The one my grandmother had angrily marched out of when Fanny had challenged her about the birth control device? And which of the fire hydrants on Last Chance Gulch was the one my grandmother had backed her Model T into?

Fanny had given me the address of the house where my mother grew up. I found it on Hayes Street, on a hill above the city. It was a fairly small, yellow-painted Victorian house with a bay of windows to the right of the front door. I recognized it immediately from the picture I had seen in the photo album so long ago. Lacy wrought-iron supports had replaced the wooden pillars that once held up the roof over the front porch. In the picture there were some small elm trees lining the street. The trees were still there, but now they towered above the houses. To the right of the house was a small garden. Maybe that was where my mother was married. I remembered a garden from the photo album, and my mother, standing among the flowers in her white bridal gown, a crown of orange blossoms anchoring her long lace veil. Beyond the garden was a vacant lot. On the other side of the house stood a large, rambling white house with a glassed-in sunporch across the front. That must be where Fanny lived, where my grandmother had gone mornings for coffee and talk.

The next morning I checked out of the motel. I got out my Montana guidebook and looked in the town index. Listed under "Ghost Towns" was Marysville—the storied gold camp I had heard so much about. It was 30 miles away. I drove out to where a small sign at the edge of the highway directed me to turn off onto a dusty dirt road. I bumped along for some miles up into the mountains until I came to a jumble of dilapidated structures. It wasn't entirely a ghost town; a few people apparently still lived there, or maybe lived there again. In the distance I could see a couple of newer houses. Some of the ramshackle buildings seemed to be inhabited; a few old cars—maybe dead, I wasn't sure—were parked in front of them. Several scruffy dogs wandered around. One offered a couple of barks in my direction, then gave up; the others paid no attention to me. I saw some clothes hanging on a line, but I didn't see any living bodies. And I didn't recognize anything in the town that looked like it might ever have been a resort, although recently a ski resort had been developed not far away on Belmont Mountain. Could this once have been a town of 3,000 souls, as the guidebook said? With theaters, an opera house, and three score saloons? I walked along the deserted, false-fronted buildings down what a sign said was Main Street. The place looked like the movie set for a western. John Wayne might come galloping up the middle of the street at any moment, six-shooters blazing. I poked around in the dilapidated stores. They smelled of rotting wood, damp from rain that had leaked in from holes in the roofs. In one a floorboard gave way under me, and I almost fell through into a cellar. There weren't signs on the buildings anymore, and I wondered which of these broken-down storefronts, almost a century ago, might have once sported a shingle that announced: MARY BABCOCK MOORE, MD. PHYSICIAN AND SURGEON.

On the drive back home, I stopped to see my mother in Berkeley. Having touched her past, I felt a compassion for her that I had not felt before. I hoped that maybe, after so many years of conflict, I could express this to her. She was eager to hear about my trip. She fixed coffee for us, and we took it out to the little table on the balcony of her apartment. Now a widow, she had long since sold the big house in Berkeley where my brother and I grew up, and where, forty years before, my grandmother had died. I told her I had met Fanny, and thanked her for giving me the address. She was delighted to hear that the little yellow house in up on Hayes Street was still there. And I described how tall the elms had grown. Then ever so subtly—so I thought—I suggested she might have had a difficult time growing up with such a powerful woman as my grandmother. The anger I remembered so well flashed to the surface.

"Absolutely not!" she exclaimed hotly. "Your grandmother was the most wonderful woman in the world!"

The State of Medicine in Dr. Atwater's Times

DR. MARY ATWATER'S LIFE SPANNED a period of major medical discoveries. Yet she did not live to see smallpox virtually eradicated from the United States, nor the development of antibiotics that would conquer many bacterial diseases, such as pneumonia, scarlet fever, typhoid, and whooping cough. With the development of streptomycin and later other drugs, the "white plague" she had worked so hard to bring under control ceased to be the threat it had once been.

At her graduation from medical school in 1887, certain tools in common use today were available to her: the stethoscope, the thermometer, the otoscope for the examination of ear passages. At that time the fever-reducing effects of quinine were known, and in 1898 aspirin was discovered. Ether and chloroform were used as anesthetics; iodine, alcohol—worst case in the form of whiskey—and carbolic acid were the disinfectants, the last especially useful in the houses of ill repute. Calomel and castor oil were used as purges; ipecac, to induce vomiting; and laudanum, a morphine derivative, for pain.

In the 1880s Louis Pasteur, and later Robert Koch, developed the "germ theory." Prior to that time, some doctors were still "bleeding" their patients. In 1895 Emil von Behring developed diphtheria and tetanus antitoxins, a development that finally convinced the medical establishment of the importance of bacteriology. Immunization against these diseases was developed in the 1930s. Almroth Wright discovered a vaccine for typhoid fever in 1897, and diabetes was brought under control with the discovery of insulin in 1922. A smallpox vaccine had been developed as early as 1795 by Edward Jenner, but immunization was not lasting, and the vaccine sometimes had serious side effects; during Dr. Atwater's lifetime smallpox remained a deadly scourge. The mortality of women after childbirth had been reduced by 90 percent with the realization by Ignaz Semmelweis that the infectious, and often fatal, agents of puerperal fever were transmitted by unclean hands. Joseph Lister had introduced antisepsis into surgery in 1867, which allowed the development of the appendectomy in the 1880s by William Byford, Dr. Atwater's teacher and the director of the Woman's Hospital Medical College of Chicago. It was an operation that Dr. Atwater was often called on to perform in the mining camps.

Wilhelm Roentgen developed the X-ray in 1895. Despite all the urging of the Montana Tuberculosis Association, however, the legislature refused to authorize the funds for Galen to acquire this important diagnostic tool until 1920. With the discovery in the 1930s of methods of growing viruses in tissue culture, the way was opened for the discovery of vaccines for yellow fever, poliomyelitis, measles, mumps, and rubella. However, the virus has still not been isolated that was responsible for the 1918 flu that killed more Americans in a few months than were killed in four years of bloody carnage in the Civil War, and that killed at least fifty million people worldwide (some researchers estimate as many as one hundred million). For all the concern taken to wear masks during the 1918 flu pandemic, it is now thought that these masks were probably ineffective. Flu epidemics have been kept under control largely by vaccines that were not available when Dr. Atwater was working with flu victims. She could reduce the fever, but it wasn't until the discovery of penicillin in the early 1940s, shortly after her death, that the pneumonia that tends to follow the flu could be adequately controlled. Given the ability of flu viruses to mutate from year to year, if an exceptionally virulent strain occurs again, the world population is as susceptible to another pandemic today as it was in 1918.

The federal Comstock Law of 1873, permitting the seizure of contraceptive devices and information from the mail, was mitigated somewhat in the 1930s, but not finally repealed until 1971. And of immense importance to the medical profession and to society as a whole was the 1906 passage of the Federal Food and Drugs Act. Among many things, this act required a listing on drug labels of the presence and amounts of dangerous ingredients, such as alcohol, cocaine, and heroin. The act was expanded in 1938 to mandate pre-market approval of all new drugs.

In light of the advances in today's medicine—the specialized drugs and diagnostic machines, the radiation and chemical therapies—the medical practices of Dr. Atwater and her physician colleagues may seem to us almost primitive. Yet often they were surprisingly successful. Perhaps it was the personal touch—the intimate bedside manner; the willingness to make house calls; the years of association with a patient and his ills; a certain watchfulness on the part of the physician leading to early warning of potential problems—that accounts for this success. These are qualities of the medical profession that today many find lacking from the "caring" part of managed care.

Dr. Volney Steele, a historian of frontier medicine, made the following comment in a letter to the author about early woman doctors in Montana: "I think that one of the reasons that most women were licensed so readily was that they were generally extremely qualified. Handicapped by their sex in the masculine world, women had to have a lot on the ball to graduate in the first place, and many of them had at least some post-graduate training. In some fields such as pathology and radiology, women were the first to specialize. Many of the men were not so well educated, and, as you know, there were a lot of them who had no schooling at all."

This was the medical world that Dr. Atwater entered on her graduation from the Woman's Hospital Medical College of Chicago in 1887, and in which she worked, off and on, till her death in 1941.

Bibliography

Alderson, Mary. "A Half Century of Progress for MT Women." Helena: Montana Historical Society, unpublished manuscript, 1934, 13.

Allen, James B., and Thomas G. Alexander. *Mormons and Gentiles: A History of Salt Lake City* (Boulder, CO: Pruett Publishing Co., 1984).

Anthony, Susan B., and Ida Husted Harper. *History of Woman Suffrage, Volume 4: 1883–1900* (Rochester, NY: S. B. Anthony, 1902).

Askin, Kacey. "Marysville, MT." Helena: Montana Historical Society, unpublished manuscript, no date.

Atwater, Mary B. "The Borderland of Insanity." *The Woman's Medical Journal* 5, no.7 (July 1898).

———. "The Etiology of Pneumonia." Unpublished manuscript, 1886.

Axline, John. "Mill's Destruction by Fire Severed Vital Link to Past." *Independent Reporter* (September 7, 1995).

Blackwood, W. R. D. "The Prevention of Conception." *Medical and Surgical Reporter* 59 (1888), 396.

Bonner, Thomas Neville. *To the Ends of the Earth: Women's Search for Education in Medicine* (Cambridge, MA: Harvard University Press, 1992).

Bradbury, Dr. Robert. *An Encyclopaedia of Practical Information and Universal Formulary* (Chicago: The Century Book & Paper Co., 1890).

Brodie, Janet Farrell. *Contraception and Abortion in Nineteenth Century America* (Ithaca, NY: Cornell University Press, 1994).

Bibliography

Brown, David. "Lessons from 1918." *The New Mexican* (June 8, 2003).

Cassedy, James H. *Medicine in America: A Short History* (Baltimore: The Johns Hopkins Press, 1991).

Chicago Medical Society Council. *History of Medicine and Surgery and Physicians and Surgeons of Chicago* (Chicago: Biographical Publishing Co., 1922).

Cornell, Virginia. *Doc Susie* (New York: Ivy Books, 1991).

Cowan, David L., and William H. Helfand. *Pharmacy* (New York: Harry Abrams, Inc., 1990).

Crosby, Alfred W. *Epidemic and Peace, 1918.* (Westport, CT: Greenwood Press, 1976).

Cutler, H. G., ed. *Medical and Dental Colleges of the West: Chicago* (Chicago: Oxford Publishing Co., 1896).

Dillon (MT) Tribune. 1891–1893.

Ehrenreich, Barbara, and Deidre English. *Complaints and Disorders: The Sexual Politics of Sickness* (New York: The Feminist Press, 1973).

———. *Witches, Midwives, and Nurses: A History of Women Healers* (New York: The Feminist Press, 1973).

———. *For Her Own Good* (New York: Doubleday Anchor, 1978).

Flexner, Eleanor, and Ellen Fitzpatrick. *Century of Struggle: The Woman's Rights Movement in the United States* (Cambridge, MA: Harvard University Press, 1996).

Getz, David. *Purple Death* (New York: Henry Holt, 2000).

Graves, F. Lee. *Bannack: Cradle of Montana* (Helena: Montana Historical Society, 1991).

Great Falls (MT) Tribune. January 3, 1919.

Gunn's New Family Physician (Cincinnati: Moore, Wilstach & Baldwin, Publishers, 1864).

Haller, John S., and Robin M. Haller. *The Physician and Sexuality in Victorian America* (New York: W. W. Norton, 1977).

Helena (MT) Independent. October 1914; October–November 1918; Mary B. Atwater obituary, June 2, 1941.

Helm, Ernest C. "The Prevention of Conception." *Medical and Surgical Reporter* 59 (1888), 646.

Henig, Robin M. "Flu Pandemic: A Once and Future Menace." *New York Times Magazine* (November 29, 1992).

Hersey, A. H. "Rich Mines Near Helena." *The Northwest Magazine* (July 1895).

Howard, Joseph Kinsey. *Montana: High Wide and Handsome,* 1943 (New Haven, CT: Yale University Press, 1959).

Ingman, Aurlette D. "Marysville Was One of the Liveliest Gold Camps in Treasure State." *Rocky Mountain Husbandman* (February 13, 1936).

Jepson, Jill. "Medicine Women: Montana's Pioneer Doctors." *Montana* (January–February 1995).

Kolata, Gina. *Flu* (New York: Farrar, Straus & Giroux, 1999).

Korting, Ann. "Marysville, Montana." Unpublished manuscript, no date. (gift of author.)

Lamar, Howard R., ed. *The New Encyclopaedia of the American West* (New Haven, CT, and London: Yale University Press, 1998).

Larson, T. A. "Montana Women and the Battle for the Ballot." *Montana* 23 (winter 1973), 24–41.

"Little Black Bag." *MD* (September 1965).

Luchetti, Cathy. *Medicine Women* (New York: Crown Publishers, 1998).

MacKnight, James A. *The Mines of Montana* (Helena, MT: prepared for National Mining Conference, 1892).

Marysville (MT) Gazette. 1894.

Marysville (MT) Messenger. 1895–1897.

Marysville (MT) Mountaineer. 1893–1897.

"Marysville's Mining Revival." *Helena Journal* (March 19, 1891).

McLaren, Angus. *A History of Contraception* (London: Basil Blackwell, Ltd., 1990).

Medical and Surgical Directory of the US (R. L. Polk & Co.). There are editions for 1886, 1890, 1898. Later editions, called *Polk's Medical Register and Directory,* 1900, 1906, 1917, 1936.

Mergler, Marie J. "History of the Northwestern University Woman's Medical School." In *Medical and Dental Colleges of the West,* H. G. Cutler, ed. (Chicago: Oxford Publishing Co., 1896).

Miles City (MT) Daily Star. November 11, 1918.

Mitchel County (IA) Press. January–May, 1889.

Mola, Jessie Wilhoit. "Historic Marysville, Montana." Marysville Pioneers Association: unpublished manuscript, 1971 (in Montana Historical Society).

Montag, Leona. *Mitchel County History* (Iowa) (Dallas: Curtis Media Corp., 1989).

Montana Medical Association. Minutes of Annual Meetings, 1894–1905. Helena: Montana Historical Society.

———. *First Hundred Years* (Missoula: Montana Medical Association, 1978).

Montana State Board of Health. *Tuberculosis.* Special Bulletin no. 3 (Helena: Montana State Board of Health, 1915).

———. *First Biennial Report, 1901–02.* (Helena: Montana State Board of Health, 1901–1910).

———. *50 Year History,* 1901–1951. (Helena: Montana State Board of Health, 1953).

Montana State Department of Fish, Wildlife and Parks. "Bannack Documentary Reference Project. Historic Themes and Research" (January 1995).

———. *Bannack*. Visitor's Guide. No date.

Montana State Tuberculosis Sanitarium. *Fifty Years of Progress, 1913–1963* (Galen: Montana State Tuberculosis Sanitarium, 1963).

Montana Woman. December 1925, 1, 8–9; September 1928, 16; December 1928, 7.

Montana Woman Suffrage Association. "Minutes of the First Convention, 1895." Helena, MT.

More, Ellen S. *Restoring the Balance: Women Physicians and the Profession of Medicine, 1850–1995* (Cambridge, MA: Harvard University Press, 1999).

Mullen, Pierce C., and Michael Nelson. "Montanans and the Most Peculiar Disease: The Influenza Epidemic and Public Health, 1918–1919." *Montana* 37 (spring 1987), 50–61.

One Hundredth Birthday Medical Committee. "Medicine: The Early Days" (Billings, MT: One Hundredth Birthday Medical Committee, 1983).

Osler, William. *The Principles and Practice of Medicine* (New York and London: D. Appleton & Co., 1910).

Paladin, Vivian, and Jean Baucus. *Helena: An Illustrated History* (Helena: Montana Historical Society Press, 1983).

Petrik, Paula. *No Step Backward: Women and Family on the Rocky Mountain Mining Frontier, Helena, Montana, 1865–1900*. (Helena: Montana Historical Society Press, 1987).

Phillips. Paul C. *Medicine in the Making of Montana* (Missoula: Montana University Press, 1962).

Pivar, David J. *Purity Crusade: Sexual Morality and Social Control, 1868–1890.* Contributions in American History 23 (Westport, CT, and London: Greenwood Press, 1973).

Polk's Gazetteer (R. L. Polk Co., 1892–1925).

Polk's Helena City Directory. 1899–1925.

Price, Ester G. *Fighting TB in the Rockies: A History of the Montana Tuberculosis Assn.* (Helena: Montana Tuberculosis Association, 1943).

Pridmore, Jay. *Northwestern University: Celebrating 150 Years* (Chicago: Northwestern University Press, 2000).

"Rich Marysville Gold Mining District." *Montana Record* (April 8, 1916).

Riddle, John. *Eve's Herbs: A History of Contraception and Abortion in the West* (Cambridge, MA, and London: Harvard University Press, 1997).

Roberts, Richard C., and Richard W. Sadler. *Ogden: Junction City* (Northridge, CA: Windsor Publications, Inc., 1985).

Rothstein, William G. *American Physicians in the Nineteenth Century* (Baltimore: The Johns Hopkins Press, 1985).

Sagstetter, William, and Elizabeth Sagstetter. *The Mining Camps Speak* (Denver: Benchmark Publishing, 1998).

Scholl, B. Frank, John Forsyth Little, and Frank E. Miller. *Library of Health: Complete Guide to Prevention and Cure of Disease* (Philadelphia: American Health Society, 1916).

Schwantes, Carlos A. *Railroad Signatures Across the Pacific Northwest* (Seattle: University of Washington, 1993).

Schwidde, Jess T. "Medicine in the Yellowstone Country." In *Medicine: The Early Days* (Billings, MT: One Hundredth Birthday Medical Committee, 1983).

Shikes, Robert M. *Rocky Mountain Medicine* (Boulder, CO: Johnson Books, 1986).

Shirley, Gayle E. *More than Petticoats: Remarkable Montana Women* (Helena and Billings, MT: Falcon Press, 1995).

Shrady, George F. "Women's Chances as Breadwinners." *The Ladies' Home Journal* (May 1891).

Shryock, Richard H. *Medicine in America: Historical Essays* (Baltimore: The Johns Hopkins Press, 1966).

Staudohar, Connie. "Food, Rest, and Happiness: Limitations and Possibilities in the Early Treatment of Tuberculosis in Montana." *Montana* 47, no. 4 (winter 1997) and 48, no.1 (spring 1998).

Steele, Volney. "Doctors at the Battle of the Big Hole." *Military History of the West,* 32, no.1 (spring 2002).

———. "Women Physicians of the Frontier." *Charting Montana's Medical Past.* Video recording, 1997.

Tuchscherer, Mabel E. "Petticoat and Stethoscope." Missoula: Montana Medical Association, unpublished pamphlet, 1978.

Tuttle, Thomas D. *Report of the Executive Board of the Montana State Tuberculosis Sanitarium, 1913–14.* Helena: Folder 7, Box 330, MC 35, Governor's Papers. Montana Historical Archives.

United States Census, 1880, 1900.

Waite, Susan. "An Historic Inventory of Marysville." Missoula: Bureau of Land Management, unpublished manuscript, 1974.

Waite, Thornton. *Union Pacific: Montana Division* (Columbia, MO, and Idaho Falls, ID: Brueggenjohann/reese and Thornton Waite, 1998).

Walker, Giles E. *Geology and History of Marysville Mining District.* U.S. Geological Survey: Open File Rept. 254, 1992.

Ward, Doris B. "The Winning of Woman Suffrage in Montana." Bozeman: Montana State University, unpublished thesis, 1974.

Weir, James Jr. "The Effects of Female Suffrage on Posterity." *American Naturalist* 29 (1895), 824–825.

White, Mollie A. *Looking Back from Beulah* (Bound Brook, NJ: Pillar of Fire, 1909).

Whitefish (MT) Pilot. October–November 1918.

Wilde, A. H. *Northwestern University: A History 1855–1905* (New York: University Publishing Society, 1905).

Wolle, Muriel S. *Pay Dirt: A Guide to the Mining Camps of the Treasure State* (Athens: Ohio University Press, 1963, 1983).

Woman's Medical College of Chicago. *Eighteenth Annual Announcement, Session of 1887–8* (Chicago: Chas. J. Johnson, Publishers, 1887).

———. "Minutes of Faculty Meeting," May 12, May 14, May 25, September 13, 1886, April 1, 1887.

Yalum, Marilyn. *A History of the Wife* (New York: Harper Perennial, 2002).

About the Author

In 1988 Mari Graña left a career as an urban planner in California and retreated to New Mexico to write. Her recent book of New Mexico regional history, *Begoso Cabin,* won the 2000 Willa Cather award from Women Writing the West. Ms. Graña works as a freelance editor in Santa Fe.

AWARD-WINNING TwoDot Titles

THE WOMEN WRITING THE WEST WILLA LITERARY AWARDS RECOGNIZE OUTSTANDING LITERATURE FEATURING WOMEN'S STORIES SET IN THE WEST.

2006 WINNER— MEMOIR/ESSAY

The Lady Rode Bucking Horses: The Story of Fannie Sperry Steele, Woman of the West
Dee Marvine

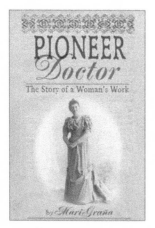

2006 FINALIST

Pioneer Doctor: The Story of a Woman's Work
Mari Graña

2006 FINALIST

More Than Petticoats: Remarkable Nevada Women
Jan Cleere

2003 FINALIST

Strength of Stone: The Pioneer Journal of Electa Bryan Plumer, 1862–1864
A Novel by Diane Elliott

Available wherever books are sold

Orders can be placed on the Web at www.GlobePequot.com, by phone at 1-800-243-0495, or by fax at 1-800-820-2329

TwoDot® is an imprint of The Globe Pequot Press